Praise for

HOW WE LEAD

"Joe Clark brings a wealth of experience to his observations on the Canadian political scene. . . . A former prime minister and foreign secretary, Clark . . . has seen Canada's presence on the international scene diminish in a worrying way since Stephen Harper became the Conservative leader and assumed power. . . . This is a thoughtful book, one that will interest anyone who cares about Canada's place in the world." *The Record* (Kitchener-Waterloo)

"The next federal election will be in October 2015. All Canadians should read this book before then and ask themselves what our role as a democracy should be in relation to the rest of the world and how we citizens can achieve that." *Calgary Herald*

"Clark's views should command serious respect as he was arguably the most outstanding Canadian foreign minister since the age of Lester Pearson." Brian Stewart, CBC News

"Joe Clark's *How We Lead* is like the honourable man: thoughtful, intelligent . . . worth the effort. . . . Who would have thought that Joe Clark could turn out to be Canada's Cassandra?" *Toronto Star*

"[A]n impassioned argument for Canada to reassert its international position as an agent of change, diplomacy and peace. Drawing on our history, successes, and the unique qualities that we possess today, Clark describes an ambitious but vitally important role for Canada—for the world's benefit, but also for our own." *Ottawa Life*

"The various criticisms he makes of the Harper government may often be familiar, but they carry weight because of who Clark is and how well he illustrates, from his personal experience, what impact a more engaged brand of Canadian diplomacy can have on the world stage. Whether readers will agree with him will depend a lot on their own politics, as one might expect of any political memoir. But they will get more out of *How We Lead*, an insightful commentary on a pressing topic of national significance, than they would from any run-of-the-mill, self-congratulatory autobiography." *Literary Review of Canada*

HOW
WE
LEAD

To Harry
with best wishes

J. Clk

CANADA IN A
CENTURY OF
CHANGE
JOE CLARK

VINTAGE CANADA

VINTAGE CANADA EDITION, 2014

COPYRIGHT © 2013 RIGHT HONOURABLE JOE CLARK

Published in Canada by Vintage Canada, a division of Random House of Canada Limited, Toronto, in 2014. Originally published in hardcover in Canada by Random House Canada, a division of Random Houseof Canada Limited, in 2013. Distributed by Random House of Canada Limited.

Vintage Canada with colophon is a registered trademark.

www.randomhouse.ca

Library and Archives Canada Cataloguing in Publication

Clark, Joe, 1939–
How we lead : Canada in a century of change / Joe Clark.

ISBN 978-0-307-35908-7

1. Canada—Foreign relations. 2. International relations.
I. Title. II. Title: Canada in a century of change.

FC242.C53 2014   327.71   C2011-902991-X

Text and cover design by Five Seventeen
Printed and bound in the United States of America

2 4 6 8 9 7 5 3 1

To my grandchildren,
Alexandra and Charlie, citizens of the future

CONTENTS

INTRODUCTION

An essential question for citizens of lucky countries is not simply who we are or what we earn, but what we could be. That question implies others: To what do we aspire? What are our talents and advantages and assets? How can we be better than we have been, in our impact on events both inside and outside our country?

Such questions are not just for the lucky. They can be asked—they are asked—in the world's hard places, where despite chaos or conflict or endemic poverty and despair, extraordinary individuals emerge and prevail—a Mahatma Ghandi; a Simón Bolivar; a Nelson Mandela. These are usually individual accomplishments, rare explosions of genius or character, but sometimes, on dramatic occasions, they occur across whole communities: South Africa during the 1980s; Europe's Eastern Bloc upon the collapse of Soviet communism; the "colour revolutions" of Central Asia; or more recently, the uprisings of the Arab Spring.

These and similar examples aside, it may not be reasonable to expect such things to happen in a desperately poor country like a Niger, where 75 percent of the population earns less than

$2 per day.[1] But aspiration *is* a reasonable expectation for Canadians, who are among the most prosperous people in any nation, and who have historically responded successfully to the challenge of making ourselves better citizens of our country and of the world. We are a geographically huge and diverse country; but for all the ways that geography defines us, Canada was formed not by accidents of nature but by acts of national will.

The magnitude of Canada's accomplishments warrants recounting: a remarkable confederation of former British colonies that resisted the economic gravity and the evangelic mission of their much more powerful neighbour; innovations that connected the country across a daunting continent—first a railway, later a national airline, a national broadcaster and cultural institutions like the Canada Council; national guarantees in the Bill of Rights and the Charter of Rights and Freedoms; programs of equalization, pensions and medicare, which confirmed that we are a society as well as a geography; free-trade agreements that facilitated our entrepreneurial instinct; and, from early days, and continuing vibrantly now, millions of wrenching individual decisions to leave family and homelands and become citizens of this evolving immigrant country. Where many nations are shaped by geography or history—islands separated from mainlands, borders drawn by colonial strangers—Canada is a *built country* that has prospered through acts that have shaped our natural assets into national strengths. The risk we face today is that, having built well on lucky ground—rich with natural resources and fertile soils, and located far from the world's conflicts—we will now take that prosperity and security for granted and forget how much we still require aspiration and foresight and accomplishment if we want our prosperity to continue.

This book is a reflection on what Canadians have accomplished at our best, specifically in international affairs. And it is a warning that this outward-reaching country could gradually turn inward, and, in the process, depreciate national and personal assets that will become more valuable in the world that is taking shape than they have ever been before.

I will focus on Canada's international potential—what we can do to be better off and better respected in a world that is becoming more turbulent and unsettled. The "we" in question is not just governments; it is also, emphatically, Canadian citizens and organizations ("non-state actors"), and more generally, the example and the reputation of our country. Any consideration of Canada's international role is also a domestic discussion, because what Canada does in the world is intimately related to who we are at home.

I have had the unusual privilege of learning about our country from two almost-opposite perspectives—from the "inside" as prime minister, minister of constitutional affairs and leader of a national political party that had to compete in every region of Canada in order to form a government. I became the national leader of the Progressive Conservative Party of Canada at age thirty-six, and was so young and so new that the ever-gentle *Toronto Star* immediately christened me "Joe who?" I had a lot to learn, so I plunged into the cultures and communities of this country, literally neighbourhood by neighbourhood, interest by interest, learning French, learning the facts, hearing hopes and fears. Fifteen years later, as minister of constitutional affairs, I took our most essential national debate out of the halls of Parliament and into Canada's communities, leading the inclusive and public discussion of the Charlottetown Constitutional Accord. That was Canada from the inside.

At the other extreme, from 1984 to 1991, I experienced a privileged view of Canada as we are assessed from outside our borders. My title was Secretary of State for External Affairs, and I learned first-hand how and why Canada is seen so positively in the eyes of other nations, and came to understand the impact we can have in the wider international community. Those seven years were a period of unusual activity and change in the world: the fall of the Berlin Wall; the end of apartheid; an expanding Canadian presence in Asia and Latin America; and a highly productive time in the relationship between Canada and the United States that produced major treaties on both acid rain and free trade. Canada was an active force literally around the world, from Punta del Este, to Pretoria, to Peshawar, to Paris. That incomparable assignment ended on April 21, 1991, when Prime Minister Brian Mulroney shuffled his cabinet, and I took up responsibility for constitutional affairs. Our daughter, Catherine, described it best that day when she said, "So long Paris, hello Moose Jaw."

This book draws upon lessons that I learned in Paris and in Moose Jaw, and in many places between. It is not a memoir but a reflection and a prescription—an attempt to consider who we Canadians are and have been, and an invitation to envisage what we might become in a world where Moose Jaw and Paris and Peshawar, and everywhere else, are crowding in on one another.

I will concentrate on two challenges that are becoming more imperative in the modern world, and coincidentally for which Canada possesses natural strengths. The first is to help resolve conflict before it explodes. The second is to be a catalyst of co-operation between states and the growing ranks of non-state actors, which are often better than governments at understanding problems and innovating solutions.

Clearly, this focus on these specific Canadian capacities does not constitute a whole foreign policy. We have vital economic, trade, environmental and security interests to pursue. But those broader interests are all in jeopardy if conflict thrives, or if Canada's reputation declines. Our proven skills in building partnerships and respect can again become a critical and distinguishing Canadian credential in the world that is taking shape. These qualities address the most challenging issues of the future. And they represent capacities where Canada's ranking in the world is not diminished by the economic growth and dominance of other countries. These are assets in which Canada's place is among the leaders—if we give them high priority.

In exploring Canada's challenges, I will advance and rely upon several propositions, each of which reveals what kind of country we have been, are now and could yet aspire to be.

- As a nation, Canada still enjoys a strong and positive international reputation, won first on the battlefields of two world wars and then enlarged by skill, initiative and consistency in building and respecting international institutions and co-operation in the seven decades after the Second World War.
- Behind this reputation, Canada possesses a palpable identity that distinguishes it from comparable countries, and does so to both international onlookers and our own citizens. Our characteristics as a country— diverse, respectful, constructive, modern—are significant assets that become more relevant, not less, in a turbulent, globalizing and self-consciously multicultural world. But they need to be recognized, valued and asserted or they will wither.
- The present Canadian government has aggressively narrowed Canada's official international policy to concentrate on trade and military initiatives, diluting

Canada's traditional signature contributions to both international development and multilateralism, and rejecting conciliation, most notably in the tinderbox of the Middle East. That has happened without much public discussion, and could lead to a serious slide away from Canada's tradition of international activism and influence.

- More than most nations, Canada possesses a combination of "hard power" assets—quantifiable strengths like our natural resource wealth and military power—as well as "soft power" assets—skill at managing diversity, reputation as a trusted interlocutor, capacity to conciliate. If we remain preoccupied, as we are today, with the imperatives of hard power—pursuing economic growth and developing military heft—and mute our soft power capacities, Canada's relative position in the world will decline.

- The Cold War was animated by ideology, but many of the conflicts that threaten lives and order today are rooted more basically—in the fears of different groups that their values or identities are under siege. These fears are as old as humankind, but can be inflamed more easily in an age when information travels rapidly, showing different practices, challenging sacred assumptions, creating new aspirations, stimulating anger or stirring anxiety and tension. In such a world, the ability to bridge conflicting identities and hostile groups, and patiently seek enough common ground to build trust and collaboration, is critically needed. At home and abroad, no one is better at this than Canada.

- In the past, the extent of Canada's international engagement tended to be calculated in terms of our formal or official representatives—our diplomats, armed forces and development workers. Increasingly, now, Canada's international presence is also defined by the thousands of its citizens who work abroad in non-governmental organizations (NGOS), multilateral agencies, transnational corporations, faith groups, service clubs, diaspora organizations, or as entrepreneurs or volunteers serving causes they believe in—Oxfam, Amnesty International, Greenpeace, the Bill & Melinda Gates Foundation, the Grameen Bank, thousands of NGOS. While their influence is great and growing, the actual power of these forces is limited. They can propose, but they can't decide public policy or rules: this is still an institutional world and, by definition, non-governments are rarely at the head table. So the challenge and opportunity now is to marry mandate with imagination—to combine the capacity-to-act of governments and other institutions with the creativity and scope of these independent forces.

- Canada's influence expands through alliances, and we can make more of our role in the United Nations (UN), the G20, the North Atlantic Treaty Organization (NATO) and existing alliances. But we should also look to new partnerships that could amplify Canada's and the world's capacity to anticipate and mediate deadly conflict, and imagine new responses to deep-rooted tensions and modern challenges.

- Many of Canada's own defining initiatives flowed from serious national conversations—royal commissions on cultural institutions, or health care, or free trade; first ministers conferences; parliamentary

debates and election campaigns that reached beyond
mere personalities and into the realm of ideas.
Those conversations lifted us over our usual divides
of culture and geography and specific interests. But
for two decades now, our country has gone silent.
We need to renew pan-Canadian conversations,
and a discussion of our presence in the world is
an excellent place to start.

I am conscious of the challenge presented to Canada in
1968, almost half a century ago, by the late British economist
Barbara Ward, who wrote in *Canadian Forum*:

> It is perhaps in her external relations that the greatest
> opportunities lie. Of all the middle powers, Canada has the
> greatest resources, the most central position, the finest web
> of contacts and influence and, relatively speaking, the highest
> proportion of experts . . . of any nation in the world. If all
> these advantages were used . . . to . . . develop Canada as a
> model-builder, then with the hind-sight of history . . . the
> citizens who helped re-create the world's image of itself
> might be recognized to have been citizens of Canada. . . . It
> is a truism that one person who wants something is a
> hundred times stronger than a hundred who want to be left
> alone. A Canada prepared to pioneer with lucidity and
> daring the role of the first "international nation" in history
> would not only have an immense impact on its fellow states.
> It might also transform its own political life.[2]

I

LEADING FROM BESIDE

In a single year, 1989, two huge walls came down and changed profoundly the way the world works. The famous fall was of the Berlin Wall—a physical, armed, concrete barrier, more than a hundred miles long, cutting West Berlin off entirely from East Germany, and symbolizing a Cold War that had dominated international affairs for more than four decades. On November 9, 1989, that barrier was broken and thousands of East Germans streamed into the free streets of the West, marking the end of a lethal struggle between super-powers, opening the way for a new faith in "market" econom-ics. The other was a wall no one knew was there, until it was breached by the insurgent Internet, powering a new age in which information moved instantly and everywhere. On March 13, 1989, the World Wide Web was born.[1] What a catalytic coincidence of events—in eight months, breaking the physical wall that had been the symbol of state oppression, and surmounting a wall of the mind, which launched a trans-forming instrument of individual expression.

The most immediate celebration was of the assertion of freedom in the societies of eastern and central Europe, and the death knell of the Soviet Union and its empire, after the Berlin Wall came down. But equal attention is owed to the life knell of the Internet technologies that allowed enterprise, science, social-interest groups and activists to connect creatively, reaching over traditional political and cultural boundaries, and making the world "global" in ways that were unimaginable before. Taken together, those breakthroughs transformed the lives of individuals, the nature of the world economy, the capacity to lift nearly a billion people[2] out of extreme poverty, and the traditional dynamics of international policy.

For more than four decades, two nations—the USA and the Soviet Union—and two organizations—the North Atlantic Treaty Organization of Western nations, and the Warsaw Pact, the Soviet alliance—had symbolized the deep divisions of the Cold War. In February 1990, with the totemic Berlin Wall freshly fallen, Canada hosted the first-ever meeting of foreign ministers from the member states of those two coalitions—called the Open Skies conference. I was Canada's foreign minister at the time and chaired that meeting, held among the limestone pillars and gilded arches of the retired train station in the heart of Ottawa. Our purpose was to negotiate an agreement that would authorize aerial surveillance flights by unarmed aircraft over the territory of all thirty-four nations involved.[3] The treaty that emerged was both a symbol and an instrument of the end of the rigid mutual antagonism between those previously deadly enemies. One significant and unanticipated result of that Ottawa conference was the agreement, on the margins of the meeting, on the "two plus four" formula. That agreement—between East and West Germany and the four powers that had occupied them after the Second World War (the USSR, USA, UK and France)—led six months later to the formal re-unification of Germany.[4]

But in that bright cold week in Ottawa, the telling drama

was not one of negotiating treaties and agreements; it was human. It was to watch the interaction between the Soviet foreign minister, Eduard Shevardnadze, and his counterparts from the Warsaw Pact. Within NATO, there had sometimes been disagreements, often intense, over the way the Americans led the alliance. But there was open debate, and usually a hard-won consensus. The Warsaw Pact had been much less consensual. If Washington usually prevailed in NATO, Moscow ruled in the Warsaw Pact. This was the first meeting to take place after that Soviet authority had snapped—the first meeting of a fundamentally different era.

As a person, Shevardnadze—charming, able, empathetic— was widely respected and genuinely liked by his colleagues from both sides of the wall. He was seen as a reformer. But in 1990, the high personal regard that Shevardnadze enjoyed as an individual was eclipsed by the accumulated anger and resentment of the former satellites against the Soviet centre. The Ottawa conference was the first time they had come together since the wall had come down and Moscow's dominance had crumbled along with it. I suddenly realized that one of my duties as chair—absolutely unprecedented—would be to protect the foreign minister of the Soviet Union. That was like having to protect the Rock of Gibraltar; it had never before seemed vulnerable.

Shevardnadze's predecessor—the dour, tough Andrei Gromyko—had been foreign minister for eighteen years, beginning when Stalin was still in power, and he acted with the authority of eternity. The first time I met Gromyko, in Moscow in 1985, his opening words were designed to show me my inconsequential place: "Mr. Clark, I have dealt with every Canadian foreign minister since St. Laurent" (whom Gromyko would have met when I was ten years old). The very office of Soviet foreign minister had acquired an aura of invincibility. But no more. The "satellites" of the Warsaw Pact had become states—equal in status, independent in attitude, determined to set their own course. That had also been the exuberant personal response of individual East Germans, when they had flowed through to the West. But theirs had been individual affirmations. This was power changing, history changing.

Looking back, it's easy to conclude that the Berlin Wall divided more than east from west. It divided the past from the future. Its collapse ended an era when two military powers dominated the wider world, and it opened another era, when a multitude of powers, formal and informal, found their voices, and then their authority. Parallel processes had been gaining strength in several countries. In 1960, the United Kingdom stepped back from its colonial control of states in Africa, its prime minister noting that, "The wind of change is blowing through this continent, and whether we like it or not, this growth of national consciousness is a political fact. We must all accept it as a fact, and our national policies must take account of it."[5] In 1988, in Chile, General Augusto Pinochet stepped down from his presidency after a national plebiscite in which 55 percent of Chileans voted against his continuing in office.[6] In South Africa, the momentous changes were in train that led to Nelson Mandela's release from Victor Verster Prison, and consequently to the peaceful end of apartheid. But the Berlin Wall had become the widely recognized symbol of totalitarian control, and its breaching was a catalyst and symbol of reform.

The real change, it turned out, was psychological. All across the world, people felt freer. They began to act more independently, as individuals and as communities, and to imagine futures they hadn't considered before. According to Freedom House,[7] the number of electoral democracies in the world has risen from 69 out of 167 in 1989 (41 percent of the world's countries) to 117 out of 195 in 2012 (60 percent). Those are dry statistics, but the human and political impacts are unquestionable. I have been privileged to lead international observation teams in countries where elections had previously been forbidden or rigged—the Democratic Republic of Congo (DRC) in 2006, with its first free election in over 40 years; Mexico in 1994 when the long-controlling PRI (Institutional Revolutionary Party) was defeated—and have seen for myself the exuberance and hope—the sense of worth—in the long lines of citizens suddenly empowered by the ability to cast a free vote.

In the tempestuous years since 1989, other walls have come tumbling down. Science changed the way we think about life, and possibility. On July 5, 1996, "Dolly" the sheep was the first mammal to be cloned from an adult cell. Space travel became routine. Commerce has been transformed by technology and the sheer speed of communications, facilitating "new business models, new processes, new inventions, new . . . goods and services . . . competitiveness and flexibility in the economy," to quote the Organisation for Economic Co-operation and Development (OECD).[8] The Internet had been in limited specialist use until the mid-1990s, and then blew open the world. The communications revolution that followed gave wings to profound social movements that had been building momentum for decades: notably, the demand for the rights and equality of women, and the campaign to sustain the physical environment.

Instant communication is so commonplace now that we forget the silos, slowness and separateness of the world before the 1990s. We lived literally in our own backyards, connecting rarely with ideas or events beyond our immediate reach, and had little real sense of our options or our futures. Businesses that called themselves international had huge disconnects between their head office and the field, and little "real time" capacity to consult or innovate or respond to local developments. Telehealth and distance learning were primitive or limited. Diplomats reported key international developments by telegram. Nothing was online—citizens who wanted to change repressive regimes had no knowledge of, or contact with, others who shared their hopes or anger, so there was far less capacity for an Arab Spring. Today, in a world population of 7.1 billion people, nearly one in three use the Internet or web.[9] In the words of Calestous Juma of Harvard's Belfer Center for Science and International Affairs, that has "changed the way people interact with each other and conduct business. . . . dramatically changed governance by improving transparency, accountability and communication between leaders and followers . . . [and] fundamentally expand[ed] . . . education [and health] opportunities."[10]

This is change in a rush, very different in velocity from the episodic changes of a Gutenberg and his printing press, a Ford and his Model T, even a Los Alamos. Nothing can be taken for granted. Ask ousted Egyptian president Hosni Mubarak. Ask former chairman of the Federal Reserve Alan Greenspan who, after the market collapse of 2008, told Congress: "Those of us who have looked to the self interest of lending institutions to protect shareholders' equity—myself especially—are in a state of shocked disbelief."[11] The observation of the cowboy humorist Will Rogers, almost a century ago, in another era of rapid change, has never been more telling: "It's not what people don't know that hurts them, it's what they know that ain't true."

Some of the starkest signposts of contemporary change are in the growth rates of major economies. In 1976, Japan and six Western nations—Canada, France, Germany, Italy, the UK and the US—accounted for over 60 percent of global GDP.[12] That was the year Canada was invited to join the "group of

NOTE study released in 2011   1.62 Billion Muslims in the world of which - 75% - 90% Sunni.

LEADING FROM BESIDE   15

orthodox version of ISLAM

seven" leading world economies. By 2050, according to projections by Goldman Sachs, "the United States will be the only Western [nation] to make it into the top five." It will trail a distant second behind China. Next, in order, will be India, "Euro Area," Brazil, Russia, Japan and Mexico. Canada will rank sixteenth, a little behind Egypt, a little ahead of Italy.[13]

Population 80 million
Egypt 80 million Muslim
90% Sunni
ultra majority

In *The Post-American World*, author Fareed Zakaria is careful to emphasize that the shift in power among states is not about any nation's decline, but reflects rather the rise and assertion of new forces.[14] The so-called BRIC nations (Brazil, Russia, India, China) and the combined clout of the European Union (EU) are followed by a range of other countries whose influence is pushing them toward centre stage. Think, for example, of Indonesia, Turkey and Nigeria, whose economies are all growing—and which are all resource rich, all strategically placed geographically, all with significant Muslim populations, all with strong militaries, all innovative in governance, all with ambitious and able populations: Indonesia, 246.9 million;[15] Nigeria, 168.8 million;[16] Turkey, 74.0 million.[17] All will become more effective in asserting their will as their skills and education grow.

Indonesia — 87% muslim
Sunni's 99%

NIGERIA
50% Muslim
majority
Sunni.

Turkey
96-99%
muslim
72% of those
are Sunni.

The significance of this change is not simply that *the rest* are rising. It is that the world views of many of those newly powerful nations are significantly different from that of the largely Western nations that were the architects and the active leaders, for so long, of so much of the international system, from the rules on trade, to military dominance, to the five permanent members of the Security Council who each have the power to veto actions of the United Nations. The imbalance in the Security Council makes the point. Of the five nations with a veto, three—the US, the UK and France—are at the deep roots of the West, two of them former colonial powers, the third a practiced superpower. Leaders from far outside of that Western

IRAQ   22 million   37% Sunni muslim
SYRIA   87% muslim   74% Sunni

ISIS is primarily Sunni
the Remnants of Saddam in IRAQ.

core have different views on basic issues ranging from the sanctity of the market system to concepts of human rights. If they are regarded as *emerging* powers now, their recent lineage has been as *outsiders*—unquestionably part of the world, but less powerful than their numbers would warrant. In the exercise of real international power—shaping the decisions, driving the agenda—those outsiders could have been described, in parliamentary terms, as the official opposition. They could speak, and object, and propose alternative policies, but they remained largely bystanders to power. The world's governing party, for a long time, was the Organisation for Economic Co-operation and Development, with the G8 as its cabinet, and the US as its prime minister. To extend that parliamentary analogy, the governing West has recently seen its status reduced to that of a minority government, compelled suddenly to take serious account of forces we have counted as marginal before and to consider permanent coalitions. For the time being, Western powers still lead, but, more than ever, we must act in concert with others, for the simple and inescapable reason that their collective impact is increasing, and ours is not.

If countries like Canada sit back complacently, or close our pores, the series of changes occurring today could turn out to be much more challenging, to us, than the changes that occurred when the Berlin Wall fell, or when the Second World War ended, with Europe devastated. There was a firmer consensus then on what to do, and on who would lead. Among Western nations, with their innovative nature and forward-reaching economies, the leadership of the US was asserted and accepted. It was symbolized by the breathtaking and pragmatic generosity of the Marshall Plan—the American program to rebuild Europe after the Second World War—but extended beyond that, shaping the basic architecture of a new international order, reflecting market economics and a Western view of human rights. When the Cold War ended, there were ardent proposals to turn swords to ploughshares, but that rarely happened. Instead, fuelled by technological change, the guiding priority became trade and economic growth. Western governments, Canada's included, chose to believe that trade would defeat poverty, that market models would release energies that were inherently democratic, and that the "shock and awe" of modern military technology would ensure a more orderly world. Some of the baseline certainties of a decade ago are now going or gone. For example:

- the most entrenched regimes in the Middle East have been chased from office and their successors reflect different priorities and face daunting new challenges;
- the BRIC and other nations are demonstrating that they are not just emerging economies but emerging societies with different world views and a confident determination to assert themselves;
- the nature of conflict has changed, as cultural differences become more influential and insurgents baffle modern armies;
- consensus is more difficult now, as more nations affirm their capacity to lead international initiatives, or to block them.

The dynamics of leadership have changed, because the world has changed.

Sometimes a small controversy drives home a large truth. In March 2011, as internal conflict grew in Libya, Britain and France were pushing for a Security Council resolution authorizing a "no-fly zone," which would protect civilians from further aerial attacks by the Gaddafi regime.[18] Secretary of State Hillary Clinton "insisted that the U.S. had to have

regional support before it took action" and agreed to a resolution once "U.N. action had been supported by the Arab
League."[19] She went on to say "for those who want to see the
United States always acting unilaterally, it's not satisfying. But,
for the world we're trying to build, where we have a lot of responsible actors who are willing to step up and lead, it is exactly what
we should be doing."[20] A "White House advisor"—the person
has never been named—described the American actions in
Libya as "leading from behind."[21] That provoked an outraged
reaction among conservative commentators: "appeasing those
who revile us";[22] "abdicating";[23] "leaving our destiny at the
mercy of events."[24] President Obama realized that "leading
from behind" fails the testosterone test, and quickly disavowed
that language. But while the phrase was unfortunate, the facts
are indisputable. As power disperses in the world, so does the
capacity to lead—and, in almost every case, the most effective
leadership will have to be shared, not only among states, but
with other entities and, often, with citizens. For all nations in
virtually every conflict, the model now should be "leading from
beside," combining the different assets of different partners to
achieve common goals.

In 1990, Harvard professor Joseph Nye identified a crucial
element of this type of leadership when he coined the phrase
"soft power."[25] He defined it as "getting others to want the
outcomes that you want. . . . [A] country may obtain the
results it wants in world politics because other countries—
admiring its values, emulating its example, aspiring to its level
of prosperity and openness—want to follow it."[26] Nye argues
that the soft power of a country "rests primarily on three
sources: its culture (in places where it is attractive to others),
its political values (when it lives up to them at home and
abroad), and its foreign policies (when they are seen as legitimate and having moral authority)."[27] On their own, Canada's

reputation and example constitute significant soft power assets. And they can operate, in compelling partnership, with the hard assets of our economic and military strength to yield a sum that is much greater than its parts—and which make Canada a desirable partner for international initiatives.

This concept of "leading from beside" is crucial to Canada and Canadians. Co-operation is a Canadian practice and instinct, and is the way we have often met challenges, at home and abroad. Internationally, it inspired our signature commitment to building multilateral institutions, and was at the heart of the concept of peacekeeping, which Canada championed and made work after the Suez Crisis. That mentality is even more relevant in this present period where the power of persuasion is often more potent than the power of arms. From Vietnam on, and in Afghanistan most recently, it has become evident that wars are virtually impossible to win by military means alone; Iraq demonstrated that high-tech weapons of "shock and awe" don't change that equation. Indeed, one of the ways Canada "led from beside" in Afghanistan was to deliberately draw together the different strengths of defence, diplomacy and development—the "three Ds"—which have together defined Canada's international policy. As Edouard Shevardnadze discovered in the Ottawa conference, and as Secretary Clinton recognized in seeking the support of the Arab League on Libya, no nation is powerful enough now to command consensus, or lead alone. Citizens in this Internet age are less docile and compliant. They unearth and determine the facts on their own, create communities that reach across national and traditional boundaries, and pursue their interests adamantly, often contesting those who presume to speak for them. In every sphere, power has changed, and so must the way that we exercise power.

2

SOFT POWER

AND HARD POWER

Canada ranks today among the world's most successful countries. We are a member of the G8 group of the world's largest "free market" economies and of the enlarged and new G20, which includes Brazil, China, India, Indonesia and other emerging economies. The Canadian troop contribution to Afghanistan was one of the largest in NATO, and our forces regularly undertook the most perilous and dangerous missions. Our "quality of life" is ranked among the highest in the world by the OECD,[1] trailing only Australia and Sweden. Economically, Canada is ranked the fourteenth most competitive economy[2] on the globe, and for five years in a row, the Canadian banking system has been rated the strongest in the world by the World Economic Forum.[3] Transparency International's Corruption Perceptions Index ranks Canada the ninth least corrupt of the 176 nations it assessed.[4] The state of our democracy is ranked eighth out of 167 countries.[5] The World Economic Forum ranks Canada seventh for health and primary education and fifteenth for higher education and training.[6]

Some other signs are more troubling. Canada's Human Development Index ranking recently slipped as low as sixteenth when account was taken of "internal inequalities in health, education and income."[7] That is due in no small part to the widespread poverty and inequality of Canadian aboriginal communities. On child poverty, the Conference Board of Canada ranks us fifteenth out of seventeen "peer countries," and notes a worsening trend, stating that "more than one in seven Canadian children live in poverty."[8] It gives Canada an equally poor ranking on the environment, citing Canada's poor record specifically on "climate change, energy intensity, smog, and waste generation."[9] In 2011, the OECD found "Canada still lags behind in productivity performance, ranking in the bottom half of OECD countries."[10] In 2012, Bank of Canada governor Mark Carney warned that "since 2000, Canada's export growth. . . . has been the second worst in the G20," trailing only the UK, largely because "our exports are concentrated in slow-growing advanced economies, particularly the United States, rather than fast-growing emerging markets."[11]

But resolving even the most stubborn of those problems is within our reach. Canada has an extraordinary combination of wealth and capacity. We can do things other countries can't, including some of the powerful emerging societies—China, India, Brazil—whose problems of internal adjustment may prove as big as their potential for growth,[12] and including some established Western countries, whose institutions and confidence have been severely shaken.[13] We can be much stronger than our population size, or economic growth rate—if we choose to refine and invest Canada's full range of assets and advantages. In a globalized, Internet age, that must happen in our international policy, as much as our domestic. Yet we are devaluing, and putting at risk the soft power that has so effectively bolstered our strong international reputation and contributed to our traditional capacity for leadership.

Some of the most significant changes introduced by the government of Stephen Harper have been in international policy, often with scant public discussion or debate. Changes in domestic policy attract more attention in Canada, and voters focus most strongly on issues that affect them directly. But if international issues are relatively less visible, they are highly important to Canadians: for example, questions of climate change, whether distant conflicts explode into violence and spread, how pandemics and crime and terrorism are confronted, whether the world's economy will slow or grow.

Taken together, Canada's current international policies mark much more fundamental changes in our relations with the rest of the world than usually occur when a new federal government comes into office.

Every two years, the leaders of 54 very different countries gather at the Commonwealth Heads of Government Meeting (CHOGM). These countries range from tiny Tuvalu in the Pacific with 10,000 citizens, to India, with more than a billion, and include some of the world's most developed countries—Britain, Canada, Australia—and some of its poorest—Mozambique, Sierra Leone. The link between these widely divergent Commonwealth nations is the legal and political tradition rooted in democracy's first charter, the Magna Carta, and then spread around the world. CHOGM discussions often reflect the frankness and familiarity of a family and, at its best (for example in the campaign against apartheid) the Commonwealth of Nations is a compelling example of "leading from beside," respecting and mobilizing vastly different capacities.

In August 1979, External Affairs Minister Flora MacDonald and I represented Canada in the CHOGM in Lusaka, the capital of Zambia. At the end of the first day's discussion, the president of Zambia, Kenneth Kaunda, who chaired those meetings in his country, said privately to me: "I'm surprised that the positions you are taking are very similar to those which Mr. Trudeau took." I replied, "Naturally they are. We represent the same country."

Historically, there have only been a few significant differences on foreign policy between the two national political parties— Liberal and Progressive Conservative—that formed governments in Canada through the twentieth century. The Suez Crisis was one example, where leading Progressive Conservatives accused the St. Laurent government of "knif[ing] Canada's best friends [the UK and France] in the back";[14] conscription, another; and the "free trade" elections of 1911 and 1988. But those were dramatic exceptions; the rule has been a high degree of continuity in the policy and approach of different Canadian governments to international policy across a wide spectrum: multilateralism, collective security, human rights, international development, freer trade, the environment, close co-operation with the United States, serious engagement with China, a balanced role in the Middle East, active support of the United Nations and other international organizations, and partnership with civil society and NGOs.

Some significant political parties that did not form governments—the CCF/NDP, the Progressives, the Bloc Québécois— advocated distinctive positions on membership in NATO,[15] or other security or defence issues, or social justice, but vigorously supported other aspects of Canada's foreign policy consensus. International issues were not prominent in the evolution of the Reform/Alliance party, or in the "merger" that created the present Conservative Party of Canada.

In the six decades after the end of the Second World War, this country's international policy was *Canadian*, not partisan. After his election in 1957, and despite his discomfort with some Foreign Service officers whom he deemed "pearsonalities," Prime Minister Diefenbaker pursued the same international principles and policies that had guided Prime Minister St. Laurent—a little more aggressive with the Americans, more nostalgic toward the British, more assertive against apartheid, but reinforcing and enhancing the established "Canadian position," and planting several seeds that blossomed into distinctive policy under later governments, including the opening of large grain sales to China and the creation of the External Aid Office,[16] which in 1968 became the Canadian International Development Agency (CIDA). In January 1963, the Liberal Party under Lester Pearson clearly embraced the acquisition of nuclear warheads[17]—which had divided, and helped defeat, the Diefenbaker government[18]— but basic attitudes toward international development, security alliances, the Cold War and other foreign policy changed only in degree. In 1979, my government may have been more emphatic and innovative in opening Canada's doors to the "boat people" cast adrift to die by Vietnam, but that initiative had begun with a Trudeau minister.[19] In 1984, the Mulroney government gave more priority to relations with the United States than its Liberal predecessors, but also vigorously enhanced Canada's activist reputation in the Americas, Africa and Asia. In 1993, despite the overwhelming electoral loss by the Progressive Conservative Party, Prime Minister Chrétien continued the major international initiatives of the Mulroney government, adding only environmental and labour clauses to NAFTA, maintaining a leading role on international environmental issues, and remaining engaged and creative in the Americas.

In fact, the transition that most seriously questioned established Canadian policy occurred after Pierre Trudeau took the
place of his Nobel Prize–winning predecessor, Lester Pearson
as leader of the Liberal Party in 1968. Mr. Trudeau "questioned the department's attachment to Pearsonian internationalism and demanded a foreign policy rooted in a more limited,
often economic notion of the national interest."[20] He appointed
Ivan Head, a member of his own staff, as his foreign policy
advisor, a "'Mini-Kissinger' competing with the country's diplomats."[21] In the event, the Trudeau government's significant
innovations—like the diplomatic recognition of China, and
the "north-south dialogue" between wealthy and developing
countries—were firmly in the tradition of that Pearsonian
internationalism. Pierre Trudeau enlivened Canada's image in
the world, but foreign policy ended up, by and large, where it
had begun. Over the course of sixty years, from 1945 to 2006,
issues, personalities and priorities changed, but there was a
general continuity in Canada's approach to world affairs.

Significant continuity remains today on the so-called "hard"
issues—international economic policy, trade, continental security,
even military policy. The government's signature international
priority has been military. But even there, what is distinct is not
so much the policy of military engagement in Afghanistan—
that decision was taken by the Chrétien government—but
rather the much higher levels of spending, profile and priority
assigned to the military side of Canada's role in the world.
Canadian international policy was once characterized by a
rough balance among diplomacy, trade, defence and development, with diplomacy usually in a lead role. Today, defence
has been placed decisively in the lead of that quartet, with
trade next, while the roles of diplomacy and development
have declined sharply.

The distinction between hard power and soft power was

coined in 1990; but, for most of the last half century, Canadian foreign policy regularly combined both. That ended after 2006. One of the current government's defining characteristics has been a sharp turn away from the soft power assets that had helped earn Canada's respected reputation in international affairs. This has been a consistent pattern, reaching across a range of major issues.

- International development: The basic purpose of Canadian development assistance—popularly called "foreign aid"—was changed from addressing poverty to promoting trade. Some of the world's poorest nations,[22] such as Niger and Rwanda, were removed from the "countries of focus" of what was then CIDA, in favour of countries like Peru and Honduras, where trade or commercial interests are stronger.[23] The share of Canada's gross national income directed to foreign aid has fallen to half its peak level in 1986–87[24] and will reach only a projected 0.25 percent in 2015.[25] That moves Canada away from the focus on fighting poverty and encouraging human development, which still guides the international agendas of the Dutch, the Nordics, the British,[26] the Americans[27] and other Western nations with whom Canada once stood in the vanguard of international development. The *coup de grace* was the elimination in March 2013 of CIDA—the stand-alone development agency— which for forty-five years had symbolized Canada's multi-partisan commitment to international develop-ment,[28] and whose mandate had been steadily eroded before the agency was absorbed into the newly named Department of Foreign Affairs, Trade and Development.

- The environment: In the 1980s and 1990s, Canada was regarded as a leader on international environmental issues. Today, our country has become the first nation in the developed world to withdraw from the Kyoto Protocol on climate change;[29] the only member of the United Nations to announce its withdrawal from an international agreement to fight drought, which earlier Canadian governments had vigorously supported and promoted;[30] and is often divisive and derided in international environmental discussions.[31]

  Earlier Canadian governments had been praised for environmental leadership—at Rio de Janeiro in 1994[32] and Montreal in 2005.[33] Now, at consecutive climate change conferences, international environmental organizations regularly name Canada "Fossil of the Day," designating "countries that do the most to disrupt or undermine UN climate talks."[34]

- Peacekeeping: At the same time that our war-fighting capacity was deployed extensively in Afghanistan, Canada's involvement in the equally critical military role of peacekeeping continued to decline. Historically, Canada was often the single largest contributor of troops to United Nations peacekeeping operations. In 2013, we ranked 58th[35] Yet the demand for effective international peacekeeping grows. There is an acute need for troops with sophisticated training to use their advanced military capacity as "force multipliers," able to buttress the physical presence of soldiers from other countries. France, Germany and Italy have been responding to that need for leadership on the ground.[36] The emphasis on active combat has pushed Canada's peacekeeping tradition virtually out of sight.

- The United Nations and multilateralism: Canada officially describes the United Nations as an "indispensable global organization for a globalizing world,"[37] and goes on to say "Canada continues to uphold the UN by actively participating in the organization's activities and providing financial support."[38] In fact, ministers of the current government are uncomfortable with the United Nations, and sometimes hostile to it. Instead of leading internal reforms to the organization, Canadian ministers have made a point of leading opposition to the UN—boycotting conferences they call "hatefests,"[39] withdrawing from important UN agreements, like those on climate change and drought relief, threatening "all available next steps" when Canada loses a vote on Palestine in the General Assembly.[40] When the national leaders of other countries attended the UN General Assembly in 2009, Prime Minister Harper made a point of going instead to the Tim Horton's Innovation Centre in Oakville,[41] and then, in 2012, travelling to midtown Manhattan during a General Assembly meeting, but bypassing the United Nations to receive an award from an interfaith group.[42] That disdain for multilateralism was evident from the government's early days,[43] and was only reinforced when Canada was defeated in its 2010 bid to be elected to the Security Council.[44] This attitude is not specific to the UN but is also reflected in a generally passive presence in other multilateral organizations like the Commonwealth, La Francophonie and the Organization of American States (OAS), where Canada has previously been an active leader.

That sharp preference for hard power over soft power is a curious attitude for our times. Almost no one denies the need for organized police or military force in this age of conflict, but fighting modern wars is futile unless it is accompanied by winning "hearts and minds," addressing root causes of conflict, and building the prospects for durable peace. In the private sector, increasing numbers of corporate leaders accept that the "bottom line" is more than merely economic, and has to include, at the least, healthier communities and sustainable environments. Institutions that seek to bind communities together—from governments to religious bodies—have to rely increasingly on dialogue, not deference, for their authority.

Compared to many other nations, Canada was a forerunner in the capacity to blend and balance different kinds of assets in international affairs. There were two reasons, principally. One was necessity: there were clear limits to our hard power, whether economic or military, compared with the US, the Soviet Union and several others. But the other reason was our nature—our experience, success and example as a community built by consensus and inclusion. That balance in attitude and in capacity became our trademark, part of our distinction—long before the terms "hard" and "soft" power came into vogue. The question is: why would a government of Canada dilute that particular trademark and reputation at precisely the time when other nations are moving to the model where Canada had become a forerunner?

Canada has choices in foreign policy. Those choices make a difference, precisely because we are a strong, successful and potentially influential country. We start with a much stronger hand than the great majority of other nations. Our options should include two basic tests: first, will a policy add to, or subtract from, the inherent value of Canada's distinctive assets; and, second, will it invest those assets creatively, in ways that add measurably to human progress and security?

The current government's movement away from Canada's soft power assets has grown more pronounced with each year in office. There is every reason to believe this view of Canada reflects the heartfelt and deep convictions of at least the prime minister and whichever colleagues or associates constitute his most trusted advisors. But these changes occurred with little public—or, for that matter, parliamentary—discussion or attention. There is no question that they reflect a significantly different view of Canada. There are, however, real questions as to whether this is a direction that Canadians would have chosen had the option been put to them in clear terms, and whether it is the appropriate policy for a country with our strengths in a complex and troubled world.

3

SEEING MORE

AND FEELING LESS

During the Cold War, the sense of threat was pervasive. With nuclear weapons in play, the target was everywhere. In retrospect, it seems bizarre that North Americans would actually build and stock a bomb shelter in their basement or backyard. But that is what happened, because the threat was personal, likely to strike you and your family at home, not a symbolic Twin Tower or strategic Pentagon far away. Now, when terrorist threat levels are high, we might postpone a trip to the airport, but we won't hustle our kids and our emergency rations into a hole in the ground. Like so many things that have changed since the Cold War, the external threats Canadians face today are real but not necessarily personal.

Some of those changes have been so dramatic and so frequent that we are tempted to focus on their details, like the rate of GDP growth in a developing nation, rather than the direct impact on the aspiration and innovation of millions of people who are suddenly able to do more than merely survive; or the contagious frustration of others still caught in poverty who see new wealth around them and become envious or angry; or the nationalist aspirations, the muscle-flexing, of nations themselves, who feel suddenly empowered and can now indulge pride and ambition that had long been curtailed. We tabulate the number of authoritarian regimes that have been toppled or threatened—Tunisia, Egypt, Libya, Yemen; 1, 2, 3, 4—almost as casually as sports fans check last night's scores. But this is not a game. More to the point, none of us are spectators. We are all on the field, sharing unprecedented opportunities and accomplishments—from the International Space Station to exploration of the oceans' depths—but also pandemics, financial crises, climate change and the instability and ambition that can incite neighbouring nations to seek nuclear arms.

Western publics respond to crisis differently than we did before modern media channelled so much outrage, protest and violence, every day and instantly, into our lives and consciousness. That drumbeat of violent images intensifies our exposure, but almost anaesthetizes our responses. I'm old enough to remember a phonograph recording—a phonograph recording!—of radio news reports filed from battlegrounds in the Second World War by CBS correspondent Edward R. Murrow.[1] The phrase that distinguished those reports was "You are there," and Murrow's skill was to instill in his listeners, in a North America remote from the fighting, the sense of actually hearing the bombs dropping, the troops marching, the world changing. There was nothing else like it—not in the daily lives of North Americans at home, not in the images or impressions they received from other media. Today, we see more and feel less, because the recurrent images of tragedy—actual tragedy—are so frequent as to seem commonplace. And "we" are not "there." So many dramatic events flash across our ubiquitous screens, yet life seems to go on largely as it had before.[2]

But our lives are not as they were before. The same media

that might tranquilize Western audiences can mobilize populations in the developing world to seek change themselves. And the flip side of uprisings against oppressive regimes is the lifting of a billion people out of poverty, or the erosion of the advantages that were previously enjoyed—indeed, seen as a matter of right—by nations and individuals who benefited from the old status quo. Some benefited directly, like the recently fallen elites in the Middle East and North Africa once did. Others benefited indirectly, like Western nations who thought their oil supplies were secure, or established industries that had never faced competition from "offshore," or like Israel's leaders and advocates who depended on their modus vivendi with authoritarian Arab leaders to contain the anger roused in the Arab streets by the plight of the Palestinians.

Another change: we live in an age when citizens can't be kept out of public decisions.

Before the Arab Spring came revolution in Hungary, Czechoslovakia, Poland, Romania and other countries of the former Eastern bloc—all changes rooted in the deep desire of citizens to have some control over their future. Those instincts will only intensify in a period of catalytic growth in information, education, confidence, and compelling contemporary examples of regimes and attitudes that have been forced to change. If citizens, aware through technology of the world's heights of wealth and individual freedoms, are shut out of decisions, their recourse will be opposition, not acquiescence. That is especially true in societies where the population is young, and without work, and able to be mobilized. If nothing else, simple prudence dictates that societies find ways to work with that citizen instinct and seek to channel it on actual reform. That course is also more than prudent or defensive; it is the best guarantee of developing modern social structures and public policy in ways that citizens might respect—critical, a Canadian might say, to "peace, order and good government."

An early result of this move toward citizen independence has been referred to as a "decline of deference."[3] This phenomenon has changed profoundly the traditional authority of our bedrock institutions—governments, churches, banks—and of such ingrained practices as the routine discrimination against women.[4] We've come a long way. But if the extent of some of those changes is significant, so is the degree of institutional resistance to deep change. By definition, institutions provide order, predictability, a reliable framework. Traditionally, in the disappearing past, successful institutions would accommodate modest change at the margins, but remain inherently protective of what they saw as their purpose and prerogatives. This resistance has specific implications for public institutions— governments, parliaments, courts, police forces and armies.

A private company that resists change can be replaced by a competitor and the system will chug along, because those companies are only a component of that system, not its custodian, not its core, not its embodiment. More is at stake when public institutions lose their authority—and the reality today is that more of those institutions, in more parts of the world, are losing the respect and standing that give them legitimacy. Egypt is one example; but, witness the difficulty throughout the Middle East and North Africa of harmonizing the revolutionary instincts behind the Arab Spring into coalitions able to govern. And there is a quieter drama, more widespread—the gradual erosion of the legitimacy of democratic governance, including in countries whose models of governance have been the most celebrated, and whose examples we routinely recommend to societies emerging from authoritarian regimes. We see it in

- the US, the most admired model—"government of . . . by . . . for the people"—where the most central democratic institutions appear implacably incapable of compromise;
- the UK, the most durable model, source of the Magna Carta and the "mother of parliaments," torn more frequently now by disorder in its streets;
- India, the largest democracy, which is debilitated by massive and endemic corruption;
- even Canada, where the prime minister prorogued parliament in December 2008 to avoid accountability and defeat.

One of the most profound new factors in this changing world is the rising role of cultural identity in lethal conflict. If the Cold War was animated by ideology, many of the upheavals that threaten lives and order today are rooted in the perceived, or real, threat to identity. Everywhere—from the contested grazing lands of Darfur, to the congested cities of Brazil or China, to most of Canada's major cities, different groups with different languages or traditions are increasingly drawn together, either virtually or directly and physically, living in the same territory, advancing competing claims, potentially alarmed or offended by different practices or cultures, and sensing their basic values or vital interests are threatened. Tensions like that are much easier to manage in Canada, with our wealth, opportunity and security, and it would be foolish to assume that our relative success can be transferred easily to more contentious societies. But our example and experience can help in more difficult places.

I don't subscribe to the idea of an inevitable clash of civilizations. In fact, one of the most important examples bilingual, multicultural Canada offers the world is precisely that diverse cultures can work together, to mutual advantage. But frictions and flashpoints are inevitable. If Cold War conflict was often contained by the same superpowers that drove it, today's conflicts can metastasize quickly, as in Iraq, Afghanistan, Libya and Syria. The Cold War mindset required to navigate an ideological conflict between two economic and military superpowers cannot successfully navigate the fears and grievances of different groups who perceive their interests and very identities to be under threat. That challenge is multiplied as these grievances are so often rooted locally but expressed transnationally. The issue now—the talent needed now—is the ability to identify shared interests between conflicting identities and hostile groups, patiently seeking enough common ground to build a truce, build some trust, and start talking.

4

CANADA'S INTERNATIONAL

HISTORY AND TRADITION

No one expected Canada to become an independent influence in international affairs. Sir John A. Macdonald, the visionary architect of Confederation, spoke for his generation in saying: "A British subject I was born; a British subject I will die."[1] We saw ourselves more as a colony than as a country, our only territorial ambition to fill our own space—to create a transcontinental country. Yet this domestically oriented country became a nation that has made a very significant contribution to the international community, in diplomacy, on the battlefield, in international development and, most fundamentally, through the international engagement of our citizens. Since 2005, the polling organizations GlobeScan[2] and PIPA (Progam on International Policy Attitudes) have conducted a "country ratings poll" for the BBC. It asks respondents around the world to rate whether the influence of several countries is "mostly negative" or "mostly positive." In 2012, that scientific sampling of 24,090 people in 22 quite different nations[3] ranked the relative influence of each of sixteen countries—Brazil, Canada, China, France, Germany, India, Iran, Israel, Japan, North Korea, Pakistan, Russia, South

Africa, South Korea, the UK, the US—and the European Union. In the category of countries whose influence was seen as "mostly positive," Canada placed third, behind Japan and Germany.[4]

How and why did Canada acquire that high reputation? In our colonial stage, we had no independent international standing and, for a long time, sought none—it was no accident we called Britain and France "mother" countries. Nations usually evolve gradually, but in our first century two watershed events changed the way Canada viewed its role in the world—the First World War, during which enormous Canadian casualties led to a direct role in negotiating the peace, and the resolution of the Suez Crisis, a Canadian solution that became a symbol of our country's new international capacity.

The First World War killed or wounded over two hundred thousand Canadians and seriously threatened Confederation, yet it also marked a significant step toward Canadian sovereignty and a more independent identity. Canada's population in 1914 was a little under eight million. From 1914 through 1918, more than 600,000 of those citizens enlisted with the Canadian Expeditionary Force, and approximately 424,000 were sent overseas, 59,544 of whom died during the war. An additional 1,500 died serving in other forces, and more than 170,000 Canadians were wounded.[5] It is noteworthy that the great majority of those volunteers were Canadians who had been born in the British Isles. They constituted only 10 percent of the total Canadian population in 1914, but "by the armistice in 1918, [accounted for] nearly half of all Canadians who served during the war."[6] Many other Canadians, from across the country, did not volunteer, including a disproportionate number of French-speaking Canadians. As the war intensified, and voluntary enrolment fell, Prime Minister Robert Borden concluded that conscription—forced service—was necessary, and called the "conscription election" of 1917. His new Unionist

Party coalition won a solid majority, but not in Quebec. "The result," to quote historian Dr. Serge Durflinger, "was profound alienation in French Canada."[7]

As the war was ending, the prime ministers of Canada, Australia, India, New Zealand and South Africa, "who had once tiptoed reverentially around the mother country,"[8] insisted on a role in the peace that was commensurate to their sacrifice in war. They "had seen too much of what . . . Borden called the 'incompetence and blundering stupidity of the whiskey and soda British h.q. staff' . . . [and] were infuriated . . . that the British [were going] . . . to settle the German armistice terms . . . without bothering to inform the dominions."[9] Borden wrote his wife that the British considered Canada "a nation that is not a nation. It is about time to alter it."[10] The result was that Britain, Canada and the other "dominions" attended the historic Paris Peace Conference together as members of a "British empire delegation." It was a landmark step toward Canadian sovereignty. And finally, in 1931, the passage of the Statute of Westminster in the British Parliament formally established Canada's independent voice in world affairs.[11]

Decades later, particularly after the Second World War, Canada put to good and innovative use its newly won international voice. The Suez Crisis in 1956 and the creation of international peacekeeping that the crisis engendered became symbols to the world of Canada's considerable ability to contribute to the solution of global problems.

After the first Arab-Israeli War, in 1948, the UN had established its small United Nations Truce Supervision Organization (UNTSO) in Palestine. Nationalist and anti-colonial sentiment had been rising in the Arab world, and in 1952 Egyptian General Gamal Abdel Nasser and his forces overthrew their country's monarchy. In June 1956, General Nasser was officially elected the first president of the new republic of Egypt.

A month later, he announced the nationalization of the Suez Canal, which had been owned by British and French interests, and provided the colonial powers with a significant commercial and strategic link between the Mediterranean Sea and the Indian Ocean. Egypt also closed the canal to Israeli shipping.

In late October, Israel bombed and invaded Egypt, followed closely by British and French forces. Their combined troops occupied large swaths of Egyptian territory. The invasion was sharply criticized by most of the world, including President Eisenhower of the United States. On November 6, 1956, strong international pressure forced a withdrawal. By this time, UNTSO's chief of staff was Canadian lieutenant-general E.L.M. Burns, a veteran of both world wars.[12]

A critical factor in Britain's withdrawal was Canada's proposal to create a buffer zone, which would be policed by a new United Nations Emergency Force (UNEF). Canada's foreign minister, Lester Pearson, proposed and negotiated that first UN peacekeeping force. General Burns was invited by UN Secretary-General Dag Hammarskjöld to organize that force and become its first commander. Canada's leading diplomat and our leading soldier combined their skill and influence to become the principal architects of the new idea of United Nations peacekeeping.

Diplomatic innovations are rarely singular and, in the critical days between invasion and withdrawal, Canadian officials worked closely with counterparts from the United States, Britain and others in formulating the UNEF plan.[13] Nonetheless, Canada's standing and skill were at centre stage when the world moved from crisis to compromise. As significantly, we were more than the innovators of an idea—*we made the new idea work*, and created an institution that would calm dozens of crises[14] and save thousands of lives in years to come.

When Mr. Pearson was awarded the Nobel Peace Prize for

his, and Canada's, critical role, the Nobel Committee noted that "never, since the end of the last war, has the world situation been darker than during the Suez crisis, and never has the United Nations had a more difficult case to deal with."[15] The Suez Crisis became a symbol of Canadian diplomacy and, by any standard, successful innovation. And our response enhanced Canada's standing among our allies as a country that punches above its weight.

A different but related "Suez factor" has helped shape Canada's reputation in the developing world. Starting with the Suez Crisis we played a leading and consistent role in peacekeeping around the world. Canadian soldiers—over 125,000 to date[16]—came to represent stability, and often rare hope, in conflicted societies from Kashmir to Congo, from Indochina to Cyprus, from Central America to Angola to Yemen.[17] In many of these countries, across Africa, Asia and the Americas, that peacekeeping role confirmed a positive Canadian reputation that had been seeded generations before by Canadian missionaries and teachers, whose presence was characterized by personal interest or commitment, not by colonial or imperial design.

Though the Statute of Westminster formally established Canada's independent voice in 1931, during the 1920s and '30s it was not often a voice we raised. In each of Britain, the us and Canada, the public reflex after a brutal war was to count losses and put domestic interests first. The war ended nearly nine years of Borden's rule in Canada, as well as Woodrow Wilson's Democratic era in the us, and led to four different governments in a decade in the United Kingdom. For Mackenzie King, who came to dominate Canadian politics during the next thirty years, the clear lesson was that foreign engagements would fracture unity at home.

Borden's goal had been to assert Canada's autonomy from Britain, but there was no taste in his young country for an activist international role. On the contrary, Canada turned viscerally away from "the feuds and fears" of Europe.[18] Canada was a signatory to the League of Nations, but wanted "a league that is a *method* of diplomacy and is not an *institution* with fighting compacts."[19] Canada sought vigorously to delete Article X, which would require all member states to come to the aid of another member if it were attacked.[20] The most dramatic phrase of that period of Canada's life was uttered by senator Raoul Dandurand, speaking for Canada to the League of Nations in 1924: "We think in terms of peace, while Europe, an armed camp, thinks in terms of war. . . . We live in a fire-proof house, far from inflammable materials. A vast ocean separates us from Europe."[21]

Two forces weighed heavily on our thinking at the time—one was the brutal memory of huge losses of Canadian life during the Great War, and the second, the growing power and attractiveness of Canada's neighbour. If the death toll and distaste for the "whiskey and soda British" amounted to a push away from old Europe, the same war that had devastated Europe had generated growth and ingenuity in the United States. By 1929 the Americans were building an "international financial centre. . . . [holding] more than 30 per cent . . . of the world's long-term investments."[22] Some of that American investment spurred the growth of Canadian natural resource and manufacturing industries, and Canadians were in turn drawn to the vitality of American society, media and universities.

Successive Canadian governments focused on building Canada's strengths within its own borders—regional rail lines were consolidated into the Canadian National Railway;

and manufacturing grew in the Windsor–Toronto–Montreal corridor. The most influential official of that period, Deputy Minister of External Affairs O.D. Skelton, believed that "the foreign affairs of every country . . . took place mainly at the fence lines that separated it from its neighbours, and largely arose from everyday matters of trade and economics." Therefore, Canada's "foreign policy ought to concentrate on the United States [rather than the] deeply entrenched British connection."[23]

Skelton drew able people, with broader views, to Canada's foreign service, but cautious Mr. King resisted creating "more foreign missions . . . partly . . . because his diplomats might find trouble abroad, getting him into trouble at home. Nor, more fundamentally, would the prime minister take the steps that were needed to separate Canada once and for all from Britain and its interests."[24]

Internally, Canada changed dramatically between the two world wars, from the growth and innovation of the 1920s, through the desperation of the Depression. New instruments of nationhood were established. Citizens became more active in their own society, through caisses populaires and credit unions, farm and labour organizations, and new political parties. Internationally, however, the country with the second largest land mass in the world was still barely on the map. Sometimes our citizens were active in the world, as missionaries, teachers or traders, but not often Canada's government. McGill University professor of military and political history Desmond Morton refers to Mackenzie King's "eternal 'no' in external relations and defence."[25]

The Second World War changed that. Canada mobilized more than a million men and women in full-time duty, and Canadian soldiers, sailors and airmen played significant and visible roles in the war. Our manufacturing industries were stimulated and reshaped by the heavy demand for both military and civilian goods, and our public service was focused and effective. Our international networks were enlarged as Canada opened trade or diplomatic posts in more than forty countries across Europe, Asia and Latin America.

But in terms of shaping strategy and decisions, we were still a junior partner, first, as usual, to the British and then, after Pearl Harbor, to the Americans as well. The US was still *the* North American power. That had been demonstrated sharply in August 1941, when British Prime Minister Winston Churchill and US President Franklin Delano Roosevelt met on warships off the coast of Newfoundland to draft the Atlantic Charter. They did not invite Canada, whose troops were fighting and dying in Europe, and would soon be on their way to Hong Kong. Dalhousie political science professor Denis Stairs explains that Prime Minister King "saw little point . . . in attempting to carve out for Canada a special place of influence in the councils of the great. . . . [he wanted] a visible recognition and acknowledgement of Canada's economic and military contribution . . . [but not] . . . a share in the responsibility for making significant strategic and political decisions, bearing on the conduct of the allied campaign."[26]

Canadian armed forces fought valiantly and impressively, and Canada's involvement in Allied strategic decisions increased as the war went on. But "Canada suffered a loss of status. It was no longer one of Britain's most important allies but a junior partner in a great power coalition. From now on, the war was to be run largely by Britain, the United States and the Soviet Union."[27] History, and then size, ordained that we would be a partner, not a power. But a partner of increasing capacity and influence, able to play a larger role in the post-war world, a period when much of Europe, and significant parts of Asia, lay in ruins.

By 1945 our economy and general capacity were much stronger than they had been in 1939. Moreover, the dynamics of international relations had also changed, to focus on reconstruction, whether that was the physical rebuilding of devastated countries, or the establishment of new mechanisms of co-operation. Where the six years of war had wreaked havoc, the rest of the 1940s saw the rise of international institutions that would shape the rest of the century: in June 1945, fifty-one countries, including Canada, signed the charter creating the United Nations; in December 1945, the Bretton Woods Agreement created the World Bank and the International Monetary Fund; in January 1948, the General Agreement on Tariffs and Trade (GATT), which later became the World Trade Organization (WTO), was signed into international law; in April 1949, twelve countries, including Canada, signed the North Atlantic Treaty, thus founding NATO; in April 1949, the London Declaration transformed the old British empire into the modern Commonwealth of Nations.

While larger countries drove those reforms, Canadians played significant roles in their negotiations and agreements. John Humphrey, New Brunswicker and professor at McGill University, was the principal author of the UN's Universal Declaration of Human Rights, adopted in December 1948. Dana Wilgress of Vancouver, trade commissioner and ambassador, served as the first chair of the contracting parties of the GATT. Louis St. Laurent is credited with drafting the London Declaration, defining a commonwealth and ending an empire. Lester Pearson was one of NATO's "three wise men"[28] who recommended practical measures to renew co-operation in an alliance strained by the Suez Crisis. And Canada insisted on Article 2 of the North Atlantic Treaty, adding political consultation to a mandate that had previously been only military. The former colony had become an active international partner in a post-war world where, in the words of historian Greg Donaghy, "there was much more room for initiatives by Canada,"[29] but we were also forced to face our own vulnerability in any future global conflict.

"North American geography no longer provided much in the way of real protection," Donaghy continues. "Canada sat squarely on the air routes between the Soviet Union and the United States. . . . prudence alone dictated a more active foreign policy."[30] The policy that emerged was more prudent than activist, but it marked a significant departure from the general caution and insularity of the 1930s, and the colonial deference of earlier decades. Denis Stairs characterizes the Canada of that time as "a status quo power of modest capacity. . . . [whose leaders gave] constant attention to the pragmatic task of identifying the available room for manoeuvre."[31] In fact, while Canadian capacity might be "modest" in its breadth and its budget, there were specific interests and issues in which we had an unusual potential to contribute. In the early 1940s, Canada pursued what it called a "functional principle," which argued that a country should have international "decision-making responsibilities" on issues where it "had made, or was willing to make . . . material contributions."[32] In other words, where Canadians make a difference, we should also make decisions. "Functionalism reinforced the view that multilateral institutions were particularly useful for . . . Canada."[33] We weren't a major power, but this was a different world, where there was strength in numbers, and new ways arose to influence international policy. There would be more doors to open, and more countries with keys.

As the Second World War gave way to the Cold War, Washington's instincts were moving along a spectrum from "isolation" to "superpower," its public and leaders alarmed by the threat of the Soviet Union. Canada's huge territory sat—directly and alone—between the contesting superpowers. Our interests were far more compelling than our power, which led us to be more attracted to alliances with other democracies than to a more robust independence—alliances that, whatever our will and skill, confirmed our junior partner status. We moved from one set of constraints to another—from the "mother country constraints" of our long deference to the British, to the "neighbourhood constraints" of living on the potential fight path between the Soviets and Americans. Lester Pearson was careful to say, on being sworn in as foreign minister in 1948, "of course we are independent now, constitutionally. But that independence is only relative."[34]

Those external forces constrained our interest in a more independent role. There was also a powerful constraint inside the country—namely, avoiding the potential threats to national unity that had divided French- and English-speaking Canadians over conscription during the First World War. Throughout the long and critical period when Mackenzie King was prime minister, conscription cast a long shadow. Professor Norman Hillmer says King "was determined to elaborate no policy which might provide, in the contemporary words of law professor F.R. Scott, 'a clear and positive direction.' Parliament, party and people must be kept away from external affairs. Foreign policy was dangerous. It was divisive."[35]

So, this was Canada—with a long-serving prime minister who considered foreign policy "dangerous," a country constrained first by a lingering colonial deference and then by geopolitical vulnerability, a reputation as "a status quo power of modest capacity," a country whose "independence is only relative." How did we get from there to Pearson and Burns and Suez and the Nobel Peace Prize? How did we become the country that, year after year, in careful and representative international polling, is regarded as "more positive" and "less negative" than almost any other?

One important factor was the appointment of Louis St. Laurent as foreign minister. The respected corporate lawyer from Quebec City would not create Canada's international capacity—rather, he would let it be expressed. In 1941, King asked him to run for a seat in Parliament and become minister of justice.[36] Canada was at war, there was deep concern in St. Laurent's province about conscription, and the young Quebecer felt he could not decline the prime minister's request. He ran and he won. As a cabinet minister, St. Laurent was highly competent, a moderate on divisive issues, and earned the increasing confidence of King and his colleagues. In addition to those attributes, he was a perfectly bilingual francophone (coming after almost four uninterrupted decades of unilingual English-speaking prime ministers) who looked like he would steer the ship of state, not rock it.

In 1946, King appointed St. Laurent secretary of state for external affairs—a position that, until that time, had always been filled by the prime minister. The foreign ministry itself had grown significantly during the war, establishing embassies in countries which had been our allies, or which represented strong trade or investment partners. Canada had six foreign-service missions in 1939 and twenty-six by 1946,[37] most of their officers being younger and more modern than the ever-cautious Mr. King. The country itself had become more urban, more industrialized and more connected with the world, due in part to the returning veterans whose horizons had been expanded by their experience overseas. St. Laurent, although only eight years younger than King, reflected that dynamic. He was personally committed to new institutions of international order. As important, he had the authority in cabinet to cause policy to change, and the will to mobilize the talents of modern and able officials, including his new deputy minister, Lester Pearson.

The first serious test of St. Laurent's broader view of Canada's international role came in the tense days leading to the Korean War. In 1947, St. Laurent approved Canada's participation in the United Nations' temporary commission on Korea, designed to supervise the withdrawal of American and Soviet troops and the elections in both the South and North.[38] King, ever wary of foreign entanglements, opposed the decision and ordered St. Laurent to reverse it. St. Laurent refused; he believed that the United Nations, then only two years old, had to be made to work. He threatened to resign, knowing several other ministers would join him. Mackenzie King backed down, sending the signal that Canada would follow a more activist foreign policy.[39] The renowned Canadian diplomat John Holmes described this as "the controversy in which may be seen the transition from the foreign policy of Mackenzie King to that of St. Laurent and Pearson."[40]

Most of the written record documents Canada's formal international roles, rather than the impact and activities of Canadian civilians—volunteers, teachers, entrepreneurs, members of NGOs, travellers or the swelling ranks of diasporas, who keep their active links with their countries of origin. Many of those individual Canadians had and have an enormous impact internationally:

- Cardinal Paul-Émile Léger of Valleyfield, Quebec, whose work with lepers and the handicapped in Cameroon during the 1960s and '70s symbolized the commitment of many thousands of Canadians inspired by their faith to work in the developing world;
- Dr. Norman Bethune, the Gravenhurst, Ontario, surgeon on the battlefields of the Second Sino-Japanese War, who was immortalized by Mao Zedong;

- the more than fifteen thousand people who served in developing countries with Canadian University Service Overseas (CUSO)[41] or Service universitaire canadien outre-mer (SUCO).

They acted as individuals, but the quality and character of their service contributes as much to the high reputation of their country as does that of their fellow citizens who work under formal auspices.

Among scholars and others who have considered the origins of Canada's high international reputation, two terms arise regularly. One is "the golden age," referring to the period of institution-building and change following the Second World War, which casts Canadian diplomats, personified by the late Mr. Pearson, as architects of a new international order. The other term is a single word—"myth"—that has two quite opposite implications: one positive, evoking a sense of pride and purpose, and the other pejorative, meaning wrong or, at least, exaggerated.

Historians and analysts agree that "myths are undoubtedly valuable and important: they offer a source of unity and give people a shared experience with which to define their future aspirations."[42] The hitch is that history as told in myth often differs from what hard evidence suggests really happened. In an essay politely entitled "The Foreign Policy That Never Was," historian Norman Hillmer argues that Mr. Pearson and his "golden age" colleagues "knew all too well the limits of Canadian power, even when that power was at its height."[43] While their reputations shimmer in retrospect, "the post-1945 politicians and diplomats . . . were practical and pragmatic, their goals moderate, their internationalism cautious, sometimes even reluctant."[44]

The suggestion of a "myth" is not intended to be dismissive, but rather to reveal the differences between the historic record and the popular belief that, to quote Dr. Greg Donaghy, head of the historical section of the Department of Foreign Affairs and International Trade, "later impressed a generation of historians and commentators, and, one might add, prime ministers."[45] Including, I might add, myself. As a former prime minister and foreign minister, and still an active citizen, my experience is that a sense of national pride and aspiration—call that a constructive myth—is critically important to this country. Indeed, as a former minister of constitutional affairs who sought to evoke and codify a consensus on national unity, I believe that constructive myths are essential to our future. Students of the historic record may well be right that "the hoary mythology surrounding the 'golden age of Canadian diplomacy' is based on a deeply flawed reading of our country's past and raises expectations about Canadian foreign policy that governments. . . . can rarely meet."[46] But it doesn't follow that the past dictates the future, let alone that high expectations can't be reached. To borrow a phrase from South Africa, where national will and leadership changed history, "tomorrow is another country."[47]

And it is a country where the Canadians who "serve their country" will not necessarily be found in uniform or in the formal offices of state.

5

MARRYING MANDATE

AND IMAGINATION

"When everyone is dead the great game is finished. Not before."
—RUDYARD KIPLING, in *Kim*[1]

The "great game" was the name given to the century-long conflict, beginning in the early 1800s, between the British and Russian empires to control much of Asia—including Afghanistan. In that era, international relations were overwhelmingly about conquest and the protagonists were almost exclusively nation-states or empires. Obviously conquest and brutality still mark international relations, and rapacious instincts remain, but generally the relations across borders now are much broader, and often more generous and hopeful, than during the "great game." That was the nineteenth century. This is the twenty-first. Norms that are commonplace now—human rights, the idea of respecting different cultures, treating local populations as equals, or helping them become educated and competitive—rarely surfaced in that era, or in international relations before the end of the Second World War, when those norms were consecrated in the charter and purposes of the United Nations.

One profound change is that international affairs are no longer so dominated by a handful of powerful states and empires. The mix has been leavened by thousands of new actors—some tiny and local; some linking across countries—who now have a real impact on how the world works. Some of the most influential are not even nation-states and include a growing array of non-state actors, which are not only independent of governments but sometimes are powers unto themselves. They are not bound by formal systems, so these new forces are better able to think innovatively, and to act quickly.

These organizations are on the front lines. In 1985, as foreign minister, I visited the Khao I Dang holding centre for Cambodian refugees, just inside the borders of Thailand, not far from the notorious "killing fields."[2] The fields around the camp had been sewn with land mines, which crews had tried to clear away. They missed one, and the day we were there its explosion took the leg off a 5-year-old boy, who had been playing in the field. The International Red Cross had established its first "border surgical hospital" at Khao I Dang, and, as Maureen and I watched, the youngster was rushed to the operating table. His leg was lost, but his life was saved. I was at Khao I Dang as a Canadian cabinet minister, discussing humanitarian aid and resettlement programs for refugees in that camp. But there was no doubt that the people who made the difference that day—and day after day—were the surgeons and nurses sent by a non-state actor.

The role of these "non-state actors" grew over time, and was articulated forcefully in 1997 by Jessica Mathews, now president of the Carnegie Endowment for International Peace in Washington, DC, in the article "Power Shift: The Rise of Global Civil Society":

The end of the Cold War has brought no mere adjustment
among states but a novel redistribution of power among
states, markets, and civil society. National governments are
not simply losing autonomy in a globalizing economy.
They are sharing powers—including political, social, and
security roles at the core of sovereignty—with businesses,
with international organizations, and with a multitude of
citizens groups, known as nongovernmental organizations
(NGOs). The steady concentration of power in the hands of
states that began in 1648 with the peace of Westphalia is
over, at least for a while.

. . . Increasingly, resources and threats that matter,
including money, information, pollution and popular culture,
circulate and shape lives and economies with little regard for
political boundaries. . . . Even the most powerful states find
the marketplace and international public opinion compelling
them more often to follow a particular course.

. . . the most powerful engines of change in the relative
decline of states and the rise of nonstate actors is the com-
puter and telecommunications revolution. . . . [B]y drastically
reducing the importance of proximity, the new technologies
change people's perception of community. . . . [A]bove all, the
information technologies disrupt hierarchies, spreading
power among more people and groups.[3]

The number and size of non-state actors continue to grow
significantly, and now have a momentum of their own, reaching
beyond the instrument of the Internet. They can often intervene
where governments cannot, or will not. They can provide agendas and platforms that turn angry crowds to agents of change.
They create revolutionary new financial instruments, like micro-
credit, and new standards of transparency and accountability.
They save natural habitats, and human dignity, and lives.

Yet there is still a tendency to treat these non-state actors as relatively peripheral factors, unwise to ignore but distinctly a second tier, not deciders. They are dismissed as having nowhere near the weight of the established institutions of policy-making. That is a serious misjudgement. The best of the non-state actors are more innovative than the traditional institutions, more trusted both by publics and by protagonists, and much freer of the constraints of convention and bureaucracy.

Their strength is content, innovation and public legitimacy, not just process and protest. Many of these non-state actors are thoughtful, informed, creative and, by definition, not institutional. Fueled by the Internet, education and a capacity to channel frustration into action, their members are not simply "joiners" listed passively on a national census—they are activist individuals who, year after year, decide to support a particular organization through a conscious commitment. These numbers increase even more dramatically when one takes account of the humanitarian involvement of churches and other faith groups.

Some non-state actors are already more influential than many nations. In an age when cynicism and failure corrode the authority of traditional institutions, their influence is growing. For example, over the last decade, Greenpeace has had a greater impact on international policy than most national governments. The Gates Foundation is more innovative. BRAC (formerly Bangladesh Rural Advancement Committee), rooted in Bangladesh but reaching out to Sudan, Somalia and other crisis points, is the largest NGO in the world, employing 120,000 people, most of them women.[4] World Vision is in ninety-seven countries, with over 40,000 staff and more than 100,000 volunteers. Amnesty International has offices in eighty countries—more national offices than most countries have embassies.

The Edelman Organization publishes its annual Trust Barometer, based upon international polling of thirty-five thousand "opinion leaders" in twenty-five countries, ranging from Ireland to India to Indonesia to Argentina to the United Arab Emirates. In 2012,[5] "for the fifth year in a row, NGOs are the most trusted institution in the world," ranking ahead of, in order, business, media and government. GlobeScan has conducted similar studies across a wider range of countries and concludes, "compared to global and national businesses, governments, and the media, trust in NGOs is significantly higher and continues to rise slowly."[6] So, in addition to activist members and the priceless capacity to innovate, these non-state actors enjoy public trust and respect.

According to the 2006 volume of the *International Journal of Not-for-Profit Law*:

> The real story is not the proliferation of NGOs, but how these organizations have effectively networked and mobilized their members to reshape world politics. This point was graphically illustrated by the significant NGO presence at the 1992 Earth Summit in Rio, where 17,000 NGO representatives staged an alternative forum to the un-sponsored meeting, while 1,400 were involved in the official proceedings. Emboldened by their success, an even larger group converged in Beijing for the fourth World Conference on Women in September 1995. There, an astonishing 35,000 NGOs organized an alternative forum and 2,600 NGOs participated in the official multilateral negotiations.[7]

Protest is only the most public of their activities. The great majority of these non-state actors are forces for positive change—Oxfam, the environmental movement, Amnesty International, BRAC, the Gates Foundation, Transparency

International and literally thousands of other organizations. But a minority of these new players are malign and dangerous—terrorist groups to whom no target is sacred, criminal enterprises smuggling people and drugs and other commodities, and other predators ranging from pirates to corrupt businesses. They operate deliberately and often violently as outlaws. The brutal power of both terrorists and criminal gangs is augmented by their capacity to work beyond the reach of national laws, and their mastery of modern technology. These outlaws pose a real threat to modern society, and pre-occupy governments, policy analysts, commentators and, significantly, the military and security establishments, which have enormous influence on the budgets and priority-setting of most Western nation-states.

An unfortunate consequence is that, since the 9/11 attacks on the US, Western governments and publics pay more attention to the world's "new threats" than to the world's "new solutions." The pre-occupation with terrorists, criminal gangs and other malign international forces has overshadowed our use and appreciation of the much broader range of international non-state actors, whose motives and activities are highly positive. It is easy to understand why governments focus on al-Qaeda and the drug cartels and their murderous co-conspirators—they need to be countered decisively. And it is almost always the case that "bad news" and fear trump "good news" and hope.

The danger is that this process creates its own spiral. As societies become more fearful, governments focus—and lead public discourse to focus—on the threats in the world, especially terrorism. As one result, the disproportion is enormous between the money and attention that Western governments spend on defence and "homeland" security compared to their investment in the capacity to achieve co-operation, understanding and tangible improvements in the conditions that often give rise to upheaval, crime and terrorism. Violence and extreme behaviour have several sources, but there is no doubt that desperation, poverty and prejudice are fertile breeding grounds, and addressing those conditions is precisely where the constructive non-state actors, with their roots in the ground, already make a huge difference. Non-state actors could be even more effective if the issues they address, and the forward-looking perspectives they acquire, were treated as seriously as military and terrorist issues.

No serious observer doubts the threats of modern terrorism—and no nation is immune. I was Canada's foreign minister in June 1985 when a bomb, loaded at a Canadian airport, blew Air India Flight 182 out of the skies near Cork, Ireland, killing 329 people, including 280 Canadians. This was sixteen years before 9/11, and the percentage of Canada's population killed in the bombing of Air India was just slightly higher than the percentage of the US population killed in the 2001 attack on the Twin Towers, the Pentagon and United Airlines Flight 93. For several months after the bombing, my family and I lived under close armed security, threatened by the tiny but violent group of Sikh extremists who opposed Canada's negotiation of an extradition treaty with India, designed to bring perpetrators of that bombing home to justice.

Terrorism will continue, and serious and sophisticated responses are necessary in all countries, including in Western countries. But the most significant direct threat of terrorism will not be to the wealthy countries that are now, in the name of security, building up the national walls they sought recently to bring down in the name of trade. Instead, the most devastating impact of terrorism today is more likely to be felt by populations in developing and emerging countries. Those are the societies where poverty, discrimination and desperation are most acute, and where it is more difficult to achieve change peacefully. The fear in Western societies relates to international terrorist attacks, while the more serious threat in developing societies is from internal civil conflicts whose protagonists adopt terrorist methods, and are drawn and recruited into terrorist networks.

The impact of international criminal enterprises is also becoming more destructive every day, with governments often unable to match the wealth and firepower of the gangs. In Latin America, and now in West Africa, the drug trade is fuelling this destruction. According to the United Nations, "eight of the world's ten most violent countries are in Latin America or the Caribbean. . . . Honduras, a strategic spot on the trafficking route, has the world's highest murder rate, about 80 times that of western Europe."[8] The drug trade is as mobile as it is lethal. As enforcement tightens in the Americas, "West Africa has emerged as a major hub in the global drug economy . . . [as] Latin American and southern European drug-trafficking organizations forg[e] . . . alliances and joint ventures with already-strong West African networks.[9]

It is clear why Western governments invest hugely and viscerally in defence and security—why they fight the "bad guys." What is not at all clear is why so little priority is given to supporting and mobilizing the "good guys," solution-oriented non-state actors whose swelling ranks work on the hard ground of conflict and crisis, and build the kind of trust, networks, insights and partnerships that closed borders and sophisticated weapons and "shock and awe" can't approach.

The relationship between governments and NGOs has always been wary, often mutually suspicious. When the two sides have fundamentally different premises and perspectives, as on some environmental issues, the relationship can be systematically hostile. On international issues, the differences are more often institutional. Public servants act for a country or a system, and are empowered and constrained by their formal roles. NGOs are populist and specific, acting for a cause or an interest, freer to innovate, operating with less power but fewer constraints. Nonetheless, the interests of formal state and non-state often intersect.

The inherent tension is on both sides. While foreign minister, some of my harshest critics were non-governmental organizations, whose first instinct, it often seemed to me, was deep suspicion of anything the government proposed. I ran into my first wall of skepticism just days after the Mulroney government was elected, in 1984. That was a period when US policy in Central America was intensely controversial, and many Canadian NGOs simply assumed that a Progressive Conservative government would adopt a hardline Reaganite position towards those countries. We did the opposite, opposing the US blockade of Nicaragua, finding ways to deliver development assistance that were not controlled by recipient governments, often working deliberately with local and Canadian NGOs. Sometimes, as in Guatemala and El Salvador, we entrusted those NGOs with running aid programs that we did not want the local government to co-opt or distort. Most importantly, we found ways to work together—state and non-state—ultimately allowing Canada to play a significant role in the Contadora peace process, which led to a negotiated end to civil wars in Central America,[10] through the Esquipulas process.[11]

It is neither surprising nor fatal that NGOs and public servants are often skeptical about one another. One is chalk and one is cheese. They should have differences. They serve the public interest from different perspectives. But they need not be enemies. Husbands and wives have differences. So do foreign ministries and finance ministries, employers and employees, friends and neighbours. And the rule is always that if you insist on the differences, they become deeper, and the capacity to achieve common purposes becomes more remote, to the disadvantage of everyone.

The question, for both sides, is: why do we concentrate on those inevitable disagreements between governments and NGOs rather than on common interests and common purposes? That antagonistic instinct is counter-productive whenever it occurs, but the stakes are higher when the issue is whether volatile populations will become calmer or more violent, or whether a limited conflict will metastasize into something larger and more lethal. In those circumstances, it is simply irresponsible to let differences and annoyances drive and define the relationship when there is so much benefit to be gained by working together.

I also know from experience that state and non-state organizations can work together productively and very effectively.

- In 1979, when Vietnamese, Laotian and Cambodian "boat people" were set afloat to die in the China Sea, my government—led by Flora MacDonald and Ron Atkey—established a partnership program with Canadian citizens and organizations which led to the rescue and settlement in Canada of 60,000 of those refugees. That enormous response by Canadian citizens was, per capita, the highest in the world, and gave weight and authority to the government when Ms. MacDonald led the arguments in the United Nations to enlarge the humanitarian response of other countries. The extraordinary nature of that Canadian co-operation was recognized in 1986 when Canada—not the government, but all Canadians— became the only country ever awarded the Nansen

Refugee Award of the United Nations High
Commission for Refugees.

- In 1984–85, there was a similar outpouring of citizen
and NGO engagement when Canadians responded to
the crisis of famine in Ethiopia. CBC correspondent
Brian Stewart, whose reports from Ethiopia galvanized
Canadians, wrote:

> By December, an astonishing two-thirds
> of Canadians were contributing money or
> supplies to African famine relief. In the end,
> this country supplied over 10 per cent of all
> the international aid that flowed to Ethiopia
> and was probably responsible for saving in
> excess of 700,000 lives.[12]

- In the campaign against apartheid in South Africa,
our government's indispensable partners were NGOs,
including prominently the Canadian Labour
Congress—not simply its then-president Shirley Carr
and her senior associates, but rank-and-file members
across Canada. They had knowledge, authority and
networks—through the Congress of South African
Trade Unions (COSATU)—which Canada's excellent
officials could not replicate.

- In 1989, I wanted to have informal discussions
with Faisal Husseini, Hanan Ashrawi and other
Palestinian leaders, as a step towards Canada
recognizing Palestinians' right to self-determination.
Those leaders were cautious about a formal meeting
with the Canadian foreign minister. However, they
had come to trust and respect Kent and Linda Stucky,
who ran the Canadian Mennonite Centre in East

Jerusalem. So the non-state Stuckys invited us all to
a "let's get acquainted" conversation, in the centre's
beautiful stone house in Sheikh Jarrah. Linda even
baked a cake and, in that congenial atmosphere,
on neutral ground, we took an essential step leading
to Canada's decision to formally recognize the
Palestinian right to self-determination. That was an
important development in Canadian foreign policy,
which may well not have happened without the good
offices of the Mennonite Central Committee.

Other Canadian foreign ministers, in other times, had similar experiences. In many parts of the world, working with
non-state actors has been standard operating procedure. The
difference now is one of critical mass. There are now many
more partners with whom governments can work. Moreover,
there are growing advantages to that co-operation, as government budgets shrink and stringent accountability rules dis-
courage public servants from taking initiatives without "head
office" authority. At the same time, as the world changes,
non-state actors themselves have to look for ways to move
beyond advocacy, and find new means to apply the reforms or
innovations or insights they learn on the ground.

This is an era of partnerships, to achieve specific agreed
purposes. That reality is recognized by local communities,
governments and enterprises around the world. I am not
speaking about mergers, where identity and independence can
be so easily lost, but of partnerships where, with care and
respect, each partner can retain its autonomy and flexibility.
Of course there will be compromises, some of them difficult,
but that's the case with every partnership, from a marriage to
a federation. The issue is not a surrender of independence, but
a recognition of interdependence. The situation is not simply

that states and non-states need each other if they want to make progress in this complex world. It is instead that they can enlarge each other—they can do things together that neither could do apart. In the process, it is almost certain that each will learn from the other. Moreover, an emphasis on partnering for big purposes would help shift public attention from the threats of the modern world to its hope and possibilities.

Yet, non-state actors remain the elephants in the room of foreign policy. The world accepts that big business and banks, motivated by private and profit interests, have become more influential internationally, often at the expense of formal governments. By contrast, there is relatively scant attention to the accelerating capacity of non-state organizations, which exist to serve the public interest, as they see it.

The new growth of these organizations is dramatic. In 1999, *The Economist* magazine estimated that the number of international NGOs rose from 6,000 in 1990 to 26,000,[13] and that number had grown to more than 33,000 by 2010[14]— nearly one-fifth of the world's thirty-seven thousand international non-governmental organizations (INGOs) were formed in the 1990s.[15] Those are active organizations, not just names on a letterhead. Like the Internet which nourishes them, they are a transforming symbol of a changed and globalized world, and the trend is rising.

The International Federation of Red Cross and Red Crescent Societies, representing nearly 100 million members, volunteers and supporters, also employ some 300,000 people.[16] That means they employ more people internationally than any of the world's three largest banks: BNP Paribas;[17] Deutsche Bank,[18] and HSBC Holdings.[19] Of the world's ten biggest multinational companies in 2011, as ranked by the *Fortune* Global 500, only five—Walmart, three Chinese state companies (Sinopec Group, Chinese National Petroleum, and

State Grid) and Toyota Motors[20]—employ more people internationally than Red Cross/Red Crescent.

The names of some of these NGOs are better known than the names of most of the 193 member-states of the United Nations—Oxfam, Amnesty International, Greenpeace, Red Cross/Red Crescent. But, if their individual names are known, their cumulative influence and impact are seriously and routinely underestimated. They are seen singularly, in the context of their specific commitments to humanitarian, social or other causes. They should also be recognized as part of a growing and influential category of actors who change the way the world works more than the majority of formal nation-states. Some 3,400 of those organizations already enjoy consultative status with the United Nations, through the UN Economic and Social Council.[21] Non-states are not the sidelines; they are, in more senses than one, the field.

For example, a study for the World Health Organization estimates that between 30 percent and 70 percent of the sprawling healthcare infrastructure across Africa is owned or run by faith-based organizations, with percentages varying across this range in different countries.[22] More generally, faith-based organizations play a major role in HIV/AIDS care and treatment in sub-Saharan Africa.[23] Hospitals and facilities run by faith-based organizations have historically been established where service needs are greatest, and often remain active regardless of political changes or humanitarian crises. They are often the only form of organized healthcare available, are usually well-perceived and well-trusted by the community, and their services are sometimes considered to be the best in their respective regions.

Those non-state actors invent new instruments, from microcredit to the Gates Vaccine Innovation Award. They build personal trust, which is the basis of creative partnerships. They are not constrained by a veto in the Security Council. Consider just a few examples, out of thousands:

- Médecins Sans Frontières (MSF), or Doctors Without Borders, offers emergency medical relief to people caught in catastrophe—armed conflict, natural disasters, epidemics or malnutrition—in some eighty countries. Its campaign for changes in pharmaceutical property rights resulted in a 99 percent drop in anti-retroviral drug prices from 1999 to 2007 and an increase in the number of people treated from 300 thousand in 2002 to three million in 2007 in middle- and low-income countries.[24]

- Oxfam International is a confederation of fifteen organizations fighting poverty in more than ninety countries. In 1995 it worked with Unilever on a ground-breaking "in-depth case study . . . [that] shows how, and to what extent, the operations of Unilever Indonesia have an impact on poverty—both positive and negative—in Indonesia."[25]

- In 2008, after Cyclone Nargis, the Burmese government blocked most humanitarian aid. An exception was Avaaz, which had "built a strong relationship with Burmese monks and civil society groups. . . . Avaaz members in 124 countries donat[ed] $1.6 million . . . in a matter of days."[26]

- Greenpeace ships began confronting whaling fleets on the high seas in 1973, while Greenpeace campaigners around the world urged national governments to ban whaling. By 1982, there was a moratorium on commercial whaling.[27] In 1995, Greenpeace also led the fight against Shell Oil's plans to scuttle a 14,500-ton oil storage facility called the Brent Spar in the North

Sea. The British government supported Shell's right
to sink the facility. Eventually, Shell bowed to public
protests and boycotts and, ultimately, there was an
international ban on the ocean disposal of oil rigs.[28]

- Partners in Health, in 1998, "against the advice of
global health experts . . . launched the community-
based HIV equity initiative to provide free, comprehensive HIV care and treatment in an impoverished
setting." It proved successful, and "contributed to
the formation of the Global Fund to fight AIDS,
Tuberculosis, and Malaria . . . the world's deadliest
infectious diseases."[29]

- The Bill & Melinda Gates Foundation has, since
1994, invested more than $27 billion in domestic
and international development initiatives to improve
health and alleviate extreme poverty. Its recurring
theme is that "innovation is the key to improving
the world."[30]

These non-state actors represent a huge community, diverse,
often difficult to draw together, often singular in their purposes, and suspicious of others, but with extraordinary capacity and track records of accomplishment. Others include:

- Faith groups, which may set out to proselytize,
but often become invaluable instruments of community and personal development in zones of conflict
and poverty;
- Service clubs—Rotary,[31] the Lions Club[32] and
similar organizations whose roots and agendas were
originally local;
- Problem-solvers like the International Crisis Group,[33]
the Center for Humanitarian Dialogue,[34] the Carter

Center,[35] the National Democratic Institute
(NDI),[36] the International Republican Institute
(IRI),[37] the Elders,[38] the Global Leadership
Foundation[39] and others.

There are of course some NGOs that are badly organized,
or otherwise not reliable, and can give the rest a bad name.
That is in the nature of operating on the edge, or in crisis,
where systems break down: the need and desire for help
is compelling, and the capacity to coordinate assistance is
scant. That has happened in Haiti, where the chaos of earth-
quakes, poverty and bad governance was often aggravated by
some NGOs that seemed to be driven by their own needs,
rather than Haiti's. The country was called, pejoratively, the
"Republic of NGOs."[40]

The problem is deeper than simple disorganization because
sometimes, in the onslaught of help, NGOs can replace the
state, and erode its authority. Similar concerns arise in Iraq,
Afghanistan—almost any place where NGOs are active on a
large scale. The problem of coordinating the priorities of
even the best of the international NGOs is itself significant, as
is a similar problem in coordinating the activities of foreign
governments that are development donors. These are all
undeniable challenges related to the presence and activities of
NGOs. But they pale beside the potential benefits that would
come from more active partnerships between state- and non-
state actors.

In this age of instant communication and high suspicions,
governments are under close and constant scrutiny, and so are
the individuals and agencies who act in their name. That has
generated standards of accountability for formal agencies that
can be so exacting they inhibit the initiative and risk-taking
necessary to respond quickly to crisis. That is not limited

narrowly to financial accountability. It also means responding to domestic political pressures, and adhering strictly to international treaties and international standards on critical issues like respect for human rights, due process or transparency. In rare cases of extreme threat or crisis, an exception might be justified to the principle that governments should follow the normal rules, but embarking on that slippery slope can compromise a state's essential legitimacy and authority.

By stark contrast, non-state actors can often respond to urgent need, or open and maintain lines of communication with significant leaders or groups who are "off-limits" for governments. That difference in the freedom to act should cry out for partnership, for finding areas where state and non-state, working together can save lives, or moderate crisis or deadly tension.

Non-state actors represent "citizen engagement" on a global—and a growing—scale. They express a swelling determination by citizens around the world to act on their own to accomplish social or humanitarian goals which had otherwise been left to governments, or simply ignored.

What these non-state actors do not have is the authority to change the rules. They bring the imagination the world needs, but only nation-states have the mandate and the power to change laws and regulations and treaty obligations. There is a growing need to marry mandate and imagination. Canada is one of a handful of countries which, in the past, has been able, willing and trusted enough to establish strong purpose-specific partnerships with non-state organizations—the international treaty to ban landmines, the campaign against apartheid, the agreement on blood diamonds, the responses to famine and emergencies, and a long list of other initiatives. Our skill at building partnerships and respect has been a distinguishing Canadian credential, and it complements the other critical aspects of our foreign policy. We have vital economic, trade, environmental and security interests to pursue. But these are all in jeopardy if conflict thrives and grows. A successful policy of partnerships with non-state actors could help significantly in addressing the most challenging issues of the future.

6

CANADA'S POLICY TODAY

International issues have played virtually no part in the elections won by Stephen Harper, nor in the platforms or prominent policy positions of his Conservative Party. The election results in 2006 and 2008 were driven by domestic issues, and, with three significant exceptions, the focus of the resulting minority governments was rarely on international issues or foreign policy. Those three exceptions were Afghanistan, China and the Middle East.

In Afghanistan, the Harper government continued the active military engagement that began in 2001 under the Chrétien Liberals, but stepped up Canada's profile as a war-fighting nation. Defence spending increased, as it should have, after a long drought, and that significant policy decision was accompanied by an "image" decision to reshape Canada's international reputation in more aggressive terms. The government quickly embraced the American habit of shuttling cabinet members into and out of Afghanistan, to offer direct encouragement to Canadian troops, of course, but also for "photo ops" that would incubate and encourage a more macho characterization of Canada's role in the world.

That emphasis on the war-fighting military stands in contrast to a steady and deliberate decline in the funding and priority assigned to Canada's diplomatic and development capacity. From the government's early days, the advice of officials in the Department of Foreign Affairs often was not sought on critical issues like relations with China and policy in the Middle East and, when offered, that advice was discounted or rejected.[1] At what was then CIDA, the early skepticism of Harper government insiders about the purpose and effectiveness of Canada's traditional development policy sowed the seeds for a fundamental shift in policy away from the long-established priority assigned to reducing poverty and toward trade.

With respect to China, the Harper government inherited "a long and generally positive . . . relationship with the People's Republic of China"[2] when it formed its first minority government in January 2006. That reflected the influences of, among others, the reputation of "Dr. Norman Bethune . . . a Canadian name in China's revolutionary pantheon . . . the pioneering initiative under Prime Minister Diefenbaker to sell wheat to China on a long-term credit basis . . . the formalization of relations under the Trudeau government in 1970. . . [and] the Team Canada endeavours of the 1990s."[3] In 1998, then-premier Zhu Rongji had described Canada as "China's best friend in the whole world."[4] For most countries in Europe and North America, relations with China had "started anew"[5] with the historic visit of US president Richard Nixon to Mao Zedong in China in January 1972. This was true even among the right wing in the United States, although "a furious Pat Buchanan threatened to resign from the White House staff on the grounds that the United States had done a deal with a communist regime . . . [He] did not carry out his threat."[6] Despite that general change in attitude toward

China over the intervening three decades, the Harper Conservatives brought to office a mindset and suspicions about the Beijing government that were almost pre-Nixonian. They "came to power in January 2006 committed to . . . a China policy substantially different from the engagement strategies of its Liberal and Progressive Conservative predecessors."[7] They described their harder-line position as reflecting "a principled foreign policy."[8] Expert observers of Canada–China relations argue that change introduced "two years of 'cool politics, warm economics' [which] had near disastrous consequences."[9] In this context, "warm economics" meant continued trade promotion. "Cool politics" included:

- shelving plans for the "strategic working group" that had been initiated by Prime Minister Martin and then-president Hu Jintao in 2005;
- suspending the bilateral human rights dialogue with Beijing;
- provoking China's sensitivity about territorial integrity by sending Harper cabinet ministers to celebrate Taiwan's Independence Day and by having the flag of Tibet on the prime minister's desk when he met the Dalai Lama;
- having key Conservatives pointedly contrast the importance of building relations with democratic India rather than maintaining them with a country they described as "a godless totalitarian country with nuclear weapons aimed at us";[10]
- the prime minister's response in Hanoi, in 2006, when questioned about Hu Jintao's reluctance to meet him at a gathering of Asian leaders, "I don't think Canadians want us to sell out . . . our belief in democracy, freedom, human rights . . . to the almighty dollar";[11] and

- deciding to have the prime minister not attend
  the opening ceremonies of the summer Olympics
  in Beijing.

By 2008, Prime Minister Harper realized that this deliberate "coolness" toward China was harming Canada's long-term interests, and began systematically to change his government's conduct. He set out to restore the relationship that had been built so carefully since the 1960s. In late 2009, four years after his first election as prime minister, Mr. Harper travelled to Beijing and met Premier Wen Jiabao. The government deserves credit for making what the *Globe and Mail*'s Mark MacKinnon calls "one of the most dramatic foreign policy reversals in recent memory."[12] However, when the two leaders met, Mr. Wen was careful to note, "This is your first visit to China and this is the first meeting between the Chinese premier and a Canadian prime minister in almost five years,"[13] reminding Harper that the while the "cool politics" might be over, they were not forgotten.

In the Middle East, Canada's commitment to Israel's rights and security has been unequivocal since that state was formed in 1948. Our role in helping the region resolve its inherent conflicts had been bi-partisan at home, and as even-handed as possible in the region. Our distant location, and the relatively small size of our population, mean that Canada will not be a major player in the Middle East—not the Europe next door, not a superpower. But, for seven decades we developed productive relations with both Arabs and Israelis, and helped reconcile some of their turbulent differences, both in our own right, and through the United Nations and processes like the multilateral Refugee Working Group. Over that period, we have made mistakes, including my own bravado affirmation—on my first full day as prime minister in 1979—of a campaign promise to move Canada's embassy from Tel Aviv to Jerusalem.[14] I reversed that decision, upon accepting the advice of a study I had requested by the wise and careful Robert Stanfield, my predecessor as leader of the Progressive Conservative Party. The Stanfield report also served the purpose of charting a course forward for Canada in the Middle East, and noted that we "must be regarded as fair-minded by the parties. . . . [and willing] . . . to express disapproval when actions are taken . . . which we believe are counterproductive to the peace process."[15]

Before and during the Second World War, between five and six million Jews were killed in the Holocaust,[16] and another seven to eight million were forced to flee their homes as "displaced persons."[17] The Holocaust is known as not just a terrible past event, but as a horror which could return in a world where extremism still thrives, and anti-Semitism continues to rise.[18] The threats against Israel are real[19] and there is no doubt they will grow as tensions, conflict and change accelerate in the region. Mahmoud Ahmadinejad is no longer president of Iran, but his assertion that "the regime occupying Jerusalem must vanish from the page of time"[20] reflected an influential and profound hostility to Israel among leaders of Iran that is hugely threatening. At the same time, the Arab Spring has blown away old regimes in nations neighbouring Israel, which had previously maintained an uneasy but steady modus vivendi with the Jewish state. Those circumstances had provided a sense of reasonable predictability, leading to an acceptable level of security. Those regimes have now been replaced by forces that are more ideological, more Islamist, and impelled to prove their credentials to volatile electors and populations.

For their part, Palestinians maintain that their ancestors have been in the region for centuries,[21] often "enjoy[ing] times of great harmony,"[22] though more recently of deadly conflict.

After the First World War, the League of Nations gave Britain a "mandate" over the territories occupied by Jews and Arabs and other populations that later became Israel, the West Bank, Gaza and Jordan.[23] In 1921, the eastern portion of that British mandate became the Emirate of Transjordan, which later became the independent nation Jordan. The western portion became the Palestine mandate where, in 1948, the UN proposed to create two states—one Jewish, one Arab. Arabs disagreed and, when the state of Israel was founded on May 15, 1948, "Egypt, Syria, Lebanon and Jordan invaded, but were beaten back."[24] Conflict has ensued since, and apparent breakthroughs in negotiation—the Camp David Accords in 1978;[25] the Oslo Accord in 1993[26]—brought no resolution. In July 2013, US Secretary of State John Kerry announced that "Israel and the Palestinians have laid the groundwork for a resumption of peace talks."[27]

The Israel-Palestine conflict is, of course, most contentious and dangerous in the immediate neighbourhood of the Middle East. However, it is also a lightning-rod issue between developed nations and the developing world, where many see the Palestinians as a symbol of broader exclusion. Nelson Mandela said in 1997, "We know too well that our freedom is incomplete without the freedom of the Palestinians,"[28] and that view is widespread among people and countries who feel their own aspirations are consistently rejected by the developed world. That has been emphasized in very recent votes in the United Nations. In 2011, the Palestinian Authority's application for formal membership as a state in the UN was stillborn because the United States said it would veto the required Security Council approval, and five other members including Britain, Germany and France[29] said they would abstain. The Palestinians changed their diplomatic strategy, and applied instead to the UN General Assembly for "non-member observer State" status.

That was an initiative which the Security Council could not veto, and the Palestinians won an overwhelming vote 138-9.[30]

The Harper government explicitly rejects even-handedness in the Middle East. It shows no interest in being regarded as "fair-minded," to use Robert Stanfield's term. Instead, in Foreign Minister John Baird's words: "We're not a referee. We have a side."[31] That side, emphatically, is with Israel—"Israel has no greater friend in the world today than Canada,"[32] Canada's foreign minister told the American Jewish Committee's Global Forum in May 2012. That single-minded support of Israel became evident very early:

- On January 25, 2006, in the Palestinian territories, the "Islamic militant group Hamas . . . won a surprise . . . [majority] victory in Palestinian parliamentary elections"[33] and on March 29, 2006, newly elected Hamas legislators were sworn in as the Palestinian cabinet. The Harper government, itself newly elected, immediately cut off any contacts with ministers of the Palestinian Authority, and suspended long-standing development assistance. "Not a red cent to Hamas," said then–Foreign Minister Peter MacKay."[34] Canada became "the first country after Israel to cut off aid and diplomatic ties."[35]

- On July 12, 2006, Hezbollah militants fired rockets into Israeli border towns, killing at least three Israeli soldiers, and taking two others prisoner. That attack was condemned by Human Rights Watch— "Hezbollah's explanations . . . utterly fail to justify these unlawful attacks"[36]—and triggered a massive Israeli military response. Israeli Army Chief of Staff General Dan Halutz said his military would target infrastructure and "turn back the clock in Lebanon

by 20 years" if the soldiers were not freed.[37]
During thirty-four days of military conflict, there
were "at least 1,109 Lebanese deaths, the vast majority of whom were civilians . . . [and] the deaths of
43 Israeli civilians and 12 Israel Defense Forces (IDF)
soldiers."[38] Prime Minister Harper's immediate
reaction was to say, "I think Israel's response under
the circumstances has been measured."[39] He modified
that position slightly as the conflict escalated,[40] but
opposed having the G8 call for an immediate end
to the fighting.[41]

- Later, on May 9, 2011, US President Obama proposed "while the core issues of the conflict must be
negotiated, the basis of those negotiations is clear: a
viable Palestine, and a secure Israel. The United States
believes that . . . the borders of Israel and Palestine
should be based on the 1967 lines with mutually
agreed swaps, so that secure and recognized borders
are established for both states."[42] Israeli Prime
Minister Netanyahu responded immediately that
"we can't go back to those indefensible lines."[43] The
annual G8 summit met three weeks later, and "the
Western world's leaders . . . plan[ned] to use the . . .
summit to present a united front on the conflicts . . .
of the Middle East. But one of the rare sources of
friction has turned out to be the renegade Middle
East views of Stephen Harper. . . . Alone among G8
leaders, the Canadian Prime Minister refuse[d] to
embrace the US President's plan."[44] Summit declarations require unanimity, so the summit expressed
"strong support for the vision of Israeli-Palestinian
peace outlined by President Obama,"[45] but was silent
on the essential principle that might make it work.

- On September 7, 2012, in Vladivostok, Russia,
  Foreign Minister Baird suddenly closed Canada's
  embassy in Tehran, and expelled Iranian diplomats
  from Canada. Mr. Baird gave no specific reasons
  beyond repeating Canada's view of "the government
  of Iran as the most significant threat to global peace
  and security in the world today,"[46] and accusing Iran
  of "routinely threatening the existence of Israel,
  engaging in racist anti-Semitic rhetoric and incite-
  ment to genocide."[47] Prime Minister Netanyahu
  quickly sent congratulations.[48] When Britain was
  forced to close its embassy in Tehran after it had been
  ransacked, Deputy Prime Minister Nick Clegg was
  careful to say, "that doesn't mean we're cutting off
  all diplomatic relations."[49] Former Canadian ambassador Ken Taylor, who brought American hostages
  out of Iran in 1979, was among those surprised by
  Baird's decision, saying, "given Canada's status as
  an international player, there's great value to having
  someone there on the ground who can interpret
  what is going on."[50]
- On November 29, 2012, when the UN General
  Assembly voted overwhelmingly to "accord Palestine
  non-member Observer status,"[51] Canada was one of
  only nine nations in opposition,[52] and "stepped into
  the spotlight as an unexpectedly vocal opponent."[53]
  The vote was overwhelming: 138 in favour, 9 against,
  and 41 abstentions. Foreign Minister Baird described
  the resounding majority vote as an "utterly regrettable
  decision to abandon policy and principle" and warned
  "we will be considering all available next steps."[54]
- On April 9, 2013, Mr. Baird broke international cus-
  tom by going deliberately to Arab East Jerusalem to

meet an Israeli cabinet minister. That is "occupied
territory" acquired by an annexation that the international community does not accept as legitimate.
So most visiting ministers won't visit Israeli officials
there. Palestinian spokesperson Hanan Ashrawi said,
"Either he's ignorant of East Jerusalem being occupied territory, which is unforgivable in a foreign minister, or it's a deliberate attempt to change the
international consensus."[55]

Canadian ministers are more categorical about their commitment to Israel than any other international issue. Canada's
support has become more adamant than that of other countries who are clearly "friends of Israel," including the United
States of America, which has been prepared to disagree with
the Netanyahu government on contentious issues like the
construction of housing settlements, and negotiations based
on 1967 boundaries and land swaps. Beyond the Middle
East, that fierce commitment to Israel also guides Canadian
policy on much broader international issues. For example,
the Harper government's hostility towards the United Nations
is framed regularly in the context of solidarity with Israel,
boycotting UN conferences on racism because they would
include extremist rhetoric that is anti-Semitic,[56] leading the
opposition to Palestinian observer status and describing
nations who voted overwhelmingly for that observer status as
"abandon[ing] policy and principle." Those outspoken positions limit, or eliminate, Canada's capacity as a mediator, or
even as a calming influence, on broader issues in the increasingly volatile Middle East because other countries in the
region regard the Israeli–Palestinian conflict to be the litmus
test of fairness and credibility[57]—and we unequivocally "have
a side." That reputation could easily spread to other areas of

the Islamic world, where conflicts are growing and Canada's traditional reputation for even-handedness could otherwise help relieve tensions or find compromise. In the past, when Canada was deemed to be too uncritically close to another country, that country was the US, our largest trading partner, next door neighbour and historic "best friend." It is notable that, at the 2011 summit in Deauville, when all other G8 nations wanted to support President Obama's proposal for new Middle East negotiations, Canada refused the necessary unanimity; Israel's opposition to 1967 boundaries trumped Washington's initiative for peace.

Various explanations are offered for the Harper government's determined and virtually automatic support of Israel.[58] However, a more basic question is whether this forceful and exceptional position really helps Israel during one of the most challenging periods of that extraordinary country's history. No doubt it has been comforting to the Netanyahu government to have such a prominent, vocal and predictable friend. But the real value of any close relationship is that trusted partners can provide frank and hard advice that would otherwise not be proffered or accepted. We don't know whether the high-octane public support that Canada delivers is accompanied by that kind of frank advice in private. What is clear is that the pressures on Israel's most basic interests have intensified with the collapse of neighbouring Middle East regimes—with which it had worked out a complicated modus vivendi—and the sharp rise of violence and threats in the region. As usual, within Israel itself, discussion and debate are vigorous and creative, and courageous options are being considered. This is precisely the time when Israel could benefit most from constructive examinations of its options with countries like Canada, which have proven to be consistent good friends since Israel's creation, and whose reserves of skill and reputation might help resolve a dangerous impasse.

Well beyond the emphasis on military engagement and imagery, the best guide to the Harper government's changes in international policy is the distinction between soft and hard power. It determines the international paths the government has opened or broadened, those it has narrowed or closed, and those where it has followed a Canadian status quo. The prominent example of that status quo is Canada's international economic policy, on which the government's record has been steady but cautious, generally following the lines established by the Mulroney, Chrétien and Martin governments. The strength of Canada's banking system was justly celebrated during the banking and financial crises in the US and Europe, but that was due to decisions on Canadian banking regulation that preceded the election of the current government. Similarly, trade policy had not been a priority in the Harper government's early years, compared with the innovations of the Mulroney government, or the prominence the Chrétien government assigned to trade missions. Harper ministers followed the lead of then–Quebec premier Jean Charest in exploring a "free trade accord" with the European Union,[59] but for some time did not focus on emerging trade opportunities in Asia, Africa or even the Americas, despite identifying "Latin America and the Caribbean . . . [as] . . . a top international priority"[60] in 2007. Then, as growth slowed in the United States and Europe, and after President Obama announced a "pivot" toward the Asia-Pacific region,[61] Harper ministers became more assertive in seeking trade agreements in emerging markets. Trade is now emerging again as a significant international priority for Canada.

The Harper government turned relatively more attention to international policy after winning a parliamentary majority in the 2011 election. Still, it remains a subsidiary interest in a government whose primary aim is domestic, and probably stems from a growing acknowledgement that economic strength at home is tied inescapably to international factors. The motive is pragmatism, not internationalism. Remarkably, this sense of connection to the rest of the world is confined narrowly to trade and economic policy. It is certainly not reflected in current Canadian policy on the environment or international development. On the contrary, in both fields, Canada has become a denier and an outlier. The Harper government has been withdrawing from Canada's commitments to environmental and development policy as consistently as it has been pursuing new trade agreements. Even on its chosen ground of military matters, several respected commentators argue that the government has developed no coherent and consistent approach to defence policy. Military historian Jack Granatstein[62] is characteristically direct: "It is becoming increasingly clear that the government has no defence policy."[63] Certainly, as Canadian troops withdrew from Afghanistan, it became evident that the government had given little thought as to where or how to apply this sophisticated and expensive military capacity next. Previous Canadian governments tried to set out a framework for international policy in formal documents, usually a "white paper," so there would be a context, a sense of direction and an opportunity for public discussion. There is no indication something like that is planned now.

To its credit, the Harper government has taken some clear and important international initiatives:

- Canada's extended engagement in Afghanistan was highly professional and widely respected, and consolidated Canada's military reputation and standing with NATO and other allies.

- The government has developed a sophisticated immigration policy, which helps secure Canada's advantages and capacity to innovate in an increasingly competitive world, and has become a model for other countries.[64]
- There has been a significant recent priority assigned to broadening international trade, including a late recognition of the importance of Africa and other emerging economies.
- There is a stated commitment to the Americas that could be productive, if it were exercised.[65]
- Canada's international economic policy has been steady, benefiting from our longstanding and unusually effective regulatory regimes.

A steady economy, a respected military, vigorous trade initiatives and a forward-looking immigration policy are important assets, but they draw upon only a part of Canada's proven capacity and potential as an international citizen. This government has been steering steadily and quietly away from other traditionally important areas of Canadian concern—diplomacy, pursuing broad multilateral relations, partnerships with civil society and NGOs, international development and fighting poverty, a balanced role in the Middle East and robust support for the United Nations. That narrows who we are, what we can do and what we represent—and that narrowing is no accident. On a critical range of international issues that mobilize soft power, there has been more change than continuity in the way Canada acts in the world.

In itself, change is a good thing, particularly in an age when international circumstances themselves change both quickly and profoundly. Old certainties no longer apply. Innovation is essential. But precisely because change is so prevalent, there should be evidence that old practices have become invalid before they are abandoned, and innovation should occur for a better reason than that it is different. Moreover, in a proudly democratic society like Canada, the reasons for change should be stated clearly, and discussed, and justified in open debate. That has not been how the Harper government conducts its foreign policy.

That has led to a broad departure from Canada's international tradition, established over decades and under different governments. In the China case Mr. Harper corrected that mistake. But the instinct to marginalize or repudiate past successes is frequent and significant enough to risk the strong and respected international reputation that those successes helped earn Canada. A short list:

- International organizations and agreements: Canada has been sliding to the sidelines of formal multilateral organizations, and treaties in which our country had traditionally played a central role. In December 2012, Canada became the first signatory nation to formally withdraw from the Kyoto Protocol on climate change, "abandoning the world's only legally binding plan to tackle global warming."[66] Then, in 2013, we became the only country among 194 UN members to withdraw from the United Nations Convention to Combat Desertification, "whose creation was led by the Mulroney and Chrétien governments."[67] Canada "joined the convention in 1995 to help sponsor research into effects and solutions for droughts around the world that reduce food production, drive small-scale farmers into poverty and produce millions of refugees."[68] We abandoned the convention, according to the prime minister, because it "is not an effective way to spend taxpayer money."[69]

- The United Nations: Since the institution was created in 1945, all previous Canadian governments have acknowledged its weaknesses and tried to correct them, but also emphasized the considerable success of the United Nations family. The Harper government professes support for the UN but focuses on its failings, to the point of hostility.

The General Assembly of the United Nations meets each fall, and leaders of many member countries attend. Usually, but not always, Canada's prime minister has addressed the General Assembly. That opportunity has arisen seven times since Mr. Harper's election as prime minister. As of this writing, he has attended twice, in 2006 and 2010. In 2012, while leaders of other nations addressed the General Assembly, Mr. Harper did visit New York. But instead of going to the UN, he attended a meeting of the Appeal of Conscience Foundation, which named him "world statesman of the year." In his acceptance speech he took a calculated shot at the world organization: "We also want . . . governments to be good world citizens. . . . that is, of course, not the same thing . . . as trying to court every dictator with a vote at the United Nations or just going along with every emerging international consensus, no matter how self-evidently wrong-headed."[70]

Canada's participation in UN peacekeeping missions has fallen from first in the world when peacekeeping began, to fifty-fifth in the world in 2012, despite an "unprecedented demand for

peacekeepers," a demand that is expected to rise.[71]
In 2010, Canada declined the UN's request to send
Lieutenant-General Andrew Leslie to command the
20,500-strong peacekeeping force in Democratic
Republic of Congo.[72]

In many UN committees, the chair rotates regularly
among member countries for short periods. In 2013,
Canada announced it would boycott sessions of the
UN Conference on Disarmament because that principle
of rotation meant there would be periods—of about
fifty days each—when North Korea, and later Iran,
would occupy the chair.

- The environment: From Maurice Strong's leadership
  of the first United Nations Conference on the
  Human Environment, in Stockholm, in 1972, to
  the Mulroney government's acid-rain treaty with the
  US, to the Montreal conference that led to the ban
  on ozone-depleting CFCs (chlorofluorocarbons),
  Canadians have historically been active leaders
  on environmental issues. The Harper government
  is reversing that leadership. UBC professor Simon
  Donner contrasts Canada's performances at the 1992
  Rio Earth Summit and the twentieth-anniversary summit in 2012: "The five point agenda laid out by . . .
  Brian Mulroney . . . was forward- looking, environ-
  mentally-minded, and beyond anything, internation-
  alist. The goals were to help developing nations
  formulate plans, to ratify inter-national conventions,
  to take action on international aid and related debt,
  to integrate sustainability into the goals of all existing
  international institutions, and to pursue an Earth
  Charter. . . . Canadians negotiators went into the
  Rio+20 summit arguing for only voluntary initiatives

in the final document, 'green' growth indicators which were intensity-based . . . and less focus[ed] on . . . aid to the developing world. The Canadian government hoped to shift the focus instead to two issues: energy and the oceans. Energy is obviously in the Canadian interest. . . . but Canada actually voted against . . . a system for protecting the open ocean from exploitation."[73]

- NGOS: The Harper government has been treating respected NGOS as adversaries, not allies, for example caricaturing environmental groups as driven by a "radical ideological agenda,"[74] cancelling funds for International Planned Parenthood Federation,[75] KAIROS, the Canadian Council for International Co-operation and MATCH International.[76]

One essential factor in any assessment of a country's international capacity is its reputation among other countries. Reputation is particularly important for a country like Canada, whose economic or military weight are not enough alone to defend our interests in a competitive and unpredictable world. The 2012 BBC World Service "Country Ratings Poll," conducted by GlobeScan and PIPA, recognized Canada as having the third most positive reputation of any nation it asked about. What is notable is that, in the early years of the poll, Canada often ranked *first*.[77] Similarly, Canada's ranking in the UNDP Human Development Index stood first for seven years, from 1994 to 2000.[78] In part, that reflects modification of the criteria, but nonetheless Canada is trending down, not up, by standards that have, historically, been important to us.

The most emphatic single demonstration of the decline in Canada's reputation came in 2010, when we were forced to quit before we were beaten in our campaign for a non-permanent seat on the United Nations Security Council. Professor Denis Stairs notes: "Even more alarming was the fact that the defeat [was] . . . by an impressively wide margin."[79] At the time, Canada was one of only five countries (Canada, Colombia, India, Italy and Pakistan) that had been elected regularly as a non-permanent member. Canada was elected six times, at roughly ten-year intervals: in 1948–49, 1958–59, 1967–68, 1977–78, 1989–90 and 1999–2000. The only previous loss was in 1946, when our country was in the early stages of establishing our international presence, and our competitor for the available seat, Australia, was much more assertive.[80]

Professor Stairs notes, "Canada has recently been pursuing some policies that have alienated a large number of countries that might otherwise have been willing to support the Canadian candidacy," including on the environment, the freezing of development assistance to Africa, "the somewhat ostentatious . . . support for Israel" and "highly visible . . . combat operations in Afghanistan."[81] He notes that "Prime Minister Harper has a reputation for not caring very much about the United Nations" and that "Louise Fréchette, the Canadian Foreign Service officer who served as the UN's deputy secretary-general for six years, has argued further that the real problem is that we don't seem to be *there* anymore. In effect, we have ignored Woody Allen's famous dictum on how to get ahead and gain influence: 'Show up!'"[82]

With the notable exceptions of Canada's significant engagements in Afghanistan and Haiti, we have become silent— failing to "show up"—on several questions where Canada was customarily an activist or leader: on relations between richer and poorer countries, or official development assistance, or a constructive interest in Africa. Or we have become obstreperous, as at the Copenhagen climate conference,[83] or quixotic, as in the cases of the Harper government's original policy toward China, which in its early days bordered on hostile, and its unprecedented level of support for Israel in the Middle East.

7

PUBLIC INTEREST COUNTRY/

PRIVATE INTEREST GOVERNMENT

The Harper government is skilled at conveying, and controlling, its own image among Canadians. But sometimes the most disciplined guard goes down, and the government actually says what it means. In October 2012, in the heat and fatigue of war-torn Kinshasa, capital of the Democratic Republic of Congo, and at the end of the fourteenth summit of La Francophonie, Stephen Harper said: "I hope that in the future, La Francophonie and other major organizations will decide to hold a summit only in countries with democratic standards."[1] Note the word "only," as though achieving democratic standards was some kind of external award rather than a demanding work in progress, which requires the presence and pressure and support of countries who have made their own progress in the transition from authoritarian to more democratic systems. In many cases, as in Canada's,[2] that transition took centuries.

It happens that, in 1989, at the third francophone summit, in Dakar, Senegal, I co-chaired the meeting of foreign ministers that negotiated the first resolution on human rights to be adopted by the organization. That initiative had been proposed forcefully by Prime Minister Mulroney, with the strong support of Quebec premier Robert Bourassa and others. We understood fully that many of the nations at that conference might sign or support a resolution, but would continue their terrible abuses of human rights—that included, notoriously, the regime of then-president Mobutu Sese Seko of Zaire, the country that later would become the Democratic Republic of Congo. However, we also knew that adopting international declarations on human rights was often a first essential step toward bringing legal or other pressures to bear that could change the behaviour of such regimes. That was one enduring lesson of the end of the Cold War.

The Helsinki Accords, signed in 1975 by members of NATO and the Warsaw Pact, "included promises related to the respect for and promotion of human rights."[3] They have been described as a "a political agreement . . . not a binding treaty,"[4] but they nonetheless created both leverage for pressure on offending states and, as importantly, an incentive and support for domestic advocates of rights and democracy in countries where those were denied. "Post-cold war analyses of the Helsinki Accord," says the *Encyclopedia of Human Rights*, "connect its human rights provisions to the mobilization of dissident movements throughout eastern Europe and even to the collapse of communism in 1989–91."[5] These are not instant developments. They require time, care, persistent engagement and an understanding that they cannot be achieved "only in countries with democratic standards," but also on the harder ground of the developing world and oppressive regimes.

Mr. Harper was not a new prime minister when he let slip his preference regarding the location of international summits. He had been in Canada's highest elective office more than six years, attending and hosting international summits, necessarily meeting with leaders of developing and poor and conflict-torn countries, and insisting on being the active final arbiter of what policies and priorities Canada should follow in the world. This is a notoriously controlling prime minister, who dominates and decides his government's domestic and international policy more rigorously than any of his predecessors since, at least, the Second World War. Over those three terms as the undisputed "key man" in Canada's government, he had been exposed, frequently, to the hard realities faced by countries that are nowhere near as rich or lucky as Canada, and where economic development, and social justice, and democracy, and stability must be pursued steadily, and patiently, and with the help and understanding of friends. There is no gentle way to say this: Prime Minister Harper should have known better than to suggest that issues of democracy—or development—are best addressed from a distance than in the countries where they are most acute.

Most Canadian prime ministers arrive in office with much to learn about societies more troubled than our own, and their interactions with foreign leaders offer a privileged crash course in the real nature and challenges of very different societies and sets of problems. Certainly that was my experience, in a prime ministership marked by an energy crisis, remarkable common purpose in rescuing Indochinese "boat people," a Commonwealth conference creating Zimbabwe, an Olympics boycott and a hostage rescue in Iran. More to the point, because Brian Mulroney was longer in office as prime minister, I watched him sop up information he could never have acquired in Montreal or Baie-Comeau, and use that knowledge to supplement the advice of colleagues and officials and help guide Canada's international conduct. That happened regularly, but I remember a specific circumstance with a broad and immediate impact. In 1985, Mulroney stepped out of a G7 economic summit meeting in Bonn to take an urgent call from President Kaunda of Zambia, a colleague in the Commonwealth whom he often consulted about Africa. A drought was devastating and starving Zambia, and Kaunda believed the G7 needed to better understand its urgent implications. Mr. Mulroney returned to the table and helped persuade this summit of wealthy nations to respond to drought-stricken Africa.[6] In the seven years between his first election and the time I am writing this, Stephen Harper would have been exposed directly to informed and passionate leaders describing similar challenges and opportunities in the developing countries they lead. Conversations of that kind may well have influenced his willingness to serve as co-chair, with President Kikwete of Tanzania, of the UN Commission on Information and Accountability for Women's and Children's Health. They could have informed his government's more recent interest in international trade, including with some countries in Africa and the Americas. However, there is little evidence of much impact on the government's understanding of the human and political dynamics of countries outside the West.

During the decades when Canada was earning a respected reputation in the world, part of our strength was that we felt no need to sit always at the head of the decision table. Our competence meant we often served there—on issues respecting arms control,[7] the environment,[8] human rights[9] and international development. But Canada operated as effectively from a seat at the side, becoming trusted as a reliable, respected and responsible partner, and building concentric circles of influence on issues from defence, to development, to conciliation, to trade. Perhaps to a fault, we were known for our quiet and constructive work. By contrast, the Harper government's performance in international affairs has shown more interest in the podium than in the playing field.

The tone is often confrontational—"court every dictator"; "just go along to get along"; "sell out human rights to the almighty dollar"—or marked by dramatic gestures that prove counterproductive—deliberately staying away from the Beijing Olympics; suddenly closing Canada's embassy in Iran with no credible explanation; threatening "there will be consequences" when Palestinians prevail in a General Assembly vote. During the Cold War, the Secretary-General of NATO, Lord Peter Carrington, urged the superpowers to avoid what he called "megaphone diplomacy." That was defined as "diplomacy based on assertion through the media rather than on discussion,"[10] and Lord Carrington considered it a dangerous practice between nuclear-armed superpowers. It is as counterproductive today, especially for a country like Canada, which has real skills and assets in diplomacy, when we apply them.

The case of the embassy in Iran is worth considering. What does Canada gain—what do our friends, including Israel, gain— from shutting down our channels of communication with a country that is unquestionably powerful, assertive and internally divided? What do the friends of democracy in Iran gain by having another door closed? It's not impertinent to ask what would have happened in 1979 to the six Americans who became Canadian "house guests" in Tehran if we had shut our embassy because we disapproved of the regime. Governments are regularly tempted to shut down relations with countries whose policies they find deeply offensive. That was an issue with South Africa in the 1980s, when many committed Canadian opponents of apartheid believed closing our embassy would be a powerful symbol and statement of our disapproval of an offensive regime. That's true, it would have been. But it would also have been our last effective gesture, and would have pushed Canada to the sidelines of influence. Analogies are unreliable, but the decision to stay in South Africa, or to stay engaged in China after Tiananmen Square, increased our influence. In South Africa particularly, Canada employed the podium, but our real strength was being present on the ground, reinforcing the citizens and forces who sought to change their own country.

With the exceptions of Afghanistan and trade, there is a curious and recurring pattern in the Harper government's actions. It is unusually assertive in its dramatic gestures and declarations, but it has drawn back steadily from initiatives designed to actually resolve critical problems—drawn back from the fight against international poverty, peacekeeping, Kyoto, arms control, a broad presence in Africa and Canada's customary leadership in the United Nations, Commonwealth and related multilateral institutions. It has taken virtually no new initiative to lead any significant international reform— no equivalent of the partnerships for change represented by the north-south dialogue, the anti-apartheid campaign, the land mines treaty, the International Criminal Court (ICC), the Contadora process, the diplomatic recognition of China, or Canada's early leadership on environmental issues.

Canada now talks more than we act, and our tone is almost adolescent—forceful, certain, enthusiastic, combative, full of sound and fury. That pattern of emphatic rhetoric at the podium, and steady withdrawal from the field, raises a basic question: what does the Harper government consider the purpose of foreign policy?

The government has indicated its preference for bilateral discussion[11] where, by definition, the number of factors and actors is limited and easier to predict, if not control. That seems to be a strong personal instinct, and extends well beyond international policy. It may be why he avoids the federal-provincial conferences and co-operation at home which have been key to critical Canadian accomplishments— from healthcare to the free trade agreement, the environmental round table to the Kelowna Accord. It is an ironic legacy for a party whose "reform" promise was to open a closed political system, and allow more transparency and engagement.

In the classic American film *Mr. Smith Goes to Washington,* Jimmy Stewart plays the idealistic outsider guided by a charming instinct to "do the right thing" in the cynical capital of politics. He doesn't much like what he finds there, but works his way through it, rather than taking on "the system." The guiding members of the new Conservative government elected in 2006 were not "Mr. Smith." They brought a palpable edge of resentment to office, a sense of wrongs to be righted, and a suspicion of both the public service and of the governments that had been there before them. There are reasons why political parties think and act as they do, and it is often not conventional ideology. I have never been a member of the political party shaped and led by Stephen Harper, but, naturally enough, have watched it closely, and think that attitude flows from three related sources:

- The compelling "outsider" tradition of the Reform Party. "The West Wants In" was conceived as a geographic slogan, but it also attracted other Canadians who genuinely felt their preferences were systematically excluded by governments that spent too freely, brought in a gun registry, rejected the death penalty, asserted the equality of women and expected locally elected Members of Parliament to toe a party line. They are in charge of a major system

now—a national government—but many of them
remain instinctively anti-system, outsiders.

- The aggressive and influential initiatives by some
  leaders of the US conservative movement, in and
  after the Reagan era, to attack what they considered
  to be the disproportionate influence on public policy
  of "liberal elites" and to counter those elites by
  building and funding "conservative" think tanks
  and policy institutes, encouraging candidates with
  socially conservative views, and advancing alternate
  visions of American social and cultural policy.
  Whatever their other consequences, those movements
  transformed the US conservative movement from
  complaint to advocacy, and impressed some
  Canadians who became involved in the Reform
  Party and sought to make it an agent of change
  rather than simply protest.
- Inexperience with the nature and institutions of the
  larger Canada beyond their particular communities,
  and sometimes discomfort with communities with
  which the party had little direct contact and not much
  sympathy, including Quebec and, at the time, cities
  that were increasingly multicultural and untraditional.

Those influences might seem to be a long way from foreign
policy, except they now help shape the thinking, prejudices and
priorities of ministers and partisans who determine current
Canadian international policy, and they make a significant difference. Nearly eight years in office have provided considerable
experience with the mechanics of government, and the aggressive use of power. There is much less evidence of any real
growth in a sense of connection between the government and
those Canadian voters or communities who don't vote for

their party but are nonetheless citizens of the country, with legitimate interests and concerns. While the 2011 election made the Conservatives a majority in Parliament, they remain a minority in attitude. Quite consistently, their policy thrust—as a majority government—has been designed to consolidate their own political base rather than encourage or construct any serious national consensus. By contrast, other majority governments of the last fifty years—Diefenbaker, Trudeau, Mulroney, Chrétien—all sought to evoke and embrace a country larger than their party base. They sometimes failed, in will or execution, but their response to a majority in Parliament was to seek to be "majority" in attitude as well.

After nearly eight years in office, the Harper government's legislative output has been relatively limited. The familiar explanation is that it was constrained by its minority status through its first five years, but there is a more compelling reason than caution for this limited agenda. These Conservatives do not believe in active government, and think that previous federal governments had become active in fields where they should not have been. In office, they have given as much attention to stopping or reversing the initiatives of former governments[12] as to taking legislative initiatives of their own. Public advocates of broader perspectives have either withered when funding of their organizations was cut[13] or not yet found the arguments or audience they need. That "curtail government" view is different from a positive belief in, for example, fiscal responsibility, which can sometimes lead governments to significant restraint in expenditures and programs. It reflects instead a substantially negative view of government, which contrasts sharply with Canada's historic and bipartisan creation of public institutions as essential partners and leaders in building a strong country, economy and society.[14]

Put at its simplest, Stephen Harper and his colleagues lead a "private interest" government in a "public interest" country. In their careers before politics, both Mr. Harper and his most influential minister, Jason Kenney, led interest groups whose principal purpose was to cut taxes and limit government.[15] The government is so uncomfortable with many of the social programs enacted by those previous governments that Mr. Harper himself, in 1997, described Canada as "a northern European welfare state in the worst sense of the term."[16] He later claimed the statement was "tongue in cheek," but it was his tongue.

A mindset that resists government leadership at home is less likely to take initiatives internationally because, in most cases, such initiatives would involve some degree of continuing government participation. By contrast, as individuals, Canadians have a broad view of their role in the world. When the World Values Survey[17] asked representative samples of citizens whether they agreed with the statement "I see myself as a world citizen," 85.8 percent of Canadians said they agreed or strongly agreed, compared to 68.6 percent of Americans.[18] Despite that positive attitude to the world, the public's attention to the activities of the Harper government has so far concentrated less on international affairs than domestic policy.

Moreover, when Mr. Harper and his colleagues formed a government, they were less than two years old as a national party, with shallow roots in much of the country and virtually no personal or party history in reconciling the kinetic factors of an unusually diverse nation. Their victories were due less to their inherent strength than to the weaknesses of their opponents. The Progressive Conservatives and the Liberals had both become their own worst enemies, scarred by internal battle, sometimes to the point of simply running out of steam. But at their best, they were both persistently pan-Canadian, had cultivated among their members a sensitivity toward the inherent differences and tensions that a national government must manage, and had built broad coalitions of voters whose specific interests were often quite different. Those diverse, even conflicting, interests came together in "big tents"—first, national political parties, and then national governments—in which their differences might be worked out, and they could pursue together the broader purposes they shared. There have always been serious weaknesses in that model: some important interests—including those specific to regions or minorities—could be treated as peripheral, and feel persistently excluded or marginalized, "outsiders" in their own family; the driving motive of public life could be seen to be compromise rather than principle; policies often seemed secondary to personalities, from Macdonald and Laurier to Diefenbaker and Trudeau.

The model also had significant strengths, including the encouragement of an ethic of co-operation—call it "compromise"—instead of conflict in a country of vast distances and potentially incendiary differences of language, culture, even identity. In my own experience, those "big tents" taught much more than compromise. They taught Canada, in ways that few—maybe no—other pan-Canadian organizations could. In the most competitive circumstances, those national parties had to appeal everywhere, because they would lose if they didn't. As a result, I learned more about my country from my experience as a party member than I ever could from school or books or broadcasts. National political parties, in that era, were forced to be as inclusive as possible, and to search for whatever common ground existed. Canadians from sharply different regions and communities, with different prejudices, priorities, languages, faiths and visions of what we or the country could be, were bound together in the real time and unpredictable circumstances of election campaigns and party-building. The Liberals, or Progressive Conservatives, or NDP became the national family we shared together, sometimes the only direct contact MPs had with the rest of their country. In some cases, membership in a party imparted a sense of purpose as well as history. In the 1990s, a former senior advisor to Pierre Trudeau asked me why a Progressive Conservative government had been so much more emphatic than Trudeau's Liberal government in making the struggle against apartheid a Canadian cause. Part of the answer is that, in 1960, a throng of Progressive Conservative supporters welcomed John Diefenbaker back to Canada from the London conference where he had been a leader in forcing South Africa to withdraw from the Commonwealth. Mr. Diefenbaker had promised while in London that there would be "a light in the window" for South Africa to return to the Commonwealth when apartheid was gone. Brian Mulroney and I, both then in our early twenties, were in the thick of that throng. When our government was elected in 1984, opposing apartheid was part of our "family" legacy.

The 2006 federal election was an ideal time for a "new" party to campaign for change. The Liberal Party had been discredited by scandals at the end of the Chrétien era, and the new prime minister, Paul Martin, had not established an appeal of his own. Conservative advertising attacked a "culture of entitlement," the idea that an elite was enjoying advantages without earning them, which struck a chord among Canadians whose faith in government had declined, or who had simply become persuaded that it was time for something different.

To manage his volatile minority government, Mr. Harper took near-absolute control, including tight limits on the amount and nature of information made available to Parliament and the public,[19] and an unparalleled concentration of power with the prime minister, through his personal and highly partisan

Prime Minister's Office (PMO), and through the Privy Council Office (PCO), the head office of the non-partisan public service that simultaneously answers directly to the prime minister. For nearly half a century, since at least 1967, decision-making power in Ottawa has been concentrating steadily in those offices, and the authority of cabinet ministers and government departments—not to mention the authority of Parliament— has declined seriously as a consequence. I have been involved with Canadian cabinets and ministers for more than fifty years, going back to the Diefenbaker period, and Stephen Harper has accumulated more personal power, as prime minister, than anyone else in that half-century.

I served in my own cabinet and Brian Mulroney's, was close to Kim Campbell's government, and sat watchfully across the floor of Parliament from the cabinets of Pierre Trudeau, John Turner, Jean Chrétien and Paul Martin. All had strong ministers who, from time to time, stood up to the prime minister and changed policy. The only people I can think of who came close to that in seven years of Harper governments were Michael Chong, who resigned in 2006, after only six months, when a central policy in his portfolio was changed without consultation with him, and Jim Prentice, who resigned in 2010. I know many members of the Conservative caucus, in both the elected and appointed houses, and admire some of them enormously; but, with the rarest of exceptions, that caucus has been as silent as the grave on issues on which I am sure several disagree with government policy or conduct.

More ominous than the muting of a caucus, including an elected caucus, is that this rule of emasculating silence has been extended to the public service. There is an actual rule now requiring officials to "clear" routine speeches or public statements with the PCO or PMO before they give them. Highly expert individuals, whose calling and profession is to serve the public, now need permission for public statements. In at least one case I know of directly, when killings broke out in a country where Canada has significant interests, our very capable high commissioner had to seek permission from Ottawa to condemn the killings; however, it was a weekend, and Ottawa was on weekend time, so official Canada was quiet while the British, the Americans and other defenders of human rights voiced their cautions and alarm. More seriously, I know of several occasions when expert public servants offered considered and apt advice, which government ministers—or, too often, their partisan staff—didn't want to hear, so those expert professionals fell out of favour, or were cast out of the decision-making loop on complex issues in which their training, experience and honest advice would have helped avoid bad policy or foolish mistakes.

That freezing out of professional advice has been most marked in the case of the ministry now named "Department of Foreign Affairs, Trade and Development."[20] Apart from resulting in ill-considered policy, this approach has demoralized a foreign service that, when trusted, had offered outstanding and innovative advice to ministers and governments of all parties.

Strategies to limit public discussion range from omnibus bills—single pieces of legislation that contain multiple, often unrelated propositions—that sharply limit Parliament's ability to examine legislation,[21] through to the failure to publish "white papers" on foreign policy to engage public discussion, as had been done by each of the Trudeau,[22] Mulroney,[23] Chrétien[24] and Martin[25] governments. In my period as a minister, we regularly involved Parliament in public discussions of Canada's evolving policy initiatives in both South Africa and Central America and, during the Gulf War in 1991, conducted weekly open and televised hearings where Parliament could question ministers and the most senior officials of the relevant departments. Those policy discussions and hearings kept Canadians closely involved in international initiatives and also helped change and chart Canadian policy.

Open debate allows the public to become part of the choices societies have to make, and informs them about their options for the future, which in turn gives citizens the opportunity to improve measures that governments propose. That way, it can also inform a government about consequences or options it did not foresee. That is a significant advantage in a society that is becoming more educated and more complex. If discussion is valuable on ordinary issues, it is especially important when the calculations are complex, as they are increasingly on major public policy issues, from the cost of F-35 stealth fighter jets, to the value of statistics, to aboriginal policy, to climate change.

Public discussion can also confer legitimacy on inherently contentious decisions. Beyond its economic implications, the free trade agreement between Canada and the United States was also a major change in Canadian practice and tradition. It stepped away from a commitment to commercial protectionism that was as old as the country. The initiative made Canada uncomfortably open and potentially vulnerable to global influences and a powerful and beguilingly similar neighbour that could swamp our industries and institutions and dilute our sovereignty. It was a risk—as medicare was a risk, as were official bilingualism and most other significant national policy decisions. But mitigating that risk was the highly public nature of both the discussion and decision, undertaken after an extensive and objective study and recommendations by a respected royal commission, announced by the government, pursued under intense media scrutiny and public debate, and conducted with the full participation—the extraordinary participation— of provinces and interest groups that might be affected and whose perspectives and priorities often differed from those of our government. It was a public process, one that included ultimately the judgment of voters in a general election. It was a major change, a major risk, and its legitimacy was inseparable from the way the decision was taken.

8

WHY WE HAVE A

FOREIGN POLICY

I n the late 1980s, a polite visitor suggested to one of my constituents in Jasper, Alberta: "You must be pleased to have the foreign minister as your Member of Parliament." The constituent replied: "He'd be more use to us if he were the minister of public works."

Despite such skepticism, foreign policy is not something countries do for others. Its purpose is to pursue and defend national interests in the wider world. A century ago, that wider world was limited to our immediate neighbour, and a "mother country" to whose apron strings Canada was still attached. The world we knew has changed profoundly, and it is safe to assume those changes are just beginning. A mere decade ago, we regarded countries like India and Brazil and China as the "developing world," the implication being that they were apprenticing to catch up to us. They have now become "emerging societies"—emerging as dominant and defining players, not replicas of Western nations—and at a pace that surprised us, because we weren't paying close enough attention. As significantly, very poor societies, which much of Western policy once pigeonholed as remote to our interests, suddenly appear as sources of opportunity, immigration or contagious conflict. In this age of instant communication, deprivation and inequality become combustible when mixed with anger or fervour. Global issues, like climate change or the drug trade, have direct local impacts, and foreign policy has to be conducted in real time, addressing contemporary challenges. International issues now affect virtually everything we do at home.

The recurring turbulence of the last decade—the Iraq War, terrorism, recurring financial crises, climate change, growing religious strife, the serial collapse of authoritarian regimes in the Middle East—makes it clear that diplomatic, governance and political skills are more important in this era when many of the most lethal threats cannot be resolved by economic or military means. Active foreign policy is at least as necessary as national defence or "national security" policy, because it is better at preventing problems from growing deadly. And it is as necessary as intelligent economic policy in an era when simple economic growth or material success is no guarantee of stability—or of social justice.[1]

In Canada's case, there is another, quite different, sense in which foreign policy serves a domestic national interest. It can help us understand and define who we are as a country—not simply because that is our team on the field, wearing Canadian colours, but, more fundamentally, because the things we do in the world reflect and affirm who we are at home. Traditionally, we Canadians have been citizens of an understated country, proud enough of our accomplishments, but quiet about them, often diffident, remarkably unassertive. When we describe Canada's qualities or identity, we tie ourselves in "nots"—we are not Americans, not British, not French, not aggressive, not a superpower, not a problem. Most of the rest of the world takes a far more positive view of Canada—they see us as a complex and successful society that respects and celebrates diversity, a developed country still trusted in the developing world, a strong economy rich in human and physical resources, a free society, an innovative and accomplished population, an example for others to consider. Clearly, Canada is not the only country with some of those assets, but our combination of capacity and reputation sets us apart from most other nations.

There might have been a time when what mattered most to national governments was bridges or buildings or roads. Today, however, the policy that we used to call "foreign" is not a luxury but a necessity, an investment in our own ability—and our children's ability—to live peaceful and productive lives. So the "national interest" of Canada, or any other modern country, is much broader now, in this intimately connected world. A narrow definition of "national interest" may have applied in an age when most international relations were adversarial or occasional, and international decisions were dominated by a handful of powers, but that concept is almost antique today. It has not, in fact, ever really fit Canada's experience.

We weren't around as a country when empires sent their galleons on colonial missions. Canada came to maturity in a multilateral time, at the end of the Second World War, when the costs of conflict were everywhere on display—in the physical rubble of devastated Europe, in the anguish and loss of the families of the sixty million or more[2] soldiers and citizens who died on both sides of that war, or in the horror of the concentration camps. Of course, conflict and adversarial instincts were still very strong in that post-war period, as they often are today, but the means to address them became more co-operative after 1945. The realization was growing that nations' "interests" were more shared than singular.

That is the context in which Canada's international contribution and reputation were framed. We had suffered huge human losses in the First World War, when the "interests" we defended were "Allied" or "British" interests, not our immediate borders, not our territory. In that war, Canada took up arms as part of a larger community; that means that the deep tradition of Canada acting internationally arose from an instinct to serve and protect a group, not a particular national interest. Our motivation reflected a broad definition of "interests"—not self-interests, but interests that served *us and others*. We have been the opposite of an aggressor nation—Canada's usual method has been to prevent or contain conflict, not precipitate it. To an unusual degree, we have served and asserted our national interests by reinforcing the instruments and effectiveness of the international community.

Canada assumed leadership roles often, as our history reveals; but, more generally, we have paid attention to the accomplishment itself, rather than who gets credit for it. We are multilateralists by talent and by instinct, but also by interest. A falling tide imperils all boats, so Canada, like many other nations, has a general interest in reducing conflict and its causes. But crucially, we also understand that nations of our size are not big enough to assert or protect ourselves on our own. We need systems of sensible rules and order. So, Canada's national interest requires co-operation with others. Even on the so-called hard issues of trade, and economics, and security, co-operation has been the practical centrepiece of our policy. That is why we have been active architects and members of the alphabet goulash of organizations that keep countries working together—the UN, the GATT, the WTO, the OECD, NATO, CSCE (Conference on Security and Cooperation in Europe), OAS and a long list of others—and why, traditionally, Canada has been a leader and supporter of international standards and agreements in health, human rights, the environment, equality and other fields.

Foreign policy has meant different things to different countries, and at different times. National cultures and identity profoundly influence domestic decisions about the priorities countries set, and the roles they will play. The French devote about one-third of their total foreign policy budget to cultural and academic relations[3]—teaching their language, promoting their industries and culture, celebrating and reinforcing France in the world. Other countries that believe they are the foyer of an important language or culture do so as well (with somewhat less brio), and treat that culture as an asset that distinguishes them from comparable countries, and otherwise adds to their status and advantages in the world. The British do this with their British Council, their support of the BBC World Service and their continuing investment in the Commonwealth as the political community whose common roots are in the English language, and law, and "tradition." The Spanish and Portuguese are vigorously renewing their trade and cultural connections with Latin America, most notably of late through the creation in 2005 of the Ibero-American General Secretariat to "deepen the Ibero-American identity in all its facets."[4] Germany has long maintained the Goethe-Institut to showcase German philosophers, artists and language. In 2004, the government of China established the Confucius Institute, whose stated purpose is to work worldwide with colleges and institutes teaching the Chinese language and culture; by 2012, the institute was operating in 106 countries,[5] including thirteen centres in Canada.[6] In those cases of older countries, the cultural policy celebrates a civilization stretching and adapting over time and space, and also serves to validate France, or Spain, or China as the source of an enduring identity, reinforcing their credentials for respect and influence today.

Now more than ever, countries are more than history, or lines on a map, or like-minded communities that have dominated a territory for centuries. They are a collection of human lives, hopes, fears and surprises, and a broadening of aspiration, if not always of opportunity. Even within closed societies, barriers wear down—barriers of class, or mobility, or education, barriers of wealth, often of gender. Outsiders know anecdotally, or logically, that closed or ordered societies are not as monolithic or quiescent as they seem. However, the extent of the ferment and change is often not known until an Arab Spring,[7] or the anti-Soviet revolutions of eastern and central Europe,[8] or the referendum and separation of South Sudan in 2011, or the massing of indigenous populations at the polls in the 2005 Bolivian presidential election.[9] Those changes percolate before they boil, and then societies that had been accustomed to authoritarian structures suddenly have to deal with assertive diversity. Outgoing Chinese Premier Wen Jiabao warned the National People's Congress in May 2013 that "unbalanced, uncoordinated and unsustainable development remains a prominent problem," and "social problems have increased markedly,"[10] demonstrating again that huge China is no monolith, and that its leaders are as apprehensive about the acquiescence of their own citizens as they are about the intrigues of China's rivals.

Fewer and fewer countries are in fact cultural monoliths.[11] Many other nations in the emerging world are collections of minorities—Brazil, Democratic Republic of Congo, India, Nigeria, Pakistan, for example—whose internal rivalries can become more intense as economies slow down, or inequalities grow, or local or religious leaders foment or allow emotional or violent responses. A recurring requirement, in many contemporary societies, is to manage diversity as traditional systems of order erode. So, at some level, in most countries, the challenge of bringing diversity together is an increasing priority. That is a cultural challenge where the Canadian example and experience can be instructive and significant. Of course, we are not a torn and turbulent country. We are instead a modern, orderly, Western federation. But that status was not inevitable and, indeed, is not inherent in a country of such diversity and distance. We earned our identity as a peaceable and tolerant society. That experience is part of who we are as Canadians—a culture as relevant today, and as communicable, as the Magna Carta or *liberté, egalité, fraternité,* or the other lessons and experiences of more historic cultures. If those historic cultures represent "how we have lived over time," Canada represents "how we can live now."

Cultural or soft power factors influence international decisions about which cultures to call upon and, as important, which countries to count upon. Foreign policy is more than a matter of setting and pursuing grand international strategies. That option has never been open to most countries, including Canada, and pursuing grand strategies is even more difficult now, in an age when central power is constrained by the information pulsing through the most authoritarian barriers, and mobilizing local and personal ambitions and anger.

By contrast, there is now much more opportunity for a country like Canada to guide and stimulate important change. One way, among others, is to form specific partnerships, with other nations or with non-state actors, to advance specific issues. Another way is to identify particular roles in existing initiatives where our strengths and assets can be applied effectively. Working this way is not new for Canada—we have a strong track record and even more impressive credentials in parternships like these—and this is an ideal time to broaden and intensify that contribution. It is worth considering some quick snapshots of a few past examples.

- Thousands of Canadians joined personally in the campaign to end apartheid in South Africa. Those citizens, and the groups and organizations they worked through, were the driving force of the difference Canada made in that historic campaign for equality. But individual actions and declarations needed to be matched by policy initiatives and coordination with other countries. As in the case of Canada's initiative on the land mines treaty and the International Criminal Court, our impact would be greatest if we acted in close concert with others. The Commonwealth of Nations was a natural instrument of concerted action because it was so large and diverse[12] and because, in 1960, South Africa had been forced to withdraw from the Commonwealth over apartheid.

    Most Commonwealth actions were taken via the regular Commonwealth Heads of Government Meeting). But the CHOGM met only every two years, and that time lag diluted the impact of its declarations and actions. Canada believed we needed more frequent and effective means to apply pressure, and in Vancouver, in 1987, the Heads of Government established the Commonwealth Committee of Foreign Ministers on Southern Africa.[13] I became chair and our foreign ministry took a leading role in directing the Commonwealth campaign, along with the Commonwealth Secretariat in London and the government of Australia. Our mandate was to coordinate government actions including sanctions, support the victims of apartheid and, importantly, counteract South African censorship and propaganda. Our method was to meet every three months in a different Commonwealth country, consult and publicize anti-apartheid leaders, and steadily increase and coordinate sanctions and other measures.

South Africans themselves ended apartheid. But the Commonwealth campaign was widely publicized in South Africa, provided significant financial and moral support to people on the front lines and was much more effective because it was coordinated. Our aggregate impact was greater than if each of us had acted alone, and the fact that we acted as a group encouraged several nations to step up their engagement.

- In the late 1990s, Canada played a leading role in drawing together state and non-state actors to create two landmark international institutions: a treaty leading to the widespread banning of anti-personnel landmines and the creation of an International Criminal Court. These initiatives illustrate how foreign ministries and civil society could work together to achieve common goals. Each partner had sought separately to drive those changes, and had failed. Governments couldn't overcome conflicting internal priorities, and NGOs had no power to convert their arguments into action.

In 1991 several NGOs began to petition governments, seeking an end to the use of landmines, which often maimed and killed civilians;[14] in 1992, six NGOs banded together in the International Campaign to Ban Landmines.

By 1995, governments had reached an impasse on banning land mines. So, NGOs forged partnerships with those countries that supported a ban, including Canada. These partnerships allowed the NGOs to learn from seasoned government policymakers how

to draft and negotiate an international treaty.[15] In
return, interested governments gained the vocal support of a united group of citizens around the world
who were already mobilized and highly visible.[16] In
December 1997, those partnerships resulted in more
than four hundred NGOs playing an active part in the
negotiating conference in Ottawa that led to an agreement. On December 3, 1997, representatives from
122 countries signed the "Ottawa Treaty," formally
known as the Convention on the Prohibition of the
Use, Stockpiling, Production and Transfer of Anti-
Personnel Mines and on their Destruction. The treaty
would commit all signatory nations to destroy their
stockpiles, remove all anti-personnel mines from their
territories and help other nations meet their treaty
obligations. It came into effect on March 1, 1999.

The implementation of the International Criminal
Court followed a similar trajectory. Several earlier
attempts had failed, but the successful initiative was
prompted in 1989 when Trinidad and Tobago
requested that the UN establish an international
forum for the prosecution of drug trafficking crimes.
In response the UN asked the International Law
Commission to examine the establishment of a
permanent international criminal court. The ad hoc
tribunals for the former Yugoslavia (1993) and the
Rwandan Genocide (1994) broadened support for a
permanent court, and a draft treaty was scheduled to
be debated at a Rome Conference in the summer of
1998. Civil society became heavily involved, creating
the Coalition for an International Criminal Court in
1995, which quickly expanded to involve hundreds of
organizations across the globe. That coalition then

worked with some sixty-five small- and medium-sized
states, including Canada, which supported a strong,
permanent, and independent ICC. Several NGOs played
an active and direct role in drafting the agreement in
Rome, in 1998, and consensus was found. Following
ratification by sixty states, the Rome Statute came
into effect in April 2002, granting the ICC jurisdiction
over crimes of genocide, crimes against humanity,
war crimes and the crime of aggression.

It had become commonplace for like-minded NGOs
to form coalitions among themselves to promote their
agendas, and for governments with common purposes
to do the same amongst their peers. What was unusual
about the land mine treaty and the ICC was that,
on complex and controversial issues, policy-makers
and civil society collaborated to accomplish real
change. Despite their mutual wariness and, often,
historic antagonism, state and non-state actors changed
history by changing their practice, and Canada played
a leading role in making it possible.

- In October 1991, an international conference in
  Madrid launched the Middle East peace process—
  known as the Madrid Process. The conference set up
  working groups on four topics—water resources, the
  environment, regional economic development, and
  arms control and regional security—a list to which
  Palestinian authorities would only agree if a fifth
  were added: refugees.[17] Israeli representatives were
  not enthusiastic, but told US Secretary of State James
  Baker that Israel "would tolerate it if Canada would
  chair it."[18] So Canada became chair or "gavel," as
  the term was, of the Refugee Working Group. The
  goal was to improve the living conditions of refugees

and displaced persons without "prejudice to their
rights and future status; to ease and extend access to
family reunification and to support the process of
achieving a viable and comprehensive solution to
the refugee issue."[19]

Any process is slow in the Middle East, and all
negotiations became much tougher with the 1995
assassination of Israeli Prime Minister Yitzhak Rabin,
bombings and Israel's construction of settlements in the
West Bank.[20] When the broader Madrid process hit
shoals, Canada kept the Refugee Working Group
going. It brought together academics, diplomats, civil
society, and a core group of influential Israelis and
Palestinians to develop ideas and proposals that could
be used in future negotiations.[21] With the second
Palestinian intifada in September 2000, all other multilateral discussions stopped; but still, Canada kept this
refugee network alive, and later worked with the
United States and European nations in a group that
coordinated the activities of donor countries concerned
about refugees and displaced persons.

This work was the opposite of glamorous or easy.
Almost by definition, refugees are an afterthought of
resolving crises—they are the "fifth" working group,
not the pre-occupation. Canada's reputation and dex-
terity maintained that focus on refugees when other
negotiations failed. More than that, the group also
helped to raise over US$90 million for the UN Relief
and Works Agency programs for Palestinian Refugees
in Jordan, Syria, Lebanon, the West Bank and Gaza,
including professional training, infrastructure development, building and rehabilitating of schools and hospitals, and increased direct humanitarian aid.[22]

Canadians have responded with enormous generosity to humanitarian crises around the world, whether those are triggered by tsunamis, famine, or the prejudice and oppression that create refugees. Often that response is individual—human to human—encouraged and channelled by faith groups and service clubs and citizens. But we have also established an infectious practice of partnership, combining the instinct of citizens and the organizing power and incentive of governments. I was privileged to be involved in two of those creative partnerships: first, in 1979–80 when, on a per capita basis, Canadians led the world in its response to the "boat people" of Vietnam, who had been cast adrift to die in the China Sea; second, in 1984–85, when more than half-a-million Canadians mobilized to aid the victims of drought and famine in Ethiopia and neighbouring African countries.

- The Vietnam War displaced hundreds of thousands of people. Many took to the seas in hopes of escaping political persecution, often in boats unsuitable for open water. Thousands lost their lives at sea and many who did reach land were turned away, or placed in refugee camps. Canada has a strong record of responding to refugees and, in 1976, Parliament specifically recognized refugees as a class of immigrants eligible to enter the country, and stipulated that citizens or private organizations now had the ability to sponsor refugees.[23] That law took effect in 1978, and Prime Minister Trudeau's immigration minister, Bud Cullen, had begun a response to the "boat people." My government was elected in May 1979 and, through Foreign Minister Flora MacDonald and Immigration Minister Ron Atkey, we stepped up the initiative, announcing Canada

would accept 50,000 Indochinese refugees by the
end of 1980. Our innovation came in matching the
sponsorship of citizens and private organizations.
Citizen response was so strong that we increased
our target to 60,000.

Between September 1979 and January 1981[24]
over 7,000 sponsorship groups were formed.[25]
60,000 "boat people" came to Canada. Only the
United States welcomed a higher number, and
the US population was ten times larger than ours.

• In 1984, drought and famine struck Ethiopia and its
neighbours, causing an overwhelming need for
humanitarian assistance. Civil conflict and widespread drought meant that millions of Ethiopians
were starving. That drought had depleted fresh water
supplies, resulting in massive crop failure and the loss
of livestock. We established a temporary African
Famine Office, to coordinate public and private
activities, and announced a $50 million special
Fund for Africa, part of which would be used to
match private donations.[26] Fundraising drives were
held in places of business, schools, community
centres, social clubs and churches. Many municipal
and provincial governments set goals for their
residents to meet, often promising to match
donations themselves. Haligonians organized a
Christmas Eve airlift to Ethiopia. The Kinsmen
club of Kingston funded a volunteer medical team
in Ethiopia—and so it went across Canada.

By March 1985, more than half-a-million Canadians
had personally contributed between sixty and eighty
dollars each.[27] Between 1984 and 1985, contributions
by voluntary organizations and the federal, provincial,

territorial and municipal governments totalled more
than $170 million. More than half of these funds—
56 percent—were committed to relief programs
organized by Canadian voluntary organizations,
drawing directly upon the expertise and knowledge
of civil society.

Initiatives like these are only one element of Canada's
capacity to have an active and effective influence on international affairs. But they merit high attention now, for three
compelling reasons:

- First, they constitute an asset that we have used
  only episodically before, often as an adjunct to
  traditional initiatives rather than as a valuable
  aptitude and vocation on its own;
- Second, these kinds of mobile, inclusive and
  innovative instruments are both more effective
  and more necessary in a time when conventional
  methods regularly prove inadequate, and lose
  legitimacy;
- Third, Canada's assets are better suited to this
  growing and essential role than those of most other
  countries in the world.

Ideology aside, the Cold War was about control. Each of the
two contesting alliances—NATO and the Warsaw Pact, West
and East—was led by a superpower, indisputably in charge.
And their writ was vast, extending well beyond the members
of their respective military alliances. Even though organizations like the Non-Aligned Movement—a group of strong
developing nations that came together to pursue common

interests outside the Soviet and NATO alliances—grew and were influential, the calculations that defined attitudes toward the developing world, particularly Africa, were Cold War calculations. When President Mobutu of Zaire allied with the "democratic" West, that West shut its eyes to his despotic rule at home. When the Soviet bloc opened its aid and its weapons and its schools to "independence movements" in developing countries, the dominant motive was to build alliances and spread ideology; certainly, the motive was not an intrinsic belief in "independence." Cuba's strategic importance skyrocketed not simply because of Fidel Castro's charisma and skill, but because it was Moscow's beachhead in Washington's backyard. That Cold War competition also drove events in Asia, the Middle East and elsewhere in the Americas. The motives and causes may have been different in Moscow and Washington, but the instrument was the same—control.

Then the Cold War ended and suddenly, on the Soviet side, control broke—and on the Western side, control gradually relaxed, and shifted to economic matters. What is startling, in retrospect, is how swiftly the West moved from an approach that had been based upon control at the centre to the dynamics of a "free market," whose premise was that economic forces and interests should operate with as little control as possible. Some old habits continued—notably the peripheral attention paid initially to the challenges and potential of the developing world. But it is also the case that more countries were suddenly "free" to act with more autonomy, and to enter into new kinds of partnerships. The world had changed. That previous concentration of control was no longer possible in a world transformed by the instant spread of information, and the ability of organizations—whether they were banks, or Greenpeace, or al-Qaeda—to operate beyond the ordinary reach of national boundaries and jurisdictions. Non-state actors were growing stronger, with their worldwide memberships and missions. Sovereign states were growing weaker; their borders mattered less, their walls didn't work. The biggest threats of the new age—disease, climate change—respect no boundaries.

That creates a significant opportunity for countries with the will and ability to seize it. If the capacity of traditional sovereignty to keep things out has diminished, so has the opportunity increased to renew the vitality of nations by mobilizing and channelling the kinetic imagination and energy of this new, globalized age. Globalization is not at all the end of nations—Brazil and India and other emerging economies are harnessing the new opportunities of globalization to generate a vibrant sense of national pride and purpose. They and the great majority of their citizens are demonstrably stronger as a result; since 1990, Brazil has more than doubled its GDP per capita, while India's has more than quadrupled. At the other extreme of national size, a geographically tiny country like Qatar has embraced globalization to transform itself from an out-of-the-way emirate into a dynamic and influential country—the home of Al Jazeera, a frequent and constructive negotiator in sensitive political disputes, an international transportation hub and financial centre.[28] Globalization is sometimes cast as a purely negative force, a juggernaut of the powerful that sweeps away national identities and individual rights. Certainly it has an enormous capacity for abuse, and requires active and aggressive scrutiny and regulation. But globalization is a catalytic process, as irreversible as a change in the weather. National governments and citizens have the right to protect and assert their specific interests and identity in a changed age, but also a responsibility to make the most of new circumstances. Some changes can't be reversed, and there is no remedy in nostalgia. But national sovereignty has never been absolute. Again: "Independence is only relative," said Lester Pearson. What's pertinent is to think seriously about the values we want to define us, and the goals we want to achieve, and then devise twenty-first century means to pursue them. That is foreign policy in action—and it is grounded in who we are at home.

Serious international policy should also mobilize the capacity of globalization itself to stop or limit abuses that conventional sovereign laws could not, or would not, overcome. International agreements—whether the North American Free Trade Agreement or the European Union or bilateral agreements—carry with them reforms to environmental regulations (such as NAFTA's North American Agreement on Environmental Cooperation), human rights (the European Convention on Human Rights, established by the Council of Europe) and other practices by which sovereign governments had previously abused, or could abuse, their power. Switzerland and other countries have amended privacy practices that had allowed the powerful to evade taxation or hide ill-gotten gains. A series of transparency initiatives—from Transparency International to the Extractive Industries Transparency Initiative and Publish What You Pay—shine more light into behaviour that rulers and their cronies once kept quiet. So does rogue behaviour like that practiced by WikiLeaks. The information revolution is as unsettling to old orders as the industrial revolution once was. Too often, globalization is seen in the narrow context of its impact upon economic arrangements, and with the apprehension that it will add power to multilateral corporations or practices that are inherently harmful to national cultures and interests. Those are legitimate concerns, which need to be addressed. But globalization should be seen whole, its opportunities as clearly as its threats. There are real benefits to breaking down old barriers and repressive practices—and real opportunities for a country with Canada's talents and assets, if we are willing to look for those opportunities. A robust foreign policy allows us to counter the threats and pursue the opportunities, and to build further upon the solutions as an active, respected and independent member of the global community.

9

CANADA AND THE UNITED STATES

On November 9, 1979, just as Question Period ended in the House of Commons and MPs began to filter out, Flora MacDonald, secretary of state for external affairs, sat down beside me in Parliament to report that Canadian embassy staff in Tehran were providing sanctuary to five Americans who had escaped the recent occupation of their own embassy. Moments after Question Period began, she had received from her officials the telegram from our ambassador, Ken Taylor, advising that the Americans were "house guests" in two of Canada's official residences in Tehran. Flora and I immediately agreed that Canada should continue to shelter the Americans and help them get out of Iran. The news was held very tightly in Ottawa because any leak would endanger both the "house guests" and Canadian officials. Because the hostages were Americans, we advised US President Jimmy Carter and Secretary of State Cyrus Vance. Arranging the escape took nearly two months, with the "house guests" (now six) hiding with Ken and Pat Taylor and the head of immigration with the Canadian embassy, John Sheardown, and his wife, Zena. Two covers were devised to spirit the hostages home—one was as a visiting film crew, the other as a visiting agricultural team from the University of Guelph. The choice of cover was to be decided on the ground in Tehran by Ken Taylor and a CIA representative, who visited briefly. Flora and I told our colleagues in cabinet on January 4 that an urgent issue of national security had arisen. We asked them to approve, without discussion, the granting of twelve temporary Canadian passports—six for the film crew scenario, six for the agricultural mission. Ministers accepted the recommendation, the Governor General approved an Order-in-Council allowing Canadian passports to be issued to the Americans,[1] and the Canadians in Tehran began the dangerous work of getting the hostages home, and leaving Tehran themselves.[2]

That was a demonstration of extraordinary courage and care by Canadian officials and their spouses, in very dangerous circumstances. But the speed of Canada's decision to help— once the need and opportunity arose—reveals how deep the friendship runs between Canada and the United States, two nations who are much more than mere neighbours.

Difficult issues arise regularly between the governments of Canada and the United States. Our national interests often conflict, usually on smaller matters, but sometimes on issues of great consequence, such as the husbanding of water and other resources that straddle our borders, the nature and vitality of our cultural industries, or basic differences on international issues, from Cuba to Iraq. But generally, on both sides of the 49th parallel, the starting instinct is to help one another. I believe that instinct—to look for agreement, not disagreement—is stronger between Canada and the United States than between any other two countries in the world. We are not scarred by the divisive memories of war or conquest or ideology, which rile and divide so many other neighbouring nations. Moreover, we share a vision of ourselves as forward-looking societies, much more about the future than the past.

Our countries have substantial common interests, from the security and environmental stewardship of a shared continent, to trade, energy, and transportation infrastructure. Part of our "good luck" as a nation is where we live, and who our neighbour is, and a central element of Canadian policy must always be to build and nurture that advantage. However, despite these common interests, we are different nations—in the way we were formed, the way we act at home and abroad, and, in a growing number of cases, in the way we see the world around us.

Both Canada and the United States began as European civilizations on the move, men and women who left behind the confinements of a settled world for the space and challenge of an immense new continent. We share the heritage of building national communities founded on the promise of equality and accomplishment to all the people who settled here. We were, we are, the "new world." But, virtually from the beginning, the purposes and methods of these two new North American communities were as different as revolution is from evolution. The first sentence of the United States' Declaration of Independence refers explicitly to *separation*. The eloquent opening phrase of that unanimous declaration is clear:

> When in the Course of human events, it becomes necessary
> for one people to dissolve the political bands which
> have connected them with another, and to assume among
> the powers of the earth, the separate and equal station
> to which the Laws of Nature and of Nature's God entitle
> them, a decent respect to the opinions of mankind requires
> that they should declare the causes which impel them to
> the separation.[3]

The Americans were determined to create a new nationality, not just an improvement on what they had left behind, but a society that would be a model for the world's future. From their earliest days, the United States of America intended to set an example whose impact would reach well beyond their shores.

In significant contrast, Canada's more modest purpose was not to reject established values and traditions but to transplant them into a new and more promising land. Our way of nation-building differed markedly in both its explicit political and cultural connections with its two original European societies, the United Kingdom and France, and its founding respect for the diversity of cultures and identities which our new Confederation drew together. The closest Canada ever came to a civil war was the battle between French and English forces on the Plains of Abraham, which lasted only fifteen minutes.[4] In the aftermath, the English, who narrowly won, did not treat the French as a vanquished people, but instead established a larger society, where both communities could thrive together and variety would enrich each. That larger society was based upon a legal system that combined the French civil code with the British common law. It accepted and maintained the French language, the Roman Catholic religion, and the traditional French seigneurial system of land management. These were not trivial matters—what you spoke, what laws you were judged by, how you prayed, how the principal industry of the time was organized. Building a new country would be hard enough without fanning old divisions or discarding proven institutions. Those pragmatic and respectful decisions shaped the future of the communities which became Canada as decisively and distinctively as the high principles of the Declaration of Independence and the American Civil War defined the American republic.

Those decisions about law, language, land and cultural respect form the roots of the Canadian tradition of diversity that was extended later to waves of new citizens of other origins, admittedly with some failures along the way (the head tax for Chinese immigrants, the "none is too many" turning away of Jewish refugees and the internment of Japanese Canadians during the Second World War). That tradition of diversity and respect is as deeply imbedded in Canada's national character as the instinct to exceptionalism is in that of the US. Of course, with time our societies have become more similar; US definitions of culture have spread across the border, and our common interests—those which our shared geography lead us to nurture and defend together—have repeatedly brought us into one another's spheres.

For more than sixty years, Canada has been most effective internationally when we have pursued simultaneously two priorities that might be seen as inconsistent. We maintained as close as possible a partnership with the United States, and we pursued as independent and innovative a role as possible in the wider world. Those are not opposite positions. They are the two sides of the Canadian coin. Our access to Washington has added real clout to the standing we have earned independently by our actions in other countries. When Canada's relations with Washington are strong, other countries come to us, or listen to us, not just because of our own merits, but because we could influence the superpower. By the same token, our positive reputation in the developing world, and in the multilateral community—to name only two critical fora—has been an asset that the United States of America has not always been able to command itself. Often, in communities where the United States might generate envy or fear, Canada has built partnerships and trust.

There has not been enough attention paid to the positive opportunities that partnership opens to Canadians. Lester Pearson would have had no role in Suez without the mutual trust he had developed with senior US officials and their willingness to open the door so Canada could exercise an influence on Egypt and Egypt's supporters that none of Britain, France or the US could exercise themselves. Brian Mulroney's direct personal advice to President George H. W. Bush to go through the United Nations in the American response to Iraq's invasion of Kuwait helped shape that historic decision.

That ability—and that determination—to use both sides of the Canadian coin served us extremely well for nearly half a century, after the end of the Second World War. Canada's ability to bridge "the West and the rest" has, historically, contributed as much to our international identity and influence as our economic strength, or our skill and valour in conflict. Some other nations have that bridging capacity too, but it is sometimes constrained by their history as colonial powers, or their absence from powerful tables like the G7/G8 or NATO, where critical decisions of "the West" have been taken. When Canada gives priority to both sides of that coin, we strengthen our overall currency in international affairs; when we neglect one critical element of our international assets, we weaken Canada's currency, and risk debasing it.

It is well-known that the Mulroney government worked closely with the United States and achieved major breakthroughs, notably on free trade and acid rain. For critics, that relationship has become the caricature of our government—Ronald Reagan and Brian Mulroney, vaudevillians belting out "Irish Eyes." What is too often overlooked is that on broader international issues Canada often disagreed sharply with the position of the Reagan and Bush administrations—on issues like Cuba, Central America, the jurisdiction of the International Court of Justice, the approach to apartheid, the Strategic Defense Initiative—even as our government worked with them closely.

"Sleeping with an elephant" was the phrase Pierre Trudeau used to describe the ever-present threat that America's power poses to its much less populous neighbour. From a US perspective, that is an apt analogy because the hazard they pose for Canada is not that they are malevolent, but that they are big, preoccupied with themselves and often insensitive to the important differences between our two similar countries. But it is a false and demeaning analogy to Canada, to portray us as the puny little "mouse" whose only option is to get out of the way. Why do we demean ourselves? I am reminded of Winston Churchill's response to a similarly dismal dismissal of his country's capacity. Speaking in Canada's own House of Commons, on December 30, 1941, a time of doubt and deadly crisis, Churchill said: "[The French] generals told their prime minister and his divided cabinet, 'in three weeks, England will have her neck wrung like a chicken.' Some chicken. Some neck."[5]

Of course the Americans are tough in a fight and rigorously defend their interests when they conflict with ours. Like most big countries, they are inclined to throw their weight around and often they throw it at Canada simply because our geography and nature mean that we intersect with the Americans on so many issues. As a self-conscious democracy, prizing free speech and inherently suspicious of government, they have a domestic public opinion that is robust, influential, self-righteous and often ill-informed, not least about their neighbours. The late Tip O'Neill, when speaker of the US House of Representatives, famously observed that "all politics is local." A variation is more apt: US politics is local and the rest doesn't matter much. Our next-door neighbour—and ally, and principal economic partner, and vigorous democracy—is a superpower in its attitudes and reach, yet remains insular in its instincts and roots. So working closely with the United States—as Canada must; neither of us is going to pick up and move—is no piece of cake. But borders and neighbours are always complicated—ask the Baltic states, ask Turkey or Greece, or India or Pakistan, or Chile or Argentina, ask almost any nation in the Middle East or Africa. Canada's challenges with our neighbour pale beside those of most countries in the world.

The US doesn't act like an elephant so much as Canada sometimes acts like a mouse. Because our differences are not based on hostility, but on size and self-confidence, the responsibility to resolve them constructively lies principally with Canada. Where size is the issue, the smaller partner needs to take the initiative, and be bold and creative. Where self-confidence is the issue, the US is not likely to scale down, so Canada needs to be more assertive. On the evidence, in both bilateral and international affairs, Canadians have often been confident enough to assert and pursue our own assets and interests. In 1960, Prime Minister Diefenbaker resisted American pressure to join a commercial embargo against Cuba, and instead maintained Canada's diplomatic relations with Havana.[6] In 1965, the Auto Pact, signed by Prime Minister Pearson and President Johnson, significantly increased the proportion of automobiles and auto parts produced in Canada for the North American market.[7] But Mr. Pearson also declined US requests to send Canadian combat troops into Vietnam, and urged a pause in American bombing to permit a possible diplomatic solution.[8] In 1970, Canada established formal diplomatic relations with the People's Republic of China.[9] In 1991, despite initial strong resistance in Washington, President Bush and Prime Minister Mulroney signed the Canada–United States Air Quality Agreement—the acid-rain treaty—requiring the US to reduce sulphur dioxide and nitrogen oxide emissions by 40 percent of 1980 levels by 2010.[10]

During the Mulroney government, the most significant disagreement between Canada and the United States was about
the Strategic Defense Initiative, or SDI, known derisively as
"Star Wars," a proposal to establish a ground- and space-based
anti-missile defence system, a research program in which
President Reagan was so keenly interested that it became almost
his signature issue. The risk was that if you didn't support the
SDI policy, you were seen as being opposed to Ronald Reagan
personally. In March 1985, the Mulroney government was
invited to participate. We considered that invitation carefully
and in detail, and decided that Canada would not take part,
although Canadian companies and universities would not be
constrained from bidding on SDI-related contracts.[11] The position we adopted was clearly the right decision for Canada, but
our decision carried with it a high risk of angering Washington.
So, on September 7 we presented it to the Americans quickly,
clearly and personally, explaining exactly our reasons. Prime
Minister Mulroney called President Reagan directly to convey
news we knew the president did not want to hear. No doubt
their strong personal relationship made the message easier to
accept. What is most striking is that, less than three weeks after
Canada declined to embrace the president's vision, the White
House nevertheless accepted Canada's proposal to negotiate a
free trade agreement. Clearly, serious disagreement on one
important issue does not prevent agreement on another.

Canada's reason for being active in the wider world has
always been the objective importance of what Canada and
Canadians were doing—in Africa, in Central America, in
multilateral agencies, in official development assistance. But
a fortunate consequence of these activities is that we have had
cards to play in Washington. It is not our commonalities we
need to demonstrate to our neighbours in the United States
of America—those commonalities are generally known and

valued by US decision-makers—it is our differences; when they consider these differences, Americans understand that they are valuable to them. What the United States needs, as it exercises its immense and sometimes clumsy power, is not an echo, not a twin, but an ally, able to speak truth to the power of Washington, able on occasion to advocate or explain American positions to a wider world, able to bridge divides.

The value of Canada's international coin has been built and reinforced by both Liberal and Progressive Conservative governments in office, and generally supported by the New Democratic Party and the Bloc Québécois in Parliament. The active constructive Canadian role in the 1980s and 90s occurred under a Progressive Conservative government— working in the tradition of John Diefenbaker's outspoken opposition to apartheid, Howard Green's practical commitments to arms control,[12] Flora MacDonald's leadership on refugee. The Mulroney government was in office long enough to demonstrate that activist internationalism is broadly Canadian, not narrowly partisan, and has been a consistent Canadian practice at least since the 1950s—in effect a Canadian tradition, drawing upon a real and substantial Canadian capacity to influence international events.

Of course, it would be false to say that every Canadian international policy was rooted in a considered assessment of the two sides of the Canadian coin. The reality is that, often, US issues drive Canadian policy, just as European issues often drive United Kingdom foreign policy, or Chinese issues drive Japan's. A significant complicating factor for policy-makers in Canada is that many Canadians pay more attention to American foreign policy than they do to our own. I learned that lesson quickly in 1984, just after being sworn in as foreign minister. As a new minister in a new government, I wanted some sense of the international issues that were of most interest to Canadians, so we commissioned a poll. To our surprise, we discovered that the priority foreign policy issue for Canadians in the fall of 1984 was the situation in five relatively small and conflict-plagued countries in Central America (Costa Rica, El Salvador, Guatemala, Honduras and Nicaragua). That outweighed concerns about nuclear conflict, the Cold War, the environment, the Middle East, apartheid and other issues. Canadian NGOs had been active in Central America, but Canada's formal involvement in the region was relatively limited.[13] The Trudeau government had been considering new development programs there, but those had not been particularly controversial. The polling showed clear concern that Canada was not doing enough, but the trigger issue for Canadian opinion was President Reagan's aggressive policy in the region, which was controversial in his own country and evidently unpopular in ours. Given the clear public interest, our government looked at what we could do to be more effective in Central America. But here is the interesting dynamic: American actions shaped Canadian opinion, which would in turn encourage a more independent Canadian policy. That caused anxiety in official Washington, but had a strong positive impact on the Central American countries involved, and significantly strengthened Canada's capacity and reputation in the hemisphere. That Canadian opinion—and Canadian policy—were both significantly different from their American counterparts.

The Contadora process, through which Canada developed and exercised its Central American policy, provides an interesting snapshot of Canada's capacity for putting its soft power to use. In the early 1980s, civil wars and rising tensions intensified conflict among countries in Central America. That conflict escalated with Cold War intervention. The US saw increased Soviet involvement being chanelled through

Cuba, and so itself provided military and financial support to counter-revolutionary forces, including the Contras in Nicaragua, drawing heated criticism from the international community. Leaders of Costa Rica, El Salvador, Guatemala, Honduras and Nicaragua—the five most directly affected Central American states—had initially tried to resolve the situation themselves, but failed to devise a workable plan. A possible break to the impasse emerged in 1983, when representatives from Colombia, Mexico, Panama and Venezuela met on the Panamanian island of Contadora and launched the Contadora process. It aimed to end the militarization of the region, implement a monitoring and verification system to oversee the withdrawal of outside military personnel, and re-establish economic development and co-operation among Central American states. A Contadora Support Group formed, which included Argentina, Brazil, Peru and Uruguay.

If peace were to come, it would need to be kept. Foreign Minister Sepulveda of Mexico asked Canada, with our peacekeeping credentials, to provide technical advice on the Control and Verification Commission (cvc) to oversee the implementation of a future peace agreement.[14] Between 1984 and 1985[15] we produced four detailed reports on the security requirements for regional stability and recommended practical ways to make peace work: a clear timeframe and mandate, guaranteed access and freedom of movement, United Nations oversight, and full access by the media.[16] When I visited the region in June 1985, Canadian military officers, skilled in peacekeeping, came with me, and described their work directly to local political and military leaders.

Canada also tripled its foreign aid to the region between 1982 and 1987, and continued active support of the Contadora Group. In January 1986, we endorsed their Caraballeda Declaration, which included calling for an end to outside support for irregular forces in the region, the withdrawal of foreign military advisors and a freeze on weapons purchases. In 1987, the five presidents signed the Esquipulas II Agreement, which became the foundation for future peace negotiations. Canada was asked to join the resulting UN peacekeeping missions, and participated in the United Nations Observer Group in Central America (1989–92) and the United Nations Observer Mission in El Salvador (1991–95).

Our support was more than technical and financial. We recognized that "the root problem in Central America is poverty, not ideology; that the real need is development assistance, not military activity; and that intervention by outside powers will only aggravate the tensions."[17] Apart from the impact on peace in the region, our active and leading support of the Contadora process strengthened Canada's credentials as an independent and effective partner in Latin America, and was a major factor in our later decision to become a full and formal member of the Organization of American States.

One consequence of globalization and shifting power is that the US will henceforth have to share a leadership it previously believed it could exercise alone. It will remain the single most influential country, and the nation with which Canada will have the most in common. But those changes mean Canada must broaden our own alliances with emerging powers—our political and personal partnerships as well as the economic relations we are seeking now through trade. We must also assess carefully how the United States will respond to these clear shifts in world power and what new opportunities that might open for co-operation between our two countries. Two developments will be especially significant to Canada: first, the ambition and ability of emerging powers to take Canada's traditional place as one of Washington's principal interlocutors with the multilateral and developing worlds; and second, a resurgence of the historic American instinct to focus inward, presaging a withdrawal from the unusually active international engagement that has been a prominent American signature since the Second World War.

Canada has benefited substantially from our informal role as a bridge between the United States and other countries. In the developed world, that was one of our key contributions to NATO—we were the other North American partner, more intimately connected to Europe, more open and less daunting than the superpower. In the Commonwealth and other partnerships with the developing world, while our status was based on our own performance, we were also known to have an inside track to Washington, an ability to speak frankly, where others might be more inhibited. In Zambia in 1989, I was chairing the Commonwealth Committee of Foreign Ministers on Southern Africa, and it was clear that some of my African colleagues had something other than apartheid on their minds. When the formal meeting ended, I said: "Okay. What's up?" Nathan Shamuyarira, the Marxist-educated foreign minister of Zimbabwe, asked: "Who's going to bell the cat?" I thought something deeply serious was afoot. Then Ben Mkapa, later the president of Tanzania, said: "There's no cat. We need to get a message to Jim Baker [the US secretary of state]," on a separate issue between their countries and the US, "and we think you can reach him more easily than we can." "He'll take your call," I replied. "We'd feel easier if you called him first." So I did. Baker immediately called them and the matter was resolved.

Today Canada faces the new challenge of being displaced in our interlocutor role by several emerging countries to whom

Americans have been paying more attention lately—India, Indonesia, Mexico, South Korea, Turkey—each and all of whom would gladly fill a space, a "special relationship" with the US, that Canada occupied with little competition in eras when geography mattered more and potential competitors had less capacity. Unless Canada refreshes our status as an active force in multilateral and development affairs, linking the developed and developing worlds, several emerging countries could assume a role we had performed historically, and be enthusiastically welcomed, because Washington needs to recalibrate relations it once dominated with countries that are now becoming more powerful.[18] We are at risk of losing a card that Pearson played so effectively at Suez, and Trudeau played in gaining access to the G7, and Mulroney wove into his strong hand with presidents Reagan and Bush. It is a card Canada counts on as one of our international credentials, and a "value-added" in our relationship with our powerful neighbour. The Canadian government, encouraged by our business community, has been preoccupied by our economic and trade relation with the United States, as a partner and market within the continent. We have been paying less attention to our political relationship with Washington, including in international policy, where the Obama administration would have been drawn naturally to the traditional Canadian model of broad engagement in conflict resolution, multilateral institutions and international development. But Canada has been much less active on many of those issues, neglecting that side of the Canadian coin, and thus diminishing our value as a partner to the Americans. Apart from recent trade initiatives, Canada has been drawing back from its traditional intense and broad involvement in Africa, at a time when the Americans are actively re-engaging. The "focus on the Americas," announced by Mr. Harper in 2007, has been much less robust than

advertised—"a disconnect," in the words of former Chilean diplomat Jorge Heine.[19] On some critical issues, Canada has been
unhelpful. For example, the Israeli-Palestinian conflict is one of
the most challenging issues on President Obama's agenda,
and the US is the one country outside the region that may be
able to budge the logjam. When Obama sought support for
his proposal at the 2011 G8 economic summit at Deauville,
France, Prime Minister Harper was the only G8 leader to
deny a consensus. The White House is not likely to forget.

At the same time, the United States is itself becoming more
distracted both by internal issues and by opportunities or
challenges that have little to do with Canada. That is particularly pertinent now, because the inclination of the United
States to look inward appears to be getting stronger. An iso-
lationist instinct has always existed—it's the flip side of the
"exceptionalism" claimed by many Americans as a justifica-
tion for freeing their pioneering country from international
rules and understandings that bound other, older or less mus-
cular nations. Up until the 9/11 attacks on the twin towers
and the Pentagon, most news shown on American television
was about the United States, and often it was highly local—
car crashes, assaults, Hollywood celebrities.[20] In virtually
every other country in the world, people would wake up in
the morning to news about someplace else, usually the US. We
might not have welcomed that focus, but it made us aware of
a world wider than our own. But in the US the news was so
predominantly about events at home that it was easier to tune
out the rest of the world. The 9/11 attacks were more than an
assault upon the physical and territorial sovereignty of a
superpower. They were a shocking intrusion on the American
assumption of self-sufficiency—and those assaults have been
followed now by other shocks—a sudden sense that the nation
is constrained by its own debt, losing its capacity to summon

consensus, and less able to exercise the political and military muscle that has been the iron first in the American glove through the Cold War and much of the post–Cold War period.

It is now possible that these internal factors—magnified by fiercely partisan and divisive politics—will gradually move that powerful nation out of the commanding centre of the international stage, at least for the time being. This would not be the result, simply, of the accumulating influence of other powers—the emerging Chinas, Brazils or Indias, the European Union, the other heavyweights in a multi-polar world. It would also be rooted much more narrowly at home, in an intense debate about the nature and purpose of the United States. This would be a troubling passage, but the United States has faced those before, and has demonstrated an extraordinary resilience. In its fundamental attitudes it is still the country of the future, the innovator, the ground-breaker, the society that turns ideals into institutions—from its Declaration of Independence, to its critical role in shaping the institutions of the post-WWII world, to the Marshall Plan, to articulating and embodying the essential democratic concept of "government of the people, by the people, for the people." And Canada has deep and privileged connections to our neighbour, not only as a proven "friend" with a positive reputation, but almost as kin bound by similar aspirations and experience, as well as interests.

In the 2000 general election, my victory in the constituency of Calgary Centre was helped materially by billboards that described me as "more than just a pretty face." To the United States of America today, Canada is much more than just a strong economy, a partner in "border security" or an ally in Afghanistan. We have been an ally and partner for a long time, from the days when foreign policy was conducted "at the fence lines," through the International Joint Commission, the Suez Crisis, Iran "house guest," good counsel in Kennebunkport, to thousands of joint initiatives. In addition, despite substantial differences in our history and our nature, we have more in common with one another than either has with any other country. We share the heritage of building national communities founded on the promise of equality and accomplishment to all who settle here. We are deeply rooted democracies and complex federations that, with all our faults and challenges, respect inherent differences and function more effectively than our counterparts. We are forward-looking innovative societies, welcoming new ideas, new people, new challenges. We are still the "new world" in ways that distinguish our reputations and potential from more ancient civilizations like Europe or China or Russia.

When President Obama visited Canada in 2009 and said, unscripted, "I love this country," he expressed the instinctive sentiment that led Ken Taylor and his colleagues to embrace immediately American diplomats in peril in Tehran, and leads citizens on both sides of the 49th parallel to help unconditionally when some tragedy strikes the other side. The details of the political relationship between our two countries will change, as we both adapt to a world where "leading from beside" is more necessary and more possible. But in the world now taking shape, the easiest trust relation—for both Canada and the US—is still with one another.

10

THE POWER OF

PREVIOUS THINKING

B efore the Second World War devastated Europe, the nations of the developed world co-operated when necessary but generally focused on their own priorities. The decade after 1945 was sharply different. Developed nations saw a need to work together, and set in motion a series of international institutions pursuing basic interests that states had in common. The United Nations might have been the most notable, though it was hardly a new "vision"—a league of nations had been established a quarter-century before, and had failed because most nations, including Canada, were still skeptical about the need to change old ways. Joining the nascent UN in that catalytic post-war decade were the first global trading organization, GATT, and security organizations such as NATO and the Warsaw Pact, which, while adversarial, were each multi-national. The leitmotif of the era was "internationalization."

The Cold War, which grew out of that same period, was well named. It froze international relations into patterns driven by animosity, distrust and the fear of mutual destruction. But the end of that era, too, was characterized by bursts

of hope and freedom, whether the courageous "colour revolutions" of Ukraine, Georgia and Kyrgyzstan, or East
Germans surging through the broken Berlin Wall, or the
enthusiastic embrace of "free markets" as the economic
superhighway to the future, or the revolution in information
technology, which dissolved time and distance, and eroded
the power of national borders. The leitmotif expanded in
this era into "globalization."

The twentieth century was characterized by a continuous
adaptation of national practices in the face of new realities.
Domestic policy in different sovereign societies became more
effective by becoming more connected to the domestic practices of other nations. For instance, the management of borders
meant more co-operation and organization with neighbouring
states. Canada and the United States accomplished that impressively a century ago, in 1909, with the establishment of the
International Joint Commission to prevent or resolve disputes
that arise because "many rivers and some of the largest lakes
in the world lie along, or flow across, [our] border."[1] The same
requirement to co-operate arises steadily as neighbouring
nations increase trade and travel, build highways, resist disease, coordinate regulations, and lead separate but intercon-
nected existences. As those connections grow, that co-operation
with immediate neighbours extends to more distant countries
whose interests intersect significantly. For example, the need
for rules in growing international trade inspired the negotiation of the General Agreement on Tariffs and Trade in 1947.
A condition precedent to organizing and protecting nations'
offshore fisheries was to get some agreement with other fishing
and seafaring countries, and that led to the UN Convention on
the Law of the Sea, which came into force in 1994, nearly forty
years after the first conference to establish such a convention.[2]
Like most developed countries, Canada has signed over four

thousand international treaties or conventions[3] on matters ranging from human rights to social security to extradition to the Berne Convention for the Protection of Literary and Artistic Works. The international rules of that post-war period brought order to the thickening relations among countries, a basis for enforcing compliance with significant agreed-upon standards, and some rough sense of equality, because those standards were assumed to apply equally to the powerful and the less powerful. Those new arrangements became broadly based, but they were not compulsory. Sovereign nation-states could choose whether they would be part of these international regimes, and sometimes states chose to stand apart—for example, Mexico did not become part of GATT until 1986.[4] But most countries accepted the logic and the value of rules and systems that reached and connected beyond borders.

At the end of the Cold War, the technological revolution and the West's enthusiasm for "market solutions" had the air of a crusade. They were Western-controlled and corporate-driven. That combination quickly raised the fear that too much power was concentrated in too few hands, and that these global drivers were hostile or insensitive to the developing world, to cultural values and to environmental imperatives. "Globalization" became a Darth Vader word, evoking dark forces that pummel and stifle lively, legitimate and local identities and interests. There are certainly compelling examples of harm, from the eclipsing of small agricultural producers in countries too small to defend their interests adequately,[5] to the fuelling of climate change, to the Enron[6] and Libor scandals,[7] to other signals of jarring corporate indifference to the public interest. But that same globalizing phenomenon also transformed the individual lives of hundreds of millions of people who, thanks to their new access to the markets and opportunities of a global economy, have escaped from immobilizing poverty. The Yale Center for the Study of Globalization argues that "never before have so many people been lifted out of poverty over such a brief period of time."[8]

The ardour of that "good" or "bad" debate about globalization has overshadowed other transformations that are shaping life today. The information revolution has accelerated wide-ranging and deep social and political changes—including the mobilization of civil society, the capacity and influence of NGOs, and the concern about environmental sustainability. These developments are not corporate-driven, nor state-controlled, and many of them respect, defend and advocate the very identity and diversity that Darth Vader globalization was seen to threaten or efface.

That Western-driven "first wave" of globalization has passed its crest. It surged forward at the end of the Cold War, with the euphoric faith that free markets and Western business models would drive both worldwide economic growth and a buoyant new era of prosperity and well-being. Now growth has spread and a second transformation is occurring as those Western "market" models are being challenged, and sometimes displaced, by the dynamic performance and ambitions of emerging societies like China and India and Brazil.

There is some debate as to whether the remarkable growth rates of emerging economies will continue. That misses the point. The spike in growth signals not merely the economic expansion of non-Western nations, but their inherent capacity to compete: their levels of education, self-confidence, accomplishment and ambition. In baseball terms, call it the Jackie Robinson factor—a prejudice has been overcome, and suddenly it is talent that determines who will play and lead in the "big leagues" of innovation and growth. At the same time, as customary deference fell, and information and scrutiny spread, the weaknesses of conventional Western economic models became as celebrated as their strengths.

During the period of high enthusiasm for markets, public enterprises lost legitimacy as a development model, and so did the idea of an activist state. Now, in the combined wake of business scandals and financial crises, it is the legitimacy of market forces that is in decline. In many market-based economies, the private sector is being balanced by stronger regulation, emergency state interventions in the form of bailouts, the rescue and recapitalization of banks, and other means. There is also a more explicit acknowledgement that Western "market" models don't work well in many of the least-developed countries. Instead, they often require "a strategic collaboration between the state and the private sector,"[9] including the leading role of state enterprises in many economies.

The Chinese investment that is becoming dominant in parts of Africa and Latin America[10] is very different from the Western corporate models that shot out of the starting gates when the Cold War ended. In China's "state capitalist" model, the central government in Beijing determines major investment priorities, and those priorities set the course followed by state-owned enterprises (SOEs)—sometimes a combination of state-owned enterprises that have very different capacities, but ultimately the same boss. Among other things, this allows China to invest by a form of barter—using the capacities of one Chinese state company to secure new assets for another. The most controversial recent case was in the Democratic Republic of Congo where, in effect, one Chinese state company received rights to significant copper and cobalt deposits in exchange for another Chinese state company building key road, rail and other infrastructure.[11] China is engaged in similar "barter" arrangements in Sudan, Nigeria,

Congo-Brazzaville and Angola for oil, Guinea for bauxite, Ghana for cocoa, Gabon for iron ore and Zimbabwe for chrome.[12] Taken together, China's SOEs "accounted for around 90 percent of [the country's] cumulative [overseas direct investment] by the end of 2011."[13] That domination by direct state entities may diminish somewhat in the future,[14] but the role of the state will stay strong. And not just in China.

In 1978, China's "paramount leader," Deng Xiaoping, described his sweeping economic reforms as "socialism with Chinese characteristics"[15]—which was intended to mean an economy in the international mainstream but different from it. In that spirit, many emerging economies are "free market with distinguishing characteristics," and often those "distinguishing characteristics" are state-run enterprises, or policy priorities that show more respect for local or regional identities or differences. If free markets were once the Noah who would navigate the turbulent new seas after the flood of the Cold War, these state enterprises are the elephants in the ark. In January 2012, *The Economist* reported:

> The 13 biggest oil firms which, between them, have a grip on more than three-quarters of the world's oil reserves, are all state-backed. So is the world's biggest natural-gas company, Russia's Gazprom. . . . Saudi Basic Industries Corporation is one of the world's most profitable chemical companies. Russia's Sberbank is Europe's third-largest bank by market capitalisation. Dubai Ports is the world's third-largest ports operator. The airline Emirates is growing at 20% a year. . . . State companies make up 80% of the value of the stock market in China, 62% in Russia and 38% in Brazil. . . . They accounted for one-third of the emerging world's foreign direct investment between 2003 and 2010.[16]

There is another significant change in the world as the West knows it. For many nations, the region is replacing the globe as the arena of co-operation, sometimes with a deliberate design to limit the role of Western countries and economies. Regionalization could be the new globalization:

- In the Americas, individual state sovereignty remains jealously guarded, but "most Latin American countries have made enormous progress in managing their economies and reducing inequality and, especially, poverty, within a democratic framework. . . . [bringing] greater autonomy, expanded global links, and growing self-confidence."[17] There is more internal growth and outside trade and investment, symbolized by China, which "by 2014 it is estimated . . . will overtake the European Union as the second largest trade partner in the Americas."[18] Young people are more confident—"Latin America's 18–30 year olds . . . are nearly twice as optimistic about their future as their global peers."[19] Major countries are joining together to drive changes in international policy and practices, most recently on drugs.[20] Some initiatives, like the Community of Latin American and Caribbean States (CELAC), explicitly exclude Canada and the US. The purpose is to reduce the political and economic influence of the United States in the region, but Canada has become a collateral target.
- In Africa, more effective regional organizations are a hallmark of the growing strength of the continent. In 2002, the African Union was carefully launched to replace the old Organisation of African Unity (OAU), which, in the 1970s, then-president Julius Nyerere

of Tanzania had dismissed as a "trade union for
tyrants."[21] The new AU was "modelled on the
European Union with structures that included an
assembly of heads of state/government, an Executive
in which countries were represented by their foreign
ministers and the AU commission . . . the administra-
tive branch . . . headed by a President. The transition
from OAU to AU was clearly intended to transform
the institutional framework . . . to an action-oriented
forum."[22] The African Union now plays major roles
in coordinating economic development in the
continent and, moreover, leads conflict resolution
in, among others, Kenya, Côte d'Ivoire, Sudan
and South Sudan, and Libya. Those are extremely
complicated conflicts, where "home team"
peace-making by the AU is often more acceptable
and effective than that by international agencies,
or foreign diplomats and soldiers. In the words
of Alex de Waal, executive director of the World
Peace Foundation at Tufts University, "African and
international approaches to peace differ only. . . .
on where the centre of gravity of international
integration should lie. Africa's preference is for power
to remain in Africa, fearing that peace agreements
may become mechanisms for creating countries
dependent on foreign patronage. The UN, Europe
and America prefer for such countries to be inte-
grated directly into the global governance order."[23]
At the same time, internal regional organizations[24]
within Africa are rapidly expanding their internal
co-operation and effectiveness.

- In Asia, for some years, regional co-operation moved
  slowly. The Association of South East Asian Nations

(ASEAN) was formed in 1967, and featured two elements that continue to characterize Asian regional organizations today. The first was an interest in dialogue as distinct from integration, and the second, a defensive instinct, was ongoing concern about the economic domination of large powers within the region, initially China and Japan. The pace of regionalization picked up in the 1990s, "a decade of remarkable institutional creativity and growth."[25] The Asian Financial Crisis of 1997–98 drove countries throughout Asia to try to reduce their vulnerability to future shocks by increasing regional co-operation on financial issues. Trade arrangements followed more slowly, before a burst of activity, most of it bilateral, resulted in more than one hundred free-trade agreements in effect by September 2012.[26] That has now stimulated an interest in means to harmonize those different agreements, possibly including a region-wide free trade agreement, or ways to give existing agreements a wider scope and consistency.[27] However, there is still "shallowness to regionalism and regional cooperation"[28] in the region as a whole, reflecting an "absence of higher levels of trust among participants and . . . [a] focus [on] state and regime security [rather than] regional community-building."[29] Asian nations are increasingly active in economies beyond their region, as traders, and sources and recipients of investment,[30] but remain preoccupied by security issues and economic developments within their own region. At the same time, there is a growing interest in increasing regional co-operation on non-economic matters, including climate change and response to

the risk of disasters, as the region "has absorbed a
disproportionate share of the world's recent natural
disasters, and where settlement patterns and rapid
urbanization expose millions to possible harm."[31]

As evidence of this transformation, new international patterns of economic growth are taking shape. Between 2001
and 2010, six of the ten fastest-growing economies in the
world were African. The only BRIC country to make the top
ten was China, in second place behind Angola. The other five
African countries were Ethiopia, Chad, Mozambique, Nigeria
and Rwanda, all with annual growth rates of around 8 percent
or more. To quote a 2011 article in *The Economist*, "Over the
next five years . . . the average African economy will outpace
its Asian counterpart. Standard Chartered Bank forecasts that
Africa's economy will grow at an average annual rate of 7%
over the next 20 years, slightly faster than China's."[32]

Politically, inward-looking or nativist instincts are on the
rise in many settled democracies—the Front National in France
won 18 percent of the national vote in the first round of the
2012 presidential elections; the Tea Party has transformed the
Republican Party in the United States; the Progress Party in
Norway won nearly 23 percent of the vote in the 2011 election; the True Finns won 19 percent in the 2011 Finnish election; and several other nativist parties are showing well across
Europe. The UK think-tank Chatham House reports:

Contrary to assumptions in the 1980s and 1990s that the
emergence of [populist extremist parties] in Europe would be
nothing more than a flash in the pan, these parties continue
to rally large and durable levels of support. They have joined
national coalition governments. They have surfaced in
countries with a tradition of extremist politics, as well as

those that were previously thought immune. They emerged
before the terrorist attacks on 11 September 2001 and the
recent financial crisis. They have rallied support in some of
the most economically secure and highly educated regions
of Europe. . . . They are guided by clear and coherent goals:
they want immigration reduced and rising diversity curtailed
or halted altogether.[33]

The resurgence and encouragement of those nativist
instincts make it more difficult to achieve consensus on
domestic policy in all those countries, but the real constraints
are upon initiatives to conclude international engagements,
which are inherently "foreign."

Taken together, these new developments represent both a
clear break from the globalizing zeal of the 1990s, and a broadening of the significant forces that drive international change.
They share a striking common characteristic: these are centrifugal forces, reflecting interests or identities that strain against
central control, or even coordination.

If the fear before was that power in the world was becoming too concentrated, the spectre now is that centres do not
hold and that—from the deep problems in the euro zone, to
unprecedented public anger at corruption and exclusion in
China, to resurgent bursts of extremism in Nigeria or Pakistan
or elsewhere, to the spreading gridlock of established democratic systems—"things come apart." These changes are not
confined to one region, one group or one cause, and their
frequency is increasing,[34] often providing an outlet for frustration with social or economic systems that function badly
or seem to be unfair. In some cases, they can be exploited by
terrorist—or, more often, criminal—organizations, which
also thrive in an era when frustration is high, and the legitimacy and actual power of the state has declined. Therefore, a

growing challenge now is to address and help reconcile some of these powerful centrifugal forces. They are often popular and legitimate, are becoming steadily more assertive, and are not responding to conventional domestic, diplomatic, military or "market" remedies.

In other spheres, our conventional sense of order is coming undone, as the "rules of the game" are disrespected in both domestic and international affairs. Gradually, some of the traditional rules of international behaviour have lost their grip, in both economics and conflict. For example, one of the bulwarks of successful international trade has been a patent system that encouraged and protected invention. Yet now, in a knock-off world, the usefulness of patents is declining. The OECD estimates that the value of "international trade in counterfeit and pirated products could have been up to USD 200 billion in 2005 . . . not includ[ing] . . . domestic. . . . pirated products and . . . pirated digital products distributed via the internet."[35] At the same time, international organizations that had once been considered to be neutral or above the fray in conflict zones have become preferred targets of terrorist or insurgent attacks. The distinctive flags of Red Cross/Red Crescent or the United Nations once guaranteed safe passage to healers or to peace-makers, but are often now targeted themselves. The most dramatic breakdowns of that previous immunity were the bombings of United Nations headquarters in Baghdad in 2003, and in Algiers in 2007. But the practice of attacking the neutral or the innocent is spreading more widely. In Nigeria, Boko Haram routinely attacks congregations in churches. At Beslan School, in Chechnya, hostage takers captured 1,100 people, including 777 children, and at least 186 children died. The terrorist targeting of the United Nations is now more habit than exception. The UN's Brahimi Report, released in 2000, argues that "the deliberate targeting of the UN by extremist groups . . . [occurs] not only for what [the UN] does, but also for what it is perceived to represent. . . . especially in the Middle East."[36] Canadian diplomat Robert Fowler, who was kidnapped and held for 130 days by al-Qaeda in the Islamic Maghreb (AQIM) in 2008 says, "The hatred of the UN by the *jihadis* is profound and implacable."[37]

In the late 1980s, a similar catalytic combination of human aspiration and "how-to" capacity composed the death warrant of the old Soviet Union, whose monolithic structures could neither compete with the dynamic economic innovations and social models of the West, nor contain the demand for change at home. The most striking and prescient phrase of that era was Mikhail Gorbachev's call for "new thinking," made all the more pointed and poignant by the fact that his pioneering reforms were short-lived in the Soviet Union, but transformed the wider world. The well-known terms *glasnost* ("openness") and *perestroika* ("restructuring") described the domestic reforms undertaken within the Soviet Union. But the lead horse of the troika of Soviet reform was "new thinking," the name applied to the Gorbachev reforms in foreign affairs,[38] and it set the tone for how the world changed in the immediate post–Cold War era. Professor Robert Legvold of Columbia University described "new thinking" as the "new conceptual notion of what the Soviet Union was or could be in international politics, how it should play its role, what the fundamental mistakes had been in the past."[39] As these events were taking place, Legvold wrote: "With a lurching, creative energy, the [Gorbachev] transformation has cut wider and deeper into the rudiments of Soviet foreign policy. For three and a half years, changes have accumulated, spreading from one sphere to the next, altering not merely the workaday calculations that trapped Mikhail Gorbachev's predecessors in their Afghan imbroglio and in their leaden approach to the euromissile challenge, but altering the assumptions. . . . underlying the deeper pattern of [the Soviet Union's] actions."[40]

Toward the end of Gorbachev's government, the internal opposition to his reforms was fierce. I visited Moscow, as Canada's foreign minister, in November 1990. My principal activity was supposed to be a day-long discussion with foreign minister Shevardnadze, about both bilateral and international issues. Each of us had our thick briefing books, and our teams of experts and advisors. But minutes into the meeting Shevardnadze said: "We can finish our formal agenda quickly, but first, I want you to hear what we are facing." He took me to sit with him in the gallery of the Duma, their parliament, where parliamentarians were vehemently attacking Gorbachev's attempts to change the old practices that still had many Soviet leaders in thrall. An interpreter spared no nuance, and then Shevardnadze leaned toward me and said, "They want a czar back." That is to say: they wanted yesterday, not tomorrow.

That is an object lesson in the power of previous thinking, and it is deeply rooted in all societies, which can tend to perpetuate routines and assumptions long after they do not apply. Even when change is accepted, there is a natural inclination to embrace those elements of reform that are most familiar, to choose the changes we prefer, and slide others toward the margins. As the Cold War ended, Western leaders did not pivot toward the opportunities to address poverty or refresh international development. Swords were not turned to ploughshares, but to trade missions and market shares. Leaders in Western nations were entranced by their apparent triumph of ideology and the global embrace of market opportunities, and one consequence was that we overlooked or discounted the significant growth, in this "global" world, of civil society and other powerful actors who were not states, and not corporations.

There is a parallel between two "post-war" periods—in the late 1940s and 1950s, and now. In both cases, citizens in Western nations were becoming more connected to events beyond their immediate neighbourhood. After 1945, the dominant influences in both Europe and North America had been an international war, and the generation of returning veterans who had lived their formative years away from home. After the Cold War, exponentially more people were becoming more educated, more mobile, more aware of the wide world and more engaged in international commerce or international causes. Today, in most cases, in this intimately and instantly connected era, informed citizens remain deeply attached to their home country, but less confined to it.[41] Communication, enterprise, art, music and fashion have become ever more international, and consequently more able to enrich personal or national impulses[42]—or to overwhelm them.[43]

There is a legitimate concern about individual nations' ability to resist changes that they might not have chosen, had they not experienced significant pressure to conform to an economic wave driven largely by Western nations and Western-based multinational corporations. But events change quickly now, and more recent history is different. The Western governments and multinational corporations that recently drove "globalization" are losing both the soft power of legitimacy and the hard power of control. Public opinion polling shows a steady decline in trust of both national governments and multinational corporations—in 2011, after polling in some fifty countries, the Edelman Trust Barometer found that "52% of those polled trusted government; this year [2012], it was only 43%. . . . trust in business fell . . . from 56% to 53%."[44]

This is the modern narrative we know—the shift of power away from American and European dominance, the rise of non-state actors, the loss of grace of once-dominant institutions, the bad behaviour of some corporations, the failure of "shock and awe" as military strategy. We also know, and are unnerved by, the chilling story of modern terrorist and criminal threats that reach over borders—the frightening "bad guys" among non-state actors. But our public plans and discussions pay much less attention to the parallel growth and significance of several more positive forces which have been inspired or empowered by this globalizing information age. Consider:

- The increasing transparency of public business because organizations like Transparency International[45], Publish What You Pay,[46] Open Society Foundations[47] and the International Aid Transparency Initiative[48] can shine light into previously opaque regimes where corruption thrived.
- The overthrow, in the Arab Spring, of previously impregnable authoritarian and inhumane regimes.
- The steady progress, under United Nations auspices, toward meeting several of the Millennium Development Goals.[49]
- Innovations like micro-credit and "mHealth,"[50] which mobilize, cure and empower previously marginalized citizens of poor countries.
- The growth of discovery and scientific research, in previously improbable places, from the cellphones that propelled African development[51] to the reduction, and in some cases the virtual elimination, of HIV/AIDS, guinea worm disease and other crippling conditions.[52]

This is not a Pollyanna to-do list for making the world look better; it is a partial checklist of actual changes that are already working. In a world that has trouble breaking the habit of old, ineffective remedies, we need to take more account of these change agents of the future. Developed countries like Canada—perhaps led by Canada—should give these change agents a priority comparable to that which we assign our conventional focus on military innovation and capacity, or our preoccupation with terrorism and national security. The need for "new thinking" has never been more urgent.

I I

TWENTY-FIRST CENTURY

ALLIANCES

Alliances are shaped by their times. The two security alliances of the Cold War were characterized by the discipline and control of a powerful sense of mutual threat. More recent economic initiatives and collaborations have been rooted in the West—the Western nations and Japan who gathered annually for an "economic summit" assumed they would continue to guide the world economy for a long time to come. Then there were surprises—including the 9/11 attacks, which reshaped security concerns, and the rapid "emergence" of strong economies elsewhere in the world, with their own assumptions and priorities, and abilities to pursue them. Simultaneously, the Internet empowered social-interest groups and activists to connect across traditional political and cultural boundaries, and to become more global and independent themselves.

It stands to reason that new kinds of alliances should be considered when traditional power is dispersing, and that different talents may be required to make them work. When command and control grow less effective, consensus and persuasion become more valuable, and opportunities grow for countries and organizations that have those capacities. Looking ahead, Canada's historic formal alliances remain highly relevant, but they are not sufficient. Some, like the United Nations, the Commonwealth and La Francophonie, may become even more important, because they retain a political and cultural authority that can reach over regionalism, and the growing divides of income, development and culture. But as the world moves on, old attitudes and established alliances will not be enough.

Traditionally, Canada's international alliances were formed by three factors—geography, security and history. Despite the renewed assertion of regionalism in Europe, Asia, Africa and the Americas, geography doesn't matter as much as before—communication is instant and easy, diseases cross oceans in a single flight, and threats to security no longer come predominantly from an aggressive neighbour or superpower, to which an armed alliance may be the best response, but rather from myriad sources—each requiring a unique response. History remains important; in a Facebook age, history is the book behind the face. It informs cultures, attitudes and identity, helps distinguish the significant from the conventional, and influences the way societies respond to new challenges, opportunities and events.

To many citizens of peaceful countries, drawing their views from television images of "foreign" violence, the developing world has seemed like a relentlessly dangerous place. In fact, as Paul Heinbecker, Canada's former ambassador to Germany and representative to the UN, noted in 2012:

> . . . since the end of the Cold War alone, the number of high
> intensity armed conflicts around the world has dropped
> by 80 per cent, partly because of preventive diplomacy
> and UN interventions. Battlefield deaths have also decreased

dramatically, as has the overall lethality of conflicts,
as humanitarian law has sought to . . . restrict . . . the
means and methods of warfare.[1]

But that may be changing. There are waves of new disturbances, whether triggered by conflict, climate, extremism or
swelling populations of young people who are angry, active
and connected through social media. Nowhere is serene.
Financial crises in developed economies combine with high
unemployment and growing inequality in developing countries. In April 2012, the International Labour Organization
(ILO) reported: "More than half of 106 countries surveyed . . .
face a growing risk of social unrest and discontent. . . . Close
to five years after the global financial and economic meltdown,
our analysis shows that there is a majority of countries where
the risk of social unrest has increased. . . . The two regions
with the highest risk are sub-Saharan Africa, and the Middle
East and North Africa. However, there are also important
increases of social unrest in advanced economies and in Central
and Eastern Europe."[2]

At the same time, there is a striking age gap between the
developed world and emerging societies. The proportion of
young people is swelling in the developing world, and shrink-
ing in the West. The exception is China, where only 16 per
cent of the population was under the age of 15 in 2012.
Nigeria has the eighth largest population in the world; in
2012, 44 percent were under age 15. Pakistan's population is
sixth largest, with 35 percent younger than age 15. In many
countries already in conflict, the proportion of the population
under age 15 is remarkably high: 46 percent in Afghanistan;
45 percent in the Democratic Republic of Congo; 43 percent
in Iraq; 42 percent in the West Bank and Gaza; and 32 percent in Egypt. By contrast, among the G8 countries, which

had recently dominated the world economy, the proportion of populations under age 15 in 2012 was much lower: the USA, 20 percent; France, 19 percent; the UK, 18 percent; Canada, 16 percent; the Russian federation, 15 percent; Italy, 14 percent; Germany, 13 percent; Japan, 13 percent. Aging populations usually mean social costs go up as the workforce goes down. Younger populations can be volatile, particularly when unemployment among young people is high and growing.[3] The ILO reports that in 2012, nearly 75 million young people (age 15 to 24) were unemployed around the world, an increase of more than 4 million since 2007.[4] Furthermore, "youth unemployment has been shown to be tightly linked to . . . a sense of uselessness and idleness among young people."[5]

There is also an explosive intersection of urbanization and natural disasters. When poor people move to cities, they settle in slums—in 2010, 828 million people lived in urban slums, according to the UN-Water Decade Programme on Advocacy and Communication, and the number increases by 25 million per year.[6] "By 2040, the global number of slum dwellers will climb to two billion—nearly a quarter of humanity. . . . but the world's rapidly growing cities are increasingly at risk of natural disasters, ranging from catastrophic fires to landslides, massive floods and tidal waves," writes senior fellow of the Council on Foreign Relations, Stewart Patrick.[7] The incidence of these disasters is on the rise. These crowding mega-cities are located disproportionately in areas that are unusually subject to natural disasters: "Vulnerability is acute along coastal areas, where the strongest population growth is occurring. . . . Globally, some one hundred million people live less than one meter above sea level, many in cities like Dhaka, Lagos, Mumbai, New York, Rio de Janeiro, and Tokyo. Beyond the threat of storms and tsunamis, such low-lying cities are acutely vulnerable to climate-change induced sea level rise."[8]

Volatile demographics, unemployment, natural disasters: one could argue that none of these developments is new, except perhaps in its intensity. But occurring together they could trigger a spreading atmosphere of instability, and often violence. As those problems increase in emerging economies and poorer countries, the financial contribution of wealthier nation-states to international development is declining, because an economic pinch at home means disproportionate cuts in spending abroad. That trend will very likely intensify. Official development assistance[9] (ODA) is the term used by the Organisation for Economic Co-operation and Development to describe international aid that richer countries provide poorer countries. A United Nations' Millennium Development Goals task force reports that "In 2011, as fiscal austerity took its toll on the economies of developed countries in general . . . the total volume of ODA fell in real terms for the first time in more than a decade."[10] Out of twenty-three donor nations, sixteen cut their aid. The UN task force warns, "If history is a guide, the impact of the economic crisis on aid may persist for several years."[11]

It is important to emphasize that there is now a broader approach to aid effectiveness—building a partnership among traditional OECD donor countries and other actors, including emerging economies like Brazil, China and India, the private sector, and civil society organizations. That has been spearheaded by a series of forums on aid effectiveness, convened by the OECD, the most recent of which was in Busan, South Korea, in late 2011. The Busan forum "emphasised the newly important role of south-south cooperation, the implications of the greater willingness of the private sector to invest in a range of developing countries, new approaches towards fragile and

post-conflict states and the formation of a new global partnership for effective development cooperation."[12] These are
important and beneficial developments, but are still in their
early stages. They do not offset the impact of wealthy countries
cutting aid at the very time that needs and crises increase.

That is another broad parallel between the need for serious
"new thinking" today and the challenges the world faced at
the end of the Second World War. Clearly, there is no current
equivalent to the extent of devastation as that war ended;
nonetheless, there has been a series of changes and surprises
which demonstrate that traditional responses aren't working.
There is a need for new kinds of inclusive international partnerships, which include NGOs, international business and
labour organizations, the thousands of assertive citizens—
especially young people—whose frustration and energy could
turn disruptive if ignored. Not surprisingly, the institutions
created in the post–Second World War period are showing
cracks and limitations in a world where so much power has
moved beyond the formal states, which were the fulcrum of
those post-war innovations. We need to be as innovative now
as our predecessors were in the 1940s, and contemplate alliances and reforms that take better account of these new forces.

How, in these new circumstances, might Canada make the
most of our invaluable assets of natural resource wealth, a
strong economy, a diverse and successful society, and an historic reputation as a fair, respected and innovative actor in the
world? Two fields of opportunity stand out initially as potentially pairing an international need with Canada's credentials
as a respected nation and a diverse society.

One is to identify and encourage purpose-specific partnerships between state and non-state actors—partnerships that

marry the imagination and innovation of non-state organizations with the mandate and power of nation-states in ways that will change formal rules and refresh established institutions. The second is to pay more attention to the growing international challenge of managing diversity and reconciling cultural differences. This is a challenge where co-operation between nation-states and non-states can be unusually important. Two things are happening concurrently. First, in a global age, simple human mobility means that more nations are becoming more diverse,[13] through formal immigration, or refugees escaping conflict or oppression,[14] or higher birth rates of new populations. At the same time, the rapid spread of information, education and opportunity nourishes ambition and assertiveness among populations that had previously been passive, and erodes old barriers of class or race or deference or status.

No doubt, the experience of countries with an immigrant-receiving tradition, like Canada, Australia or the United States, is different from that of countries in Africa, Asia or Europe, where relations among different cultural communities are often marked by historic tension or conflict. Nonetheless, there is real value to the experience and example of nation-states that manage diversity successfully.[15] This is also a field where many non-state organizations have real and practical experience, and often a credibility, neutrality and flexibility that formal governments do not. One example, among several others, is the Canadian Institute for Conflict Resolution;[16] its Third Party Neutral training program brought together equal numbers of Serbs, Bosnians and Croats in Mostar in 1998 for training in conflict resolution, which led to fifteen of the seventeen participants establishing their own NGOs to help refugees resettle in their country.

Co-operation between nation-state and non-state actors has been a well-established Canadian practice. As noted earlier, it is how Canada helped transform both the International Criminal Court and the landmines ban treaty[17] from good ideas with broad public support into formal institutions of state, with binding authority on the large majority of nation-states who became formal signatories. It builds upon the practice of co-operation between interested nation-states and activist members of civil society in the Conference on Security and Co-operation in Europe,[18] which drove the inculcation of human rights and democracy as the Cold War ended; the successful worldwide "public-private" campaigns against apartheid; support for women's rights, protection of the environment and other issues that have enlarged the focus of public policy and debate. Often those were cases where public pressure had no instrument but vigorous protest and private persuasion, and interested individual states were constrained by the vetoes, or the more subtle resistance, of their status-quo allies.

That was the situation that led Sweden, in 1967 in the United Nations, to propose an international conference on "the extremely complex problems related to the human environment" and to then convene the first United Nations conference on the environment in Stockholm in 1972.[19] A similar kind of partnership led to the four global women's conferences[20] of the United Nations, which helped move gender equality to the heart of the international agenda. Those and similar initiatives helped force governments out of the ruts of outdated habit, and allowed public policy to address both old inequities and urgent new realities. Governments alone would not have initiated most of those changes—they had too little consensus around the tables where collective decisions are taken. At the same time—for all their determination and ingenuity—non-governments had too little formal power to actually change practice on issues of the environment, or gender, or apartheid, or landmines without government participation. Mandate needed imagination, and vice versa.

It is striking that many of these breakthroughs by partnership, while relatively recent, predate the Internet. They occurred in a time when the power of public opinion was more limited, the general deference to institutional leadership was still strong, and there was less danger that public frustration would combust into violence. Today, the need is more urgent to bridge the inevitable gulf between formal governments—with their conventional agendas and their growing internal constraints—and modern publics. Modern technology and communication make that easier. What is critical is the will to change. These are not new challenges, and Canada is certainly not the only country with a capacity to respond to them. But each of these opportunities requires more serious and consistent attention than it is receiving now, and each is complex and requires sensitive and constructive leadership.

Further, these are challenges where Canada is strongly placed to inspire new circles or alliances, based, to an important degree, on soft power assets that we share with other countries, and that could be more effective if they were concerted. Hard power assets, while necessary, are clearly not sufficient. Indeed, followed narrowly or blindly, they generate their own disturbances, whether brutal conflict, or social disruption, or fatal abuse of the natural environment. Therefore, befitting this different era, these would be alliances based on attitude and vocation, as distinct from the hard power imperatives that drove earlier Canadian alliances—physical security in the case of NATO, economics or trade in the case of the original GATT/WTO, or today's bilateral or regional trade agreements. These would be soft power alliances.

If Canada wanted to modernize and extend our alliances, who might our partner nations be? Three characteristics stand out:

- nations that are forward-looking and outward-reaching, seeking seriously to embrace a changing world;
- nations that are innovators or problem-solvers, at home and in how they see the world;
- nations whose wealth, or location, or cultural composition, or history equips them to understand and address these new sources of conflict.

Potential partner countries should be from both the developing and the developed world. They should include federations, or similar societies that manage diversity, or have demonstrated a capacity for mediation. They should include small nations as well as large, to help reverse the growing marginalization of small states, and draw upon their specific experiences and perspectives. Their selection could build upon the practice of partnership among very different societies within existing "family" associations like the Commonwealth, La Francophonie, Lusofonia[21] or the Organisation of Islamic Cooperation,[22] and regional organizations.

A beginning list of potential nation-states that could bring new value to this kind of alliance could include:

- Norway, Sweden and other Nordic countries, many of which have long been active in the international application of soft power. Sweden has hosted inspiring and game-changing international conferences on the environment; Norway has been a driving force behind peace proposals in the Middle East, Sri Lanka and elsewhere;

- Australia, a modern economy and multicultural society, with a history of being active and effective in its
  region and the world;
- Indonesia, a modernizing state rooted in the Non-
  Aligned Movement, a member of the G20, home to
  the largest Muslim population in the world, and host
  and initiator of the Bali Democracy Forum since its
  inception in 2008. Human Rights Watch declared in
  its 2012 *World Report*: "Over the past 13 years
  Indonesia has made great strides in becoming a sta-
  ble, democratic country with a strong civil society
  and independent media";[23]
- Mexico, the eleventh largest economy in the world,
  and projected to be the fifth largest by 2050, with
  a history of leadership in Latin America, and already
  a partner of Canada in both NAFTA and regional
  development.
- South Korea, having established its economic
  strength, has skill and capacity as a middle power,
  hosting the G20, the Nuclear Security Summit and
  the International Forum on Aid Effectiveness at
  Busan, and has won election to the Security Council;
- Ghana has been a model of political and economic
  reform in the developing world, active in international
  peacekeeping, a key leader of the West Africa regional
  organization, ECOWAS, and an innovator in a changing
  continent;
- Qatar, a young and highly innovative nation-state,
  has been an active mediator in its own region, is
  a major economic force in and beyond the Gulf
  and, through its Qatar Foundation, aims to become
  a leader in education, science and research, and
  community development;

- Turkey has growing economic and political weight in its region and the world, is a dynamic society active in international affairs, and possesses historic cultural, social and commercial links to the new nations of central Asia, as well as to Canada and its other partners in NATO.

Forming these alliances would require stepping beyond stereotypes or familiar practice. The critical characteristics would be a desire and capacity to innovate change and value diversity. To succeed as catalysts and bridges, these would need to be alliances of partners, not mirrors, and would require us to reconsider those stereotypes about countries with which we have dealt at some distance before.

Nigeria is one example. Its caricature is as an unruly and dangerous society—and too often, both those descriptions apply. But those descriptions also apply, too often, to parts of Detroit or New Orleans,[24] or to a society whose normal calm and comity is disrupted by brutality, as Sweden was by the assassination of Prime Minister Olof Palme in 1986, or Norway, by the inexplicable malice behind the seventy-seven murders committed by Anders Breivik in 2011. We accept that orderly places are becoming more troubled, yet we regard the assassination of a head of state, or the murders of youth at a summer camp, or even the school shootings in Newtown, Connecticut, as exceptions to the rule, not a new badge of endemic bad behaviour. Why, then, do we allow the outrages of Boko Haram to obscure the much better news in Nigeria, such as the significant civic reforms that are turning a once-unruly city like Lagos into a model of urban co-operation? There are alarming developments in almost every country in the world, but that is no reason to stand back from emerging societies—potential new partners with whom we could find common ground.

If the impulse to break old patterns originated with non-state actors, who were finding and feeling their oats and unhappy with old constraints, it also applies now to many small states, who might hold sovereign seats in international organizations but have been steadily marginalized by larger countries and by globalizing forces. Those small states have occasional victories in atypical cases (such as Antigua and Barbuda's challenge in the WTO to the US casino law[25]), but generally their voice is ignored, and their influence wanes in the formal system. The most striking case is climate change, where their larger "partner" states turned a deaf ear to issues as urgent as island nations like Tuvalu sinking into the sea.[26]

For seven decades, one of Canada's distinguishing assets has been the ability to sit as a decision-maker at the tables of the most powerful economies of the West—more recently, the G8 economic summit—while also maintaining trusted relations with the developing world. Unfortunately, the present Canadian government has stepped off that path, with an instinct to focus more on proven allies of the past rather than potential allies of the future, and on developed or emerging economies, rather than the developing world. A case in point: in the name of budget restraint, the government initiated in 2012 a cohabitation policy with the United Kingdom in some of our international embassies, beginning with Haiti and Burma.[27] In itself, that's not a bad idea; Canada has co-operated with Australia in sharing consular arrangements in a number of Asian, African and Latin American countries.[28] But if Canada is to contemplate cohabitation abroad with other countries, should we not also consider countries where we want to *build* a history rather than simply celebrate one? Given present dynamics in the world, and issues of conflict or opportunity that impact all societies, why not a privileged relation also with Indonesia, South

Korea, Turkey or a burgeoning federation like Nigeria? The specific countries would need to be carefully considered, but the principle is important: we must enlarge the range and scope of Canada's de facto alliances if we are to make ourselves more effective in a transforming world.

The real challenge will not be in attracting nation-states to this kind of alliance, but in engaging non-state actors, particularly non-governmental organizations. "Non-governmental" is both a description and a credential. By their nature, NGOs concentrate on critical issues, while governments are obliged to follow a broad agenda and balance conflicting interests. That means that even those governments most committed to social or humanitarian change often walk cautiously or speak quietly, or turn a half-open eye to critical issues: human rights, or the environment, or reducing the impunity of oppressive leaders. The freedom to passionately pursue a particular cause or injustice is the reason NGOs exist, and that role is essential both to the nature and health of an open society because so many of the challenges arising today can neither be ignored or resolved by "in the box" thinking.

NGOs and governments are not natural partners. Any serious NGO must be conscious of the real risk that, if it works too closely or consistently with governments, it could become (or be seen to be) co-opted. That is the challenge from the NGO's perspective, and it is rational and real. To cite just one warning flag, consider an experience of the organization Médecins Sans Frontières, with which Kevin Phelan served as a press officer.

As a famine raged in 1984, the Ethiopian government began
a policy of forcibly relocating hundreds of thousands of
people in the country from areas most affected by the
drought to more fertile regions. When MSF assisted with the

first transfer, it saw no reason for criticism. But it became clear over time that the transfers had two nefarious aims: (1) to weaken the guerilla movements in the north (in Eritrea and Tigre) by removing their grassroots supporters, (2) to place these populations in villages in order to bring them ideologically in line with government policy. Under this scheme, humanitarian aid actually became a trap, used to attract vulnerable villagers and blackmail them into going along with the program.

. . . after lodging many fruitless protests with the Ethiopian government authorities, MSF decided in November 1985 that regardless of the consequences to its ability to remain in the country, the organization could no longer remain silent. If [it stayed], MSF feared it would appear to be condoning the brutality of these transfers, already responsible for more deaths than the famine.[29]

That is just one example in which an NGO felt a partnership was abused. In Canada, in 2012, there was significant criticism of the very principle of CIDA-funded co-operation on social programs between Canadian mining companies and Canadian NGOs working in three separate developing countries.[30] That is only one of many reasons why NGOs must be cautious about partnering with government. Another is that, to effectively pursue their goals, NGOs often have to push their priorities to a point where they can be seen as not simply "non-government" but "anti-government" as well. That is often essential to their role; NGOs would be of no use if they built a compelling argument for change, and then politely and regularly allowed themselves to be rebuffed. Some NGOs are too consistently combative for my taste, but no more so than some of my more passionate former colleagues in the House of Commons. Vigorous disagreement and debate are at the heart of free and democratic systems, and passion and determination are usually essential to address wrongs or to open minds. More often, NGOs are combative only when they believe that such an approach is necessary to encourage a government to face a controversial option or reality. Still, that sticks in the craw of many governments, particularly if those NGOs also receive some kind of public funding. But public funding should not be "hush" money; in a democracy, its purpose is to broaden public options and discussion, not limit or silence them. That is especially true in a parliamentary democracy, like ours, where having fiercely opposed views is hardly a startling concept. Our system is designed deliberately to hear all sides of any case. That dynamic of opposing views is at the heart of parliamentary democracy, which is based fundamentally upon an Official Opposition whose most essential duty is to question, and doubt, and contest the priorities and performance of the government. In Parliament itself, both the opponents and the proponents draw on public funds.

Moreover, in my experience as leader of the Official Opposition and prime minister and foreign minister, the government and the Opposition often find common cause on really critical questions, despite their vigorous differences. That doesn't always happen but is how, for example, the Charter of Rights and Freedoms was strengthened and enriched by the Progressive Conservative amendment ensuring the right of women to equality "before and under the law," section 15,[31] and the NDP amendment "recognizing" aboriginal rights, section 35.[32] Co-operation is not contamination, and surely the parliamentary precedent of respecting different views and seeking common ground—which is fundamental to our system of governance—should lead governments to value constructive dissent, and to be genuinely open to important cases where the public interest requires an exceptional partnership.

Some of the best thinking about the transformations that shake and shape the modern world comes from non-state actors who live on the front line. It is worth noting that building bridges between these most effective agents of change and state actors, who have the capacity to alter the framework of international laws or institutions, is a Canadian practice with deep roots. On January 26, 1967, Maurice Strong, then director-general of Canada's external aid office, told the Empire Club of Toronto:

> We would like to see our government aid programs
> complemented and supplemented by an increasing
> amount of private initiative on the part of voluntary service
> organizations, church groups, cooperatives, and business
> and industry. Private agencies can do so much to create . . .
> direct personal channels . . . between Canadian citizens
> and the people of the developing world.[33]

Author David Morrison quotes Strong in his history of CIDA and other Canadian aid initiatives, and adds:

> Strong . . . was determined to tap the energy and
> experience of citizens by expanding voluntary work
> for international development. He persuaded his superiors
> to approve two innovative forms of financial support:
> first, core funding for Canadian University Service
> Overseas . . . and other volunteer-sending NGOs, even
> though they had considerable latitude in determining
> their own priorities, and, second, grants of public funds
> to match, on a project-by-project basis, donations raised
> by NGOs for activities they wanted to pursue.[34]

That thinking reflected the twin understandings that effective international development was critical to international stability and progress, and that the imagination and enterprise of individual citizens and organizations could make a big difference. That is much more the case today.

What has changed since Strong made those comments almost half a century ago is that NGOs today fill a much larger share of the development sky than they did then—and official development agencies a smaller share, trending down. The "energy and experience of citizens" is amplified today by the influence and respect that NGOs have earned, so the nature of the contemporary relationship would not be "assistance" but "partnership."

A marriage of mandate and imagination. How difficult a marriage would that be? And if marriage is too permanent a concept, what kind of working relationship could be designed to achieve specific goals? Take two givens: first, state actors will be wary of diluting the formal power that confirms their primacy in the international system; second, NGOs prize their independence. Both were the case when the Mulroney government and the Canadian Labour Congress worked together very closely in the international campaign against apartheid, despite their significant differences and high suspicion of one another.[35] History provides many such examples of partnership to build upon. The landmines treaty began in 1991 with a petition to the American Congress by the NGO Women's Commission for Refugee Women and Children. The creation of the International Criminal Court, brought together hundreds of NGOs under the banner of the Coalition for an International Criminal Court, and sixty-five countries, chaired by Canada.

This kind of co-operation need not be restricted to initiatives between governments and NGOs. In 2003, Oxfam Great

Britain and Oxfam The Netherlands, on one side, and Unilever Indonesia on the other—classic bitter adversaries—opened their books absolutely to each other and discovered a wide range of ways to work together in what they called "the drive towards sustainable poverty reduction." Their mutual purpose was to examine the impact—good and bad—of Unilever Indonesia's activities on that country's general economy, employment, low-income consumers and poverty, and to identify opportunities for change through co-operation.[36] A study by the European Academy of Business in Society "highlights the fact that while multi-national corporations and NGOs have different missions and strategic objectives, they can leverage each other's expertise, resources and insights around a common cause."[37]

What could be done to make this invaluable co-operation more commonplace? Almost always, for nation-states or non-state actors, a critical step to resolving an international challenge is to build down the suspicions that keep parties apart. When Ronald Reagan and Mikhail Gorbachev were negotiating the critical agreements that helped end the Cold War, a Russian proverb—*doveryai no proveryai*, or "trust but verify"[38]—was invoked regularly to leaven the corrosive and historic mutual suspicion on both sides. Trust is always difficult between habitual adversaries and, usually, the first steps have to be taken on instinct, not evidence. But distrust is a dead end, and co-operation can start with steps small enough to test caricatures and intentions—to verify—and on that evidence determine whether the future can be different from the past.

One of the classic cases of adversaries coming together was the determination by two leaders in late-apartheid South Africa—Nelson Mandela of the African National Congress and then-new president of South Africa, F.W. de Klerk—to trust the sincerity of the other. That partnership was controversial, difficult and frustrating for both leaders and their advisors, but it pulled their shared country back from a violent abyss, and demonstrated the transforming force of co-operation. I have had the unusual privilege of coming to know both men, and learning how they met that extraordinary challenge. I had chaired the Commonwealth Committee of Foreign Ministers on Southern Africa, which coordinated the Commonwealth's anti-apartheid campaign, so was one of about a hundred people invited to Lusaka, Zambia, in March 1990 when the newly freed Nelson Mandela made his first visit to reunite with the men and women who had led his African National Congress in exile. He spoke briefly, expressing his profound thanks, and then took a question from an ANC veteran about how to deal with the Afrikaner leaders who had created apartheid and imprisoned him for twenty-seven years. Mr. Mandela's answer was: "We have to understand how difficult all this is for them." I have never—before or since—heard such generosity, which was both profoundly genuine and a signal and instruction of the way to put the future ahead of the past.

Since 2006, I have worked closely with Mr. de Klerk in the Global Leadership Foundation (GLF),[39] a not-for-profit organization of former heads of government and diplomats, which he founded and chairs, and which helps government leaders in developing countries undertake difficult political and governance changes. We have spoken about the steps he took, as leader of the governing national party, to bring his ministers and colleagues to understand "that we had to change."[40] His predecessor as president of South Africa, P.W. Botha, had used private meetings of his ministers—"cabinet retreats"—to entrench their commitment to apartheid. Mr. de Klerk reversed the purpose of those meetings, and employed them and other measures to convince his governing national party to "abandon the concept of separateness . . . embrace a new vision of togetherness . . . with equal rights for all and an end to discrimination . . . [and] make sure that South Africa would not become caught up in . . . chaos."[41]

In very different circumstances, in 1991–92, as Canada's minister of constitutional affairs, I chaired a constitutional negotiation that brought together national, provincial and territorial governments and, for the first time in Canadian history, the four major organizations representing Canada's aboriginal people.[42] The aboriginal organizations did not have a vote, because they were not formal governments, but they participated directly and completely in all negotiations. The result was the Charlottetown Accord. It was defeated by popular vote in a national referendum on October 26, 1992, but was also remarkable for achieving unanimous agreement among leaders of all governments, and aboriginal groups, on a very wide range of major changes. Those included the recognition of Quebec as a "distinct society" within Canada, the creation of a "triple e" (equal, elected, effective) Senate, the principle of aboriginal self-government, entrenchment of the composition and appointment process for the Supreme Court, and changes to the division of legislative powers. As a constitutional matter, the accord failed—it was rejected by 54 percent of Canadians who voted. However, as a demonstration of finding broad agreement on complex issues, it was a signal success. Virtually everyone had come to the table with priorities so firm they defied negotiation. Yet the give-and-take of actual face-to-face discussion brought agreement, compromise and, finally, unanimity. It proved to me, and to most participants, how much can be done when former adversaries seek seriously to achieve common interests.

In 1954, speaking at the White House, Winston Churchill, no pacifist, stated the principle: "It is better to jaw-jaw than to war-war." That has never been more true than it is now, when conflicts abound, sophisticated weaponry can't contain insurgencies, and normal rules of engagement have been shattered, whether by trials and incarcerations in a Guantanamo Bay prison or attacks on civilians and aid groups and heretofore protected "neutral international organizations" like the UN or Red Cross/Red Crescent. Canada is, and has been, highly skilled in both our primary military ("war-war") and diplomatic ("jaw-jaw") capacities. Yet to the degree our history is known at all, Vimy Ridge and two world wars and our valiant soldiers in Afghanistan are more widely celebrated symbols of our international engagement than our considerable accomplishments in diplomacy or development—with the possible exception of the Suez Crisis. That imbalance is understandable and, probably, irreversible, because terrible losses of life and the courage to face an "ultimate sacrifice" strike the deepest human chords, and deserve profound respect. Yet, as Canadians assess what we might do internationally now and in our immediate future, it is useful also to understand our capacity and success in preventing or abating deadly conflict.

A question might be raised as to whether focusing on these roles with non-state actors might be seen as a diversion, an eccentricity, and thus detract from Canada's reputation as a country serious about trade and defence and traditional diplomacy. On the contrary, it would demonstrate our determination to use our multiple assets in the most effective way, and strengthen our influence in a multi-polar world. A helpful comparison is Canada's innovation of peacekeeping, which responded to a new international need in the 1950s and enlarged Canada's reputation.

In a similar way, a broad, soft power–based re-engagement with international partners of many kinds would respond to the challenges and capacities of the contemporary world, and renew Canada's international reach and credentials.

I 2

NATIONAL CONVERSATIONS

Each year since 1976, usually in June, ten nations of Southeast Asia meet to discuss developments in their region, and their positions on international events. They are ASEAN—the Association of Southeast Asian Nations. Each is a unique nation, some with ancient cultures, determinedly sovereign states, none aspiring to be a superpower, proud but not aggressive, smart, often wise, pooling their interests and resources where they can, forming a distinct community, whose perspective was often different from that heard in Western capitals. Since 1977 Canada has been one of a handful of "outside" nations[1] invited to that annual summit as a "dialogue partner."

Burma, Cambodia, Laos and Vietnam have joined ASEAN since my visits in the 1980s and '90s, but at that time there were six members: Brunei, Indonesia, Malaysia, Philippines, Singapore and Thailand. Their discussions were relaxed about the serious issues they faced, and characterized by good humour—foreign partners felt like we had been invited into the family for a weekend. The formal meetings were dark suits and hard chairs, but we got over that quickly, and were soon decked out in colourful shirts and advised that, important though we might consider ourselves, at the gala dinner we were also the entertainment. I remember American secretary of state George Shultz, the tough and avuncular ex-Marine, and his late wife O'Bie leading a singalong of "Down by the Old Mill Stream," and Maureen and I and our diplomats belting out "Alouette," with Thais and Indonesians joining enthusiastically in the chorus.

By 1990, I had been the guest—Canada had been the "dialogue partner"—of each of the six ASEAN countries. Their ministers would all be attending the September General Assembly meeting of the United Nations in New York, which, that year, ended just before Canadian Thanksgiving. So I invited my six ASEAN colleagues to stop on their way home for a two-day meeting in Jasper, the beautiful Rocky Mountain park which, just coincidentally, was in my constituency. Since golf is a lingua franca of Southeast Asia, and Jasper has a magnificent course, I suggested the ministers bring their clubs.

Of course, Alberta that year celebrated Thanksgiving with a massive snowstorm, which closed the Hinton Airport, where we had planned to land. However, as happens in the unpredictable Rockies, the first snowfall had left the Banff–Jasper highway relatively clear. So we flew to Calgary, rented a Brewster bus, and set off by road for Jasper. At the Columbia Icefields, a heavy snowstorm found us. The foreign minister of Brunei was His Royal Highness Mohamed Bolkiah, brother to the sultan, and I said, "Your Royal Highness: this is probably the first time you've ever been caught in snow." At which point, Indonesia's foreign minister, the late Ali Alatas, interjected: "This is the first time His Royal Highness has ever been on a bus."

All of us have buses we've not been on before. We see the world from our own perspective—sometimes a perspective of privilege, sometimes of disinterest in people or events outside our immediate field of vision, sometimes of acute deprivation and despair. Those of us whose buses travel in relative comfort and on well-established paths regularly underestimate the desperation of populations in the wider world who, literally, struggle every day to find food, or security in a conflict zone, or a future for their children. Even within Canada, we often have no idea of the pressures faced by the 882,000 Canadians who used food banks each month in 2012, to that date the highest rate of food bank usage in our nation's history.[2] If you are not in that number, it is just another statistic, like a hockey score or the jackpot in the latest lotto, or the breathtaking salary of some corporate CEO. But if you count on food banks for survival—and in 2012 one in almost forty Canadians did—that number has a quite different impact, on health, on hope, on your sense of fairness and opportunity. Most of us are blind in the eye that should see people whose circumstances are different from our own and, often, we can also fail to understand the harm our well-intentioned acts can cause them. I learned how easy this is to do.

In 1990, Canada played an active military and diplomatic role supporting the United Nations action to remove Iraqi forces from Kuwait. Canada had been elected to the Security Council for that term, and I travelled to the UN personally to cast Canada's vote in favour of Resolution 678, authorizing "all necessary means" to force Iraq to withdraw. The prime minister and I and others regularly condemned Saddam Hussein. Then a group of Arab-Canadian leaders, who supported the UN intervention, invited me to a private meeting in Toronto to discuss the rhetoric Canadian leaders were using. In that crowded meeting, the first question put to me was, "Mr. Clark: Do you realize how many six-year-olds in Toronto schools are named Saddam Hussein, and can you imagine what their reaction is when their foreign minister and prime minister and media say repeatedly 'Saddam Hussein is evil'?" I had not foreseen that at all, yet as a father knew full well how exclusively six-year-olds identify themselves, and no one else, with their name. We strove, subsequently, in that brief war, to reduce the rhetoric, but damage had been done—quite literally to innocents, to children. That could have been avoided. With hindsight, it is clear we could and should have brought into our plans Arab-Canadians and others who were bound to be so affected.

Ironically, as society becomes busier and more complex, we relax the priority we once assigned to understanding, persuading and co-operating with communities whose perspectives might be sharply different from our own. We are so immersed in the rapid changes that concern us directly that we have paid less attention to the transformations beyond our immediate nest. Internationally, this helps explain why our best experts are often surprised by an Arab Spring, or the assertive militancy and fundamentalism in faiths and religions, or a Tea Party in the US, or a Front National in France. Domestically, we continue to judge other provinces and citizens by what we once thought they were—an *indépendantiste* Quebec, an "outsider" Alberta—rather than the more complex and sophisticated communities they are becoming.

As a huge and diverse country, Canada has plenty of solitudes, and, despite our worsening tendencies to gaze inward, we've spent a good deal of our history trying to bridge our divides. We've done that physically, with the railway and the national airline; socially, with equalization, health care and other programs; culturally, through the national broadcaster, the Canada Council, the Official Languages Act, a sustained—if slow and frustrating—focus on First Nations, a respect for multiple cultures, and an investment in artists and formal cultural institutions; and legally, initially through our courts, and later the equality provisions of the Charter of Rights and Freedoms. We have been proactive in trying both to achieve some rough equality and to identify common ground.

Those values have also characterized our actions internationally—our diplomats and development workers, among their other skills, were often the treaty-makers, the trusted interlocutors, the moderate voice, the connectors among adversaries and interests that might otherwise stay apart. For decades after the Second World War, Canadian governments of both political parties also pursued an aggressive policy of nation-building, through physical projects such as the seaway and the "roads to resources" program, through splendid museums and galleries, through social programs, and through a recurring series of constitutional discussions and changes, like those that led to the eventual establishment of the territory of Nunavut.[3] Those were high-cost endeavours, both financially and in terms of the energy and priority they required of governments and citizens.

I am proud to have played a leading role in Brian Mulroney's activist agenda of the 1980s and '90s—acid rain, free trade, the GST, international initiatives from Asia to the Americas to the abolition of apartheid to the environment to the Gulf War, the Royal Commission on Aboriginal Peoples, and serious and sustained attempts at constitutional reform. Some of our actions made some voters angry, and the pace of government initiatives may have exhausted others. Not surprisingly, a time came when Canadians wanted some relief from high-octane nation-building.

During the 1993 federal election campaign, wily Jean Chrétien's solemn undertaking on constitutional reform was that he wouldn't talk about it. Voters rewarded him with a majority government. Following the failure to adopt the Meech Lake and Charlottetown accords, the country was grateful to put constitutions aside. I fully understand that; I was worn out too, and stepped out of politics. But, upon reflection, it's clear that Canadians underwent a broader change in conduct. As a country, we stopped talking about much at all.

The Canadian agenda turned from "unfinished business"— constitutional change, aboriginal reform, adjusting to globalization—to "get down to business"—cut costs, trim programs, put fiscal priorities ahead of virtually everything else. That reflected more than just fatigue with two decades of hyperactive government in Ottawa. Other countries too were making restraint and austerity their priority and, to our credit, Canada became a leader in that international movement toward government restraint. But our renewed focus on that issue came at a price: a narrowing of the Canadian vision and a gradual silencing of the broad and inclusive conversations that have long helped us shape and build the country.

In international affairs, there were some notable initiatives during the Chrétien government—most significantly, the world leadership on the landmines treaty and the International Criminal Court driven by Lloyd Axworthy, and vigorous international trade missions bringing together leaders of business, the provinces and the national government, serving goals of both unity and growth. Nonetheless, the Chrétien era was a time of housekeeping, not house building. I remember vividly the February night in 1980 when Pierre Trudeau defeated me in the early days of a new decade and proclaimed: "Welcome to the 1980s." Nobody welcomed anyone to the 1990s.

Some of most prolific seeds of that decline in Canadians' interest in "nation-building" were planted well before the election of the Harper government in 2006. Our political system is very different from what it was in 1972, when I was first elected to the House of Commons. Those differences go beyond the changes in courtesy and tone, which have made national public life so much more venomous and unattractive. There have also been institutional developments that changed the nature of how we decide public policy.

- First, interest groups—ranging from environmental movements to tax-cutting organizations—became a principal instrument of political involvement. That changed the fundamental dynamics of public debate, and political organization, in Canada. By definition, those groups assert a particular interest, rather than a general one. That is entirely legitimate, even beneficial. The desire to advance a specific and important interest is often driven by a belief that conventional definitions of "the public interest" discount critical issues that can only be defended by zealous and singular advocacy. But the dominance of that process diminishes the pool—and the role— of activists and institutions whose aim is to reconcile contesting claims into a broader public interest. That risks subjugating the public interest to the special interest, which would be a fundamental departure from the traditional Canadian model, one which has encouraged Canadians to look and think beyond our immediate agendas.

- Second, that change in the balance between broad and specific interests aggravates the natural Canadian tendency to live in silos—whether those silos are regions, language groups, cities versus towns, occupations or other points of distinction. The parts have become more insistent than the whole. Those tendencies in turn have been aggravated by a lobbying industry that is far more prevalent in Canada than it was twenty years ago, and which was adapted largely from a US political model that is fundamentally different from Canada's. The US model is based on a separation of powers, essentially between the Congress and the president, whereas the Canadian system concentrates power in the executive (and increasingly the prime minister). In the US, therefore, lobbyists have to address both power centres—the president and the Congress— because each has a real capacity to shape policy; as a consequence, more options get discussed more openly. In Canada, elected parliamentarians have very limited influence, except for the few who are senior ministers, so lobbyists exclusively target the executive and, increasingly, the executive then decides without much public or parliamentary consultation. While there are now some rules about the conduct of lobbyists, their impact on public policy in Canada has grown immensely over the last thirty years, and much of it is exercised privately, rather than in the more public arenas of the House of Commons or Senate.
- Third, among other consequences, that transfer of power seriously weakens Parliament as an institution by further marginalizing MPs and Senators, and

encouraging citizens or communities to take their important cases to lobbyists, not to elected parliamentarians. Beyond the impact on the content of policy, that process erodes the effectiveness and respect for Parliament, which is one of the few national institutions left in Canada whose membership represents all corners of our diverse community.

- Fourth, the 1993 federal election revealed a sea change in the way Canada's political parties won national office. Each of the traditional parties—the Liberals and the Progressive Conservatives—had a base of voters that was large, but rarely large enough alone to elect them to national office in a way that would let them be regarded as a legitimate and representative government. From 1957 to 1993, the political parties had to compete everywhere if they wanted to govern anywhere. In 1993, that model broke. The Official Opposition was formed by the Bloc Québécois, whose founding purpose was to promote the sovereignty of Quebec. The next largest party in opposition was the Reform Party, all but one of whose Members of Parliament came from western Canada. Those parties owed their victory to their narrow focus, and while each contained individual members who had broad and informed views of the larger country, the lesson for the parties was that being inclusive was a luxury they need not indulge.

Those are all institutional and political changes. Several other factors have also caused Canadians to concentrate on "housekeeping" not "house building": the 9/11 attacks turned everybody inwards and provoked both caution and a focus on protection not expansion; economic crises, while more acute elsewhere, caused Canadians to concentrate on their immediate and material concerns; political discourse in Canada became routinely divisive, both in Parliament and in relations between governments, and also with civil society.

Those are troubling trends. Canada needs national conversations that reach across interests that might divide us, or regions that might confine us, or silos that are inevitable in a vast and diverse country. That separateness can become reinforced by the ease with which we can burrow into communications with "people like us" beyond our national boundaries—our business networks, our Facebook friends, our allies in interest groups we fervently support. Ironically, the easy access to a wider world can narrow our own sights, rather than broaden them and, in that process erode our sense of connection to our actual neighbours and environment. Canada is a country that has to keep proving its worth to its parts, and national conversations have played a major role in the initiatives and experiences that have proven that worth, and, along the way, reinforced our strength as a country.

Sometimes conversations about our future were stimulated by general election campaigns—in 1958 with John Diefenbaker, for example, and 1968 with Pierre Trudeau. More regularly, they occurred in federal-provincial conferences, where the elected leaders of our different jurisdictions agreed on common Canadian purposes. Often, and seminally, those conversations have been generated by royal commissions, many of which led to initiatives or reforms that have become signature characteristics of Canada. A partial list includes:

- The Royal Commission on Radio Broadcasting (the Aird Commission), in 1929, which led to the creation of the Canadian Broadcasting Corporation;

- The Royal Commission on Dominion-Provincial Relations (the Rowell-Sirois Commission), in 1940, which led to the policy of equalization;
- The Royal Commission on National Development in the Arts, Letters and Sciences (the Massey-Lévesque Commission), in 1951, which spawned the Canada Council, the National Library and other cultural institutions;
- The Royal Commission on Health Services (the Hall Commission), in 1964, which led to national medicare;
- The Royal Commission on Bilingualism and Biculturalism (the Laurendeau-Dunton Commission), in 1964, whose recommendations resulted in the Official Languages Act;
- The Royal Commission on the Economic Union and Development Prospects for Canada (the MacDonald Commission), in 1985, which led to the Free Trade Agreement with the United States, and later to NAFTA;
- The Royal Commission on Aboriginal Peoples (the Erasmus-Dussault Commission), in 1996, which set a path for co-operation and respect between aboriginal and other Canadians.

Constitutional negotiations have often included significant public discussion and debate. Notable among these were the nationally televised parliamentary hearings that led to amendments in Parliament guaranteeing changes in the Charter of Rights and Freedoms and, during the Charlottetown Accord, the "Renewal of Canada" conferences, the six forums of two hundred participants each preceding negotiation of the Charlottetown Accord. At critical times in our history, serious policy discussions were also sponsored by national political parties—the Port Hope (1942) and Fredericton (1964) conferences of the Progressive Conservative Party; the Kingston Conference of Lester Pearson's Liberal Party (1960); the founding conventions of both the CCF (Calgary, 1932) and the NDP (Ottawa, 1961). Very often, in the past, these national conversations were led by Parliament, including government MPs not in cabinet, the Opposition and the Senate.

But that pattern is changing dramatically. The last meeting of first ministers in Canada took place on November 10, 2008. The last royal commission in Canada was the Romanow Commission into the future of healthcare, which concluded in 2002. There have been a few judicial commissions of inquiry into particular issues, like the sponsorship scandal, or the Air India tragedy. But those were investigations, not conversations. The last election campaign about issues occurred in 1988, on free trade. What is even more pertinent is that— with the notable exception of the late Jack Layton's success in 2011—election campaigns are now focused much more on the narrow and the negative—mobilizing an existing vote, attacking your opponent. In that sense, campaigns no longer speak to the whole nation, or seek common purposes that might lift Canadians up, let alone draw us together.

The purpose of these national conversations has not been just to talk. It is to identify goals and purposes that keep us moving forward as a national community, overcoming our reticence and differences in order to identify and pursue our purposes as a country. That is essential in any diverse society. The *New York Times* columnist Thomas Friedman has reflected on the link between national purpose and national performance, in the context of his own country:

Beginning with Eisenhower and continuing to some degree with every cold war president, we used the cold war and the

Russian threat as a reason and motivator to do big, hard things together at home—to do nation-building in America.[4]

Those are American references, and they reflect an American instinct to respond vigorously to threat, which is not so deeply embedded in Canada. Instead of threat as a motivator, our history has revealed a remarkable instinct for acting in order to improve ourselves as a whole national community. Medicare was not adopted simply to protect the health of each of us as individuals, but to yield a healthier society. Equalization had a similar inspiration—to lift the whole. Those of us who argued for a trade agreement with the United States were looking not for personal opportunity but for a "big, hard thing" that would strengthen the country. When the "boat people" were set adrift to die in the China Sea and then welcomed by the tens of thousands as refugees into Canada, the Nansen Award was not given for a single act of generosity but for a national response of unmatched generosity. Those are examples of "collective action" *à la canadienne*, and they have won us success at home, and respect and admiration in the world.

But to preserve that truth about ourselves we have to recognize and honour it, and also recognize the accompanying truth that, as a lucky minority in the world, we can slip easily into our silos—into our region, our immediate circle of family and friends, our self-interest. That is our easy option. Our better option, our better nature, was expressed in a phrase I heard at the very beginning of my duties as minister of constitutional affairs, and could never forget. At the opening of my first meeting with the Assembly of First Nations, in the community of Morley, on a Stoney reserve of the Nakoda Nation in Alberta's foothills, a prayer was offered by the chief of the O'Chiese First Nation. His name was Peter O'Chiese, and his invocation and challenge was: "Let us lift each other up."

As a constitutional venture, that Charlottetown process failed—its proposals were rejected decisively in a national referendum. But, as a conversation leading to consensus on important common goals, it was a success worth repeating. After months of deliberation and extensive public discussion, the elected leaders of each of the national government, the ten provinces, the then-two territories[5] and four national aboriginal groups[6] agreed unanimously on major changes.

Two unusual features of Charlottetown made that process work. First, in the negotiating room itself, the formal participants actually took the time to listen to one another, and were prepared to move away from firmly held previous positions, when counter-arguments were persuasive and agreement seemed possible. Second, before those formal negotiations, public consultation moved beyond the traditional cluster of "constitutional experts" and deliberately gave equal status to the considered views of "ordinary citizens"—thoughtful individuals who had thought about the issues and then applied to take part in one of the six "Renewal of Canada" conferences, which discussed specific aspects of constitutional change. Those citizen participants were independent, cogent and informed, and there were enough of them—roughly 25 percent of each conference, a critical mass—that they challenged the arguments and opened the minds of the governments, academics, interest groups, business and labour leaders, and others who had become the "usual suspects" in constitutional negotiations. The six conferences were televised live, and the genuine and unscripted nature of the debate generated a high level of public interest.[7]

Canada has plenty of models to guide a new round of national conversations about our assets and our future—from the tribal circles of indigenous people that pre-date European settlement, through the processes which led to the cascading agreements on Confederation, through town hall meetings, and First Ministers conferences, royal commissions and more recent broad consultations within provinces, for example on electoral reform in British Columbia[8] and "reasonable accommodation" in Quebec.[9] These all occurred in a much less "connected" age. Canadians are among the world's most active users of the Internet,[10] so technology now allows a level and breadth of discussion and engagement that had never existed before.

If we want to, we can certainly find ways to talk seriously with one another about what we can do as a nation. Of the range of opportunities open to a society like Canada, one of the most important lies outside our physical borders, in a world whose explosive tensions, and conflicts, and inequalities would benefit from the moderation, and initiative, and respect for others that have been among Canada's signature characteristics. Canada's role in an ever more challenging world is a natural place to start a serious and inclusive conversation about our assets and future. Compared to twenty years ago, there is now a torrent of informed Canadian commentary on international affairs, stimulated by the publications and discussions of active organizations like the Canadian International Council,[11] the Canadian Defence and Foreign Affairs Institute,[12] universities across the country, and excellent international sources available online through organizations like the International Crisis Group and the Carnegie Endowment for International Peace.[13] But it is still a specialist discussion and should become broader. We need to make a stronger connection between those discussions and the larger activist and interested Canadian public. I hope this book might help stimulate that broad conversation about where and how, in this turbulent and promising world, we Canadians might make a greater difference.

NOTES

INTRODUCTION

1. World Bank, Development Research Group, http://data.worldbank
    .org/indicator/SI.POV.2DAY/countries/NE?display=graph (for
    Niger poverty headcount ratio; accessed June 30, 2013).
2. Barbara Ward, "The First International Nation," in *Canada:
    A Guide to the Peaceable Kingdom*, ed. William Kilbourn
    (Toronto: Macmillan, 1970).

CHAPTER I: LEADING FROM BESIDE

1. "Twenty years ago this month, a software consultant named Tim
    Berners-Lee at the European Organization for Nuclear Research
    (better known as CERN) hatched a plan for an open computer
    network to keep track of research at the particle physics laboratory
    in the suburbs of Geneva, Switzerland. Berners-Lee's modestly
    titled, 'Information Management: A Proposal,' which he submitted
    to get a CERN grant, would become the blueprint for the World
    Wide Web." Larry Greenemeier, "Remembering the day the
    World Wide Web was born," *Scientific American*, March 12, 2009,
    http://www.scientificAmerican.com/article.cfm?id=day-the-web
    -was-born.
2. *Economist*, "Towards the end of poverty," June 1, 2013,
    http://www.economist.com/news/leaders/21578665-nearly-1
    -billion-people-have-been-taken-out-extreme-poverty-20-years
    -world-should-aim/print.
3. The formal Treaty on Open Skies was signed in Helsinki, Finland,

on March 24, 1992, and entered into force on January 2, 2002.
Office of the Spokesperson, US Department of State, "Open
Skies Treaty fact sheet," press release, March 23, 2012,
http://www.state.gov/r/pa/prs/ps/2012/03/186738.htm.

4.   On September 12, 1990, the Treaty on the Final Settlement with
Respect to Germany was signed and the formal reunification of
Germany followed on October 2, 1990.

5.   Harold Macmillan, speech to the South Africa parliament,
February 3, 1960, quoted in Michael Fleshman, "A 'wind of
change' that transformed the continent," United Nations Africa
Renewal, http://www.un.org/africarenewal/magazine/august-2010
/%E2%80%98wind-change%E2%80%99-transformed-continent
(accessed June 30, 2013).

6.   *Encyclopaedia Britannica Online*, s.v. "Augusto Pinochet,"
http://www.britannica.com/EBchecked/topic/461158/Augusto
-Pinochet (accessed June 30, 2013).

7.   Freedom House, "Freedom in the World—Electoral Democracies,"
http://www.freedomhouse.org/sites/default/files/Electoral%20
Democracy%20Numbers%2C%20FIW%201989-2013.pdf
(accessed June 30, 2013).

8.   "Broadband also enables the emergence of new business models,
new processes, new inventions, new and improved goods and
services and it increases competitiveness and flexibility in the
economy, for example by the increased diffusion of information
at lower cost, by improving market access to increasingly larger
markets, by allowing people to work from multiple locations
with flexible hours, and by speeding up procedures and processes,
boosting the economy's dynamism. . . . The benefits that accrue
from using them increase as diffusion spreads." Desirée van
Welsum, *Broadband and the Economy* (Paris: OECD, 2007),
http://www.oecd.org/internet/ieconomy/40781696.pdf.

9.   Calestous Juma, interview by Doug Gavel, "Celebrating the
Remarkable Impact of the Internet and World Wide Web,"
Harvard Kennedy School, March 21, 2013, http://www.hks.
harvard.edu/news-events/news/articles/queen-elizabeth-prize
-feature (accessed June 30, 2013).

10. Ibid.

11. Quoted in Andrew Clark, "Greenspan—I was wrong about
the economy. Sort of," *Guardian*, October 24, 2008,
http://www.guardian.co.uk/business/2008/oct/24/economics
-creditcrunch-federal-reserve-greenspan.

12. The world's total GDP was estimated by the World Bank in 1976
to be $6,328 trillion, although no data was made available by the
USSR. The G7 countries accounted for the following amounts: the

United States $1,809; Japan: $576; Germany: $503; France: $367; the United Kingdom: $227; Italy: $216, Canada: $203. This placed 61.6 percent of Global GDP in the hands of the G7. United Nations Statistics Division, World Bank, http://data.un.org/Data.aspx?q= gdp&d=WDI&f=Indicator_Code%3aNY.GDP.MKTP.CD (for 1976 GDP statistics; accessed June 30, 2013).

13. David Keohane, "Goldman Sachs: Brics in 2050," *Financial Times*, December 7, 2011, http://blogs.ft.com/beyond-brics/2011/12/07 /goldman-sachs-brics-in-2050/?#axzz2XooQyrLX.

14. Fareed Zakaria, *The Post-American World* (New York: W.W. Norton, 2008): 3.

15. World Bank, "Indonesia," http://data.worldbank.org/country /indonesia (accessed August 14, 2013).

16. World Bank, "Nigeria," http://data.worldbank.org/country/nigeria (accessed August 14, 2013).

17. World Bank, "Turkey," http://data.worldbank.org/country/turkey (accessed August 14, 2013).

18. United Nations Security Council, "Security Council approves 'No-Fly Zone' over Libya, authorizing 'all necessary measures' to protect civilians, by vote of 10 in favour with 5 abstentions," press release, March 17, 2011, http://www.un.org/News/Press/docs/2011 /sc10200.doc.htm.

19. Quoted in Ryan Lizza, "The Consequentialist," *New Yorker*, May 2, 2011, http://www.newyorker.com/reporting/2011/05/02 /110502fa_fact_lizza?currentPage=all .

20. Ibid.

21. Ibid.

22. William Kristol, "A leader from behind," *Weekly Standard*, May 9, 2011, http://www.weeklystandard.com/articles/leader -behind_558488.html.

23. Charles Krauthammer, "The Obama doctrine: Leading from behind," Washington Post, April 28. 2011, http://www.washing-tonpost.com/opinions/the_obama_doctrine_leading_from _behind/2011/04/28/AFBCy18E_story.html.

24. Mitt Romney, quoted in Alex Koppelman, "The not-Obama doctrine," *New Yorker*, October 9, 2012, http://www.newyorker. com/online/blogs/comment/2012/10/the-not-obama-doctrine.html.

25. Joseph S. Nye, Jr., *Bound to Lead: The Changing Nature of American Power* (New York: Basic Books, 1990).

26. Joseph S. Nye, Jr., *Soft Power: The Means to Success in World Politics* (New York: Public Affairs, 2004): 5.

27. Ibid.: 11.

CHAPTER 2: SOFT POWER AND HARD POWER

1. "The Paris-based organization does not give an overall ranking,
    but if all the indicators are added up and given equal weighting,
    Canada would come in third behind Australia and Sweden."
    CBC News, "Canada picked among best places to live,"
    May 28, 2013, http://www.cbc.ca/news/canada/story/2013
    /05/28/business-canada-oecd.html.

2. Canada is ranked 14th out of 144 in global competitiveness by
    the World Economic Forum, placing us between Taiwan and
    Norway. Klaus Schwab, *The Global Competitiveness Report,
    2012–2013* (Geneva: WEF, 2012), http://www3.weforum.org
    /docs/WEF_GlobalCompetitivenessReport_2012-13.pdf.

3. Foreign Affairs, Trade and Development Canada, "Harper
    Government focused squarely on jobs and economy at World
    Economic Forum meetings," press release, January 26, 2013,
    http://www.international.gc.ca/media_commerce/comm/news
    -communiques/2013/01/26a.aspx/

4. Transparency International, *Corruption Perception Index, 2012*
    (Berlin: Transparency International, 2012), http://issuu.com
    /transparencyinternational/docs/cpi_2012_report/5?e=0.

5. Economist Intelligence Unit, *Democracy index, 2011: Democracy
    under stress* (London: Economist Intelligence Unit, 2011),
    http://www.sida.se/Global/About%20Sida/S%C3%A5%20
    arbetar%20vi/EIU_Democracy_Index_Dec2011.pdf.

6. Klaus Schwab, *The Global Competitiveness Report, 2012–2013*
    (Geneva: WEF, 2012), http://www3.weforum.org/docs/WEF_Global-
    CompetitivenessReport_2012-13.pdf.

7. United Nations Development Programme, "2011 Human Develop-
    ment Index covers record 187 countries and territories, puts
    Norway at top, DR Congo last," press release, November 2, 2011,
    http://hdr.undp.org/en/media/PR2-HDI-2011HDR-English.pdf.

8. Conference Board of Canada, "Child Poverty," How Canada
    Performs, http://www.conferenceboard.ca/hcp/details/society
    /child-poverty.aspx (accessed June 30, 2013).

9. Conference Board of Canada, "Environment," How Canada
    Performs, http://www.conferenceboard.ca/hcp/details/environment
    .aspx (accessed June 30, 2013).

10. Angel Gurría, "Canada and the OECD: 50 Years of Converging
    Interests," (speech, Public Policy Forum Conference, Ottawa,
    June 2, 2011), http://www.oecd.org/Canada/Canadaandtheoecd-
    50yearsofconverginginterests.htm; in 2012, that productivity
    performance fell again to 14th place, from 12th in 2011, in the
    Global Competitive Index of the World Economic Forum. Klaus
    Schwab, *The Global Competitiveness Report, 2012–2013*

(Geneva: WEF, 2012), http://www3.weforum.org/docs/WEF
_GlobalCompetitivenessReport_2012-13.pdf.

11. Mark Carney, "Exporting in a Post-Crisis World," (speech,
Greater Kitchener Waterloo Chamber of Commerce, Waterloo,
April 2, 2012), http://www.bankofCanada.ca/2012/04/speeches
/exporting-in-a-post-crisis-world/.

12. "China faces numerous internal tensions, especially a class-divided
populace (rich-poor, urban-rural, coastal-inland) that have erupted
within one generation. Moreover, an increasingly complex society
can fracture along multiple fault lines. Pollution, corruption,
healthcare, housing, migrant workers, workers' wages, social
cynicism, changing values, among other raging issues, threaten
to fragment society—and all are exacerbated by an energetic
social media." Robert Lawrence Kuhn, "Xi Jinping's Chinese
Dream," New York Times, June 4, 2013, http://www.nytimes.
com/2013/06/05/opinion/global/xi-jinpings-chinese-dream.
html?pagewanted=all&_r=0; "All of a sudden, a country that was
once viewed as a stellar example of a rising, democratic power
finds itself upended by an amorphous, leaderless popular uprising
with one unifying theme: an angry, and sometimes violent, rejection
of politics as usual." Simon Romero and William Neuman,
"Sweeping protests in Brazil pull in an array of grievances,"
New York Times, June 20, 2013, http://www.nytimes.com/2013
/06/21/world/americas/brazil-protests.html?pagewanted=all.

13. For example, the riots in London, England, in 2011. Mary Riddell,
"London riots: the underclass lashes out," Telegraph, August 8,
2011, http://www.telegraph.co.uk/news/uknews/law-and-order
/8630533/Riots-the-underclass-lashes-out.html.

14. Howard Green, quoted in Charles Yneh, "Howard Green—a
profile," Ottawa Citizen, June 3, 1959, http://news.google.com
/newspapers?nid=2194&dat=19590602&id=XB0yAAAAIBAJ&
sjid=d-QFAAAAIBAJ&pg=5249,540290.

15. "In July 1987 the NDP released a white paper on defence. Entitled
Canadian Sovereignty, Security and Defence it confirmed the NDP's
long standing intention to pull Canada out of NATO and proposed
that the estimated one billion dollar saving be used to expand
Canada's ability to defend its own sovereignty and territorial
integrity especially in the Arctic." J.A. Bayer, "The Canadian
Press, The NDP and NATO," Canadian Journal of Communication 16,
no. 1 (1991), http://www.cjc-online.ca/index.php/journal/article/view
/581/487.

16. Foreign Affairs, Trade and Development Canada, "CIDA's Mission
and Mandate," http://www.acdi-cida.gc.ca/acdi-cida/ACDI-CIDS.nsf
/eng/NIC-5493749-HZK (accessed June 30, 2013).

17. "[Canada] should at once end its evasion of responsibility, and put itself in a position to discharge the commitments it has already accepted for Canada. It can only do this by accepting nuclear warheads." Lester B. Pearson, "On Canadian Defence Policy," (speech, January 12, 1963), in Lester B. Pearson, *Words and Occasions: An Anthology of Speeches and Articles Selected from His Papers* (Toronto: UofT Press, 1970): 202.

18. Diefenbaker was seen by the Americans as equivocating on the issue of nuclear weapons. In response the government of John F. Kennedy targeted Diefenbaker in the media and supported Lester B. Pearson in his election campaign. J.C. Bourque and Joe Martin, "How John F. Kennedy helped Diefenbaker lose an election," *Globe and Mail*, April 8, 2013, http://m.theglobeandmail.com /news/politics/how-john-f-kennedy-helped-diefenbaker-lose -an-election/article10844078/?service=mobile.

19. The late Bud Cullen, then minister of employment and immigration.

20. "Pierre Elliot Trudeau, described his government as 'new guys with new ideas,' and was openly sceptical about the department and its occupants. 'I think the whole concept of diplomacy today,' he told an interviewer in January 1969, 'is a little outmoded.' Trudeau's concerns went even deeper. He questioned the department's attachment to Pearsonian internationalism and demanded a foreign policy rooted in a more limited, often economic, notion of the national interest. And to get it, he revamped the policy-making process. He exposed foreign policy to scrutiny by other departments, and invited those with overseas responsibilities, mainly trade and commerce, immigration, finance, and the Canadian International Development Agency (CIDA) to join External Affairs on an interdepartmental committee on external relations. To keep track of these changes, Trudeau appointed Ivan Head, a member of his own staff, as his foreign policy advisor, a 'Mini-Kissinger' competing with the country's diplomats." Greg Donaghy, "DFAIT Marks Its Centennial," *Canadian Parliamentary Review* 32, no. 4 (2009), http://www.revparl.ca/32/4/32n4_09e_Donaghy.pdf.

21. Ibid.

22. Niger, the second-poorest country in the world, ranked 186th in the 2012 Human Development Index. Burkina Faso ranked 183rd, Malawi ranked 170th, Benin ranked 166th and Rwanda ranked 167th. All of these countries are rated as "low human development." United Nations Development Programme, "Human Development Index (HDI)—2012 Rankings," http://hdr.undp .org/en/statistics/ (accessed June 30, 2013).

23. Peru ranked 77th in the 2012 Human Development Index, Columbia ranked 91st, Bolivia ranked 108th and Honduras

ranked 120th. Bolivia and Honduras are listed as medium human development, while Peru and Columbia are considered to be at high human development. Ibid.

24. Measured then as a proportion of gross national development. Jennifer Paul and Marcus Pistor, *Official Development Assistance Spending* (Ottawa: Library of Parliament, May 2009), http:// www.parl.gc.ca/Content/LOP/researchpublications/prb0710-e.pdf.

25. Measured in Gross National Income. Canadian Council for International Co-operation, "CCIC Analysis of Budget, 2012," http://www.ccic.ca/_files/en/what_we_do/2012_08_CCIC_Initial _Analysis_Budget_2012.pdf (accessed June 30, 2013).

26. "The Department for International Development (DFID) leads the UK's work to end extreme poverty." Government of the United Kingdom, "Department for International Development," Inside Government, https://www.gov.uk/government/organisations /department-for-international-development (accessed June 30, 2013).

27. "Development was once the province of humanitarians, charities, and governments looking to gain allies in global struggles. Today it is a strategic, economic, and moral imperative—as central to advancing American interests and solving global problems as diplomacy and defense." Hillary Clinton, "Remarks on Development in the 21st Century" (speech, Center for Global Development, Washington, DC, January 6, 2010), http:// www.state.gov/secretary/rm/2010/01/134838.htm.

28. In March, 2013, federal budget documents announced that CIDA was being merged into the Department of Foreign Affairs and International Trade. Adam Chapnick, "The problem of international aid in a post-CIDA Canada," *Toronto Star*, April 9, 2013, http://www.thestar.com/opinion/commentary/2013/04/09/the _problem_of_international_aid_in_a_postcida_canada.html.

29. CBC News, "Canada and Kyoto," http://www.cbc.ca/news/ interactives/canada-kyoto/ (accessed June 30, 2013).

30. Formally called the United Nations Convention to Combat Desertification in those Countries Experiencing Serious Drought and/or Desertification, Particularly in Africa. Canada, under Progressive Conservative and Liberal governments, had been among the leading countries proposing the convention, which was signed in 1994. CBC News, "Canada quietly pulls out of UN anti-droughts convention," March 27, 2013, http://www.cbc.ca /news/canada/story/2013/03/27/un-droughts-deserts-convention -canada.html.

31. The 2013 Climate Change Performance Index, produced by organizations Germanwatch and Climate Action Network Europe,

ranks Canada 58th of 61 countries and comments, "Canada still shows no intentions to move forward on climate policy and thereby leave its place as the worst performer of all western countries." Jan Burck, Lukas Hermwille and Laura Krings, *The Climate Change Performance Index, Results 2013* (Berlin: Germanwatch, November 2012) http://Germanwatch.org/en /download/7158.pdf.

32. "Canadian conference chair Maurice Strong, then prime minister Brian Mulroney and environment minister Jean Charest were praised for brokering behind-the-scenes deals and setting the example for other nations to follow." Connie Watson, "Canada needs to show leadership at Earth Summit, Charest says," CBC News, June 18, 2012, http://www.cbc.ca/news/world/story /2012/06/18/f-vp-watson-earth-summit-canada.html.

33. "Other industrialized countries, chiefly Britain and Canada, deserve considerable praise." *New York Times*, "America's Shame in Montreal," December 13, 2005, http://www.nytimes.com /2005/12/13/opinion/13tue1.html.

34. Brian, Blomme "Canada sweeps up three fossil awards at the Cancun climate conference," Greenpeace Canada, November 30, 2010, http://www.greenpeace.org/canada/en/Blog/canada-sweeps -up-three-fossil-awards-at-the-c/blog/29190/ (accessed June 30, 2013).

35. 15. United Nations Peacekeeping, "Ranking of Military and Police Contributions to UN Operations," April 30, 2013, http://www.un .org/en/peacekeeping/contributors/2013/apr13_2.pdf.

36. Canadians for Peacekeeping, "Canada and UN Peacekeeping," July 2012, http://peacekeepingcanada.com /wp-content/uploads/2010/03/PKO-Eng-2012.pdf.

37. Government of Canada, "Canada and the United Nations," http://www.canadainternational.gc.ca/prmny-mponu/canada _un-canada_onu/can_un-can_onu.aspx?lang=eng (accessed June 30, 2013).

38. Ibid.

39. "Immigration Minister Jason Kenney says Canada will not attend a UN conference on racism next September because the event will be a 'charade' and a 'hatefest.'" CBC News, "Canada to boycott Durban conference," November 25, 2010, http://www.cbc.ca /news/politics/story/2010/11/25/kenney-durban.html.

40. National Post Wire Services and National Post Staff, "Canada 'considering all available steps': Baird hits out at UN's 'utterly regrettable' decision to recognize Palestine," *National Post*, November 29, 2011, http://news.nationalpost.com/2012/11/29 /canada-considering-all-available-steps-baird-lashes-out-at-un -ahead-of-utterly-regrettable-decision-to-recognize-palestine/.

41. Steven Chase, "Harper makes donut run," *Globe and Mail*, September 22, 2009, http://www.theglobeandmail.com/news /politics/ottawa-notebook/harper-makes-donut-run/article4286299/.

42. Tom Parry, "Stephen Harper accepts World Statesman of the Year award," CBC News, September 27, 2012, http://www.cbc.ca/news /politics/story/2012/09/27/pol-parry-harper-award.html.

43. "Multilateralism, whether pursued as an end in itself or the best means through which Canada can achieve its objectives, has long been a crucial component of Canadian foreign policy. Under the Harper Conservatives, however, multilateralism has not been as salient. For example, in 2011 Canada quietly withdrew from an organization focused on improving public health in the far north that it had helped establish. In 2012, the government announced that Canada would withdraw from three United Nations organizations—on tourism, on the sustainable use of tropical lumber, and on international exhibitions, and in March 2013, Ottawa withdrew from the UN Convention on Desertification. Rather, bilateralism seems to suit this government and its emphasis on international strength." Kim Richard Nossal and Leah Sarson, "About Face: Explaining Changes in Canada's China Policy 2006–2012," (paper presented to the Annual Meeting of the Canadian Political Science Association, University of Victoria, June 6, 2013), http://www.cpsa-acsp.ca/papers-2013/Nossal.pdf.

44. "Heinbecker [former Canadian diplomat] says Canada's shifting positions on climate change, our decidedly pro-Israel policy in the Middle East conflict, and our shift away from focusing aid to Africa all contributed to the loss." Parminder Parmar, "2010 'crystallized' Canada's changing foreign policy," CTV News, January 2, 2011, http://www.ctvnews.ca/2010-crystallized -canada-s-changing-foreign-policy-1.589379.

CHAPTER 3: SEEING MORE AND FEELING LESS

1. Edward R. Murrow and Fred W. Friendly, *I Can Hear It Now— 1933–1945*, radio broadcast collection narrated by Edward R. Murrow (Columbia Records, 1948), http://archive.org/details/ ICanHearItNow-1933-1945.

2. In April, 2011, I was an international observer in an important and potentially violent presidential election in Nigeria, and had a phone interview with the CBC from an outdoor polling place, an open field, in Abuja. My sister-in-law, Sunny, highly active in her own communities in Canada, sent this e-mail: "Hi Joe, it was good to hear your voice from Nigeria on CBC. To illustrate how we live in a vacuum here in Canada, we are rushing to get to Costco for

some lettuce. Please stay safe." Sunny Clark, e-mail message to author, April 9, 2011.

3. The phrase was captured by Neil Nevitte in his book *The Decline of Deference: Canadian Value Change in Cross National Perspective* (Toronto: UofT Press, 1996).

4. When I was sworn in as prime minister, I convened a meeting of the most senior officials of the Government of Canada. Sylvia Ostry, then chairman of the Economic Council of Canada, was unavoidably out of town that day, so the meeting was all male. That was in early June 1979. When I became foreign minister in September 1984, Canada had only a small number of ambassadors or high commissioners or heads of mission who were women. Not long ago, in Canada, women were scarce-to-invisible in leadership positions in the public sector, as they still are in the private sector.

CHAPTER 4: CANADA'S INTERNATIONAL HISTORY AND TRADITION

1. Quoted in *Canadian Encyclopedia Online*, s.v. "Canada and the United States," http://thecanadianencyclopedia.com/articles /canada-and-the-united-states (accessed June 30, 2013).

2. The author is an independent director of GlobeScan.

3. "In total 24,090 citizens in Australia, Brazil, Canada, Chile, China, Egypt, France, Germany, Ghana, India, Indonesia, Japan, Kenya, Mexico, Nigeria, Pakistan, Peru, Russia, South Korea, Spain, the United Kingdom, and the United States were inter-viewed face-to-face or by telephone between December 6, 2011 and February 17, 2012. Countries were rated by half samples in all countries polled. Polling was conducted for BBC World Service by GlobeScan and its research partners in each country." GlobeScan, "Views of Europe slide sharply in global poll, while views of China improve," press release, May 10, 2012, http://www.globescan.com/commentary-and-analysis/press-releases /press-releases-2012/84-press-releases-2012/186-views-of-Europe -slide-sharply-in-global-poll-while-views-of-China-improve.html.

4. Ibid.

5. Canadian War Museum, "The Cost of Canada's War," Canada and the First World War, http://www.warmuseum.ca/cwm /exhibitions/guerre/cost-war-e.aspx (accessed June 30, 2013).

6. Serge Durflinger, "French Canada and Recruitment during the First World War," Canadian War Museum, http://www.warmuseum.ca /education/online-educational-resources/dispatches/french-canada -and-recruitment-during-the-first-world-war/ (accessed June 30, 2013).

7. Ibid.

8. Margaret MacMillan, *Paris 1919: Six Months that Changed the World* (Toronto: Random House Canada, 2001): 44–45.

9. Ibid.

10. Quoted in ibid.

11. *Canadian Encyclopedia Online*, s.v. "Statute of Westminster," http://www.thecanadianencyclopedia.com/articles/statute-of -westminster (accessed June 30, 2013).

12. Lieutenant General E.L.M. Burns's military career is well detailed in J. P. Johnston, "E.L.M. Burns—A Crisis of Command," *Canadian Military Journal* 7, no. 1 (2006), http://www.journal .forces.gc.ca/vo7/no1/history-histoire-eng.asp.

13. "Pearson's experience, diplomatic skill, and impeccable timing were vital. . . . More important, however, Pearson had powerful support from both the British and the Americans. Senior British politicians and officials, distressed by their government's action, rushed to offer Pearson their support. . . . The resolution Pearson moved to create the UNEF was drafted in Washington not Ottawa." Greg Donaghy, "Coming off the Gold Standard: Re-assessing the 'Golden Age' of Canadian Diplomacy" (lecture, University of Regina, October 26, 2005), http://www.schoolofpublicpolicy. sk.ca/_documents/outreach_event_announcements/DFAIT_symposium /Coming_off_the_Gold_Standard.pdf.

14. There have been sixty-eight peacekeeping operations since 1948, as of April 30, 2013. United Nations, "Peacekeeping Fact Sheet," United Nations Peacekeeping, http://www.un.org/en/peacekeeping /resources/statistics/factsheet.shtml (accessed June 30, 2013).

15. Gunnar Jahn, "Award Ceremony Speech" (presentation speech of Nobel Peace Prize to Lester Pearson, University of Oslo, December 10, 1957) in *Nobel Lectures, Peace, 1951-1970*, ed. Frederick W. Haberman (Amsterdam: Elsevier Publishing, 1972), http://www.nobelprize.org/nobel_prizes/peace/laureates/1957 /press.html.

16. Permanent Mission of Canada to the United Nations, "Peace-keeping and Peacebuilding Operations," http://www.canada international.gc.ca/prmny-mponu/canada_un-canada_onu /positions-orientations/peace-paix/peace-operations-paix.aspx ?lang=eng (accessed June 30, 2013).

17. For a detailed look at Canada's role in peacekeeping and the international reputation it acquired, see Joseph T. Jockel, *Canada and International Peacekeeping* (Toronto: Canadian Institute of Strategic Studies, 1994).

18. O.D. Skelton, "Notes on the Protocol of Geneva," Department of External Affairs Records (NAC), vol. 813, file 629 (1), quoted in Gregory A. Johnson and David A. Lenarcic, "The Decade of

Transition," in *The North Atlantic Triangle in a Changing World: Anglo-American-Canadian Relations, 1902–1956*, ed. Brian James Cooper McKercher and Lawrence Aronsen (Toronto: UofT Press, 1996), http://auspace.athabascau.ca/bitstream/2149 /1714/1/The%20north%20atlantic%20triangle%20during%20 the%201920s.pdf.

19. Loring Christie to Arthur Meighen, December 23, 1925, Meighen Papers (NAC), vol. 64, ibid.

20. "The Members of the League undertake to respect and preserve as against external aggression the territorial integrity and existing political independence of all Members of the League. In case of any such aggression or in case of any threat or danger of such aggression the Council shall advise upon the means by which this obligation shall be fulfilled." *The Covenant of the League of Nations*, Article X, entered into force January 10, 1920.

21. Raoul Dandurand, League of Nations, "Official Journal, Special Supplement no. 23," *Records of the Fifth Assembly* (Geneva, 1924): 222, quoted in Gregory A. Johnson and David A. Lenarcic, "The Decade of Transition," in *The North Atlantic Triangle in a Changing World: Anglo-American-Canadian Relations, 1902–1956*, ed. Brian James Cooper McKercher and Lawrence Aronsen (Toronto: UofT Press, 1996), http://auspace.athabascau.ca /bitstream/2149/1714/1/The%20north%20atlantic%20triangle %20during%20the%201920s.pdf.

22. Gregory A. Johnson and David A. Lenarcic, "The Decade of Transition," in *The North Atlantic Triangle in a Changing World: Anglo-American-Canadian Relations, 1902–1956*, ed. Brian James Cooper McKercher and Lawrence Aronsen (Toronto: UofT Press, 1996): 97, http://auspace.athabascau.ca/bitstream/2149/1714/1 /The%20north%20atlantic%20triangle%20during%20the%20 1920s.pdf.

23. O.D. Skelton was undersecretary of state (deputy minister) of external affairs from 1925 to 1941. Norman Hillmer, "National Independence and the National Interest," in *In the National Interest: Canadian Foreign Policy and the Department of Foreign Affairs and International Trade, 1909–2009*, ed. Greg Donaghy and Michael K. Carroll (Calgary: University of Calgary Press, 2011): 11–13, http://dspace.ucalgary.ca/bitstream/1880/48549/4 /UofCPress_NationalInterest_2011.pdf.

24. Ibid.: 24.

25. Desmond Morton, *A Short History of Canada*, 6th ed. (Toronto: McClelland & Stewart, 2006).

26. Denis Stairs, "Realists at Work: Canadian Policy Makers and the Politics of Transition from Hot War to Cold," in *Canada and the*

Early Cold War, 1943–1957, ed. Greg Donaghy (Ottawa: Canadian Government Publishing, 1998): 94, http://publications.gc.ca /collections/Collection/E2-179-1998.pdf.

27. Foreign Affairs, Trade and Development Canada, "1939–1945: The World at War," *Canada and the World: A History*, http:// epe.lac-bac.gc.ca/100/206/301/faitc-aecic/history/2013-05-03 /www.international.gc.ca/history-histoire/world-monde/1939-1945 -1.aspx@lang=eng (accessed June 30, 2013).

28. Along with foreign ministers Gaetano Martino of Italy and Halvard Lange of Norway.

29. Greg Donaghy, "Coming off the Gold Standard: Re-assessing the 'Golden Age' of Canadian Diplomacy" (lecture, University of Regina, October 26, 2005):3, http://www.schoolofpublicpolicy .sk.ca/_documents/outreach_event_announcements/DFAIT _symposium/Coming_off_the_Gold_Standard.pdf.

30. Ibid.

31. Denis Stairs, "Realists at Work: Canadian Policy Makers and the Politics of Transition from Hot War to Cold," in *Canada and the Early Cold War, 1943–1957*, ed. Greg Donaghy (Ottawa: Canadian Government Publishing, 1998): 92–93, http://publications.gc.ca /collections/Collection/E2-179-1998.pdf.

32. "Functionalism was the principle whereby a country would be accorded decision-making responsibilities in recognition of the material contributions it had made or was willing to make to the work of the institution. In the 1940s, Canadian diplomats pressed this principle into service whenever possible because of the significant material contributions that Canada was making in many areas. Functionalism reinforced the view that multilateral institutions were particularly useful for lesser powers such as Canada in that they would provide an opportunity for these states to enhance their position in international negotiations and thus better protect their interests in dealing with other states, as long as these states were making a material contribution to the work of these organizations." Tom Keating, *Multilateralism and Canadian Foreign Policy: A Reassessment* (Calgary: CDFAI, 2003): 5–6, http://www.cdfai.org/PDF/Multilateralism%20and%20Canadian %20Foreign%20Policy%20-A%20Reassessment.pdf.

33. Ibid.

34. L.B. Pearson, "Some Principles of Canadian Foreign Policy" (speech, January 1948), in L.B. Pearson, *Words and Occasions: An Anthology of Speeches and Articles Selected from His Papers, 1924–1968* (Toronto: UofT Press, 1970): 68.

35. Norman Hillmer, "The Foreign Policy That Never Was, 1900–1950," in *Canada, 1900–1950: A Country Comes of Age*, ed. Serge

Bernier and John MacFarlane (Ottawa: Organization for the History of Canada, 2003): 151.

36. King's request to St. Laurent to run for Parliament is detailed in *Dictionary of Canadian Biography Online*, s.v. "St-Laurent, Louis-Stephen," http://www.biographi.ca/en/bio.php?id_nbr=7989 (accessed June 30, 2013).

37. Foreign Affairs, Trade and Development Canada, "'Punching Above Its Weight': 1939–1968," http://www.international.gc.ca /history-histoire/photos/punching-jouer.aspx?menu_id=39&menu= R (accessed June 30, 2013).

38. United Nations Association in Canada, "Canadian Participation in UN Peacekeeping—Chronology," http://www.unac.org/peace-keeping/en/un-peacekeeping/fact-sheets/canadian-participation -in-un-peacekeepinga-chro/ (accessed June 30, 2013).

39. "A lawyer by profession, St. Laurent was a convinced internation-alist. . . . Much more than King, he was willing to take on an activ-ist foreign policy." Steven Hugh Lee, *Outposts of Empire: Korea, Vietnam, and the Origins of the Cold War in Asia, 1949–1954* (Montreal: McGill-Queens University Press, 1995): 25.

40. John W. Holmes, *The Shaping of Peace: Canada and the Search for World Order, 1943–1957*, vol. 2 (Toronto: UofT Press, 1982): 65.

41. CUSO International, "As CUSO-VSO turns 50, international volun-teering continues to evolve," press release, June 1, 2011, http:// www.sources.com/Releases/NR1308.htm.

42. Greg Donaghy, "Coming off the Gold Standard: Re-assessing the 'Golden Age' of Canadian Diplomacy" (lecture, University of Regina, October 26, 2005): 11, http://www.schoolofpublicpolicy. sk.ca/_documents/outreach_event_announcements/DFAIT _symposium/Coming_off_the_Gold_Standard.pdf.

43. Norman Hillmer, "The Foreign Policy That Never Was, 1900–1950," in *Canada, 1900–1950*, ed. Serge Bernier and John MacFarlane (Ottawa: Organization for the History of Canada, 2003).

44. Ibid.

45. Greg Donaghy, "Coming off the Gold Standard: Re-assessing the 'Golden Age' of Canadian Diplomacy" (lecture, University of Regina, October 26, 2005): 11, http://www.schoolofpublicpolicy. sk.ca/_documents/outreach_event_announcements/DFAIT _symposium/Coming_off_the_Gold_Standard.pdf.

46. Ibid.

47. Allister Sparks, *Tomorrow Is Another Country: The Inside Story of South Africa's Road to Change* (New York: Hill & Wang, 1995).

CHAPTER 5: MARRYING MANDATE AND IMAGINATION

1. Rudyard Kipling, *Kim* (Project Gutenburg, 2009), http://www.gutenberg.org/files/2226/2226-h/2226-h.htm.

2. Cambodian journalist Dith Pran "coined the term 'killing fields' to describe the horrifying scene he witnessed on his journey to freedom in Thailand. The Khmer Rouge was the ruling party in Cambodia from 1975 to 1979, during which it was responsible for one of the worst mass killings of the 20th Century. The regime claimed the lives of more than a million people—some estimates say up to 2.5 million perished." BBC News, "'Killing Fields' journalist dies," March 30, 2008, http://news.bbc.co.uk/2/hi/7321560.stm.

3. Jessica Mathews, "Power Shift: The Rise of Global Civil Society," *Foreign Affairs* 76, no. 1 (January/February 1997): 50–66.

4. Matt Styslinger, "Small is beautiful. Big is necessary," Worldwatch Institute, http://blogs.worldwatch.org/nourishingtheplanet/small-is-beautiful-big-is-necessary-brac-bangladesh-rural-advancement-committee-grameen-bank-microfinance-poverty-social-enterprise-education-empowerment-and-livelihood-for-adolescents-program-women-e/ (accessed June 30, 2013).

5. Edelman, "NGOs Most Trusted Institution Globally," http://trust.edelman.com/trusts/trust-in-institutions-2/ngos-remain-most-trusted/ (accessed June 30, 2013).

6. GlobeScan, "High public trust in NGOs, but is it built on shaky foundations?" http://www.globescan.com/commentary-and-analysis/featured-findings/entry/high-public-trust-in-ngos-but-is-it-built-on-shaky-foundations.html (accessed June 30, 2013).

7. James McGann and Mary Johnston, "The Power Shift and the NGO Credibility Crisis," *International Journal of Not-for-Profit Law* 8, no. 2 (January 2006), http://www.icnl.org/research/journal/vol8iss2/ijnl_vol8iss2.pdf.

8. *Economist*, "Drug policy in Latin America: Burn-out and battle fatigue," March 17, 2012, http://www.economist.com/node/21550296.

9. James Cockayne and Phil Williams, *The Invisible Tide: Towards an International Strategy to Deal with Drug Trafficking Through West Africa* (New York: International Peace Institute, October 2009), 8. http://mercury.ethz.ch/serviceengine/Files/ISN/126889/ipublicationdocument_singledocument/b13d2282-4842-4c3f-a4db-f9ca3a01f04d/en/west_africa_drug_trafficking_10_2009.pdf.

10. "The Esquipulas peace agreement by five Central American presidents . . . paved the way, albeit not immediately, for a negotiated end to civil war across the isthmus. It was considered a turning point for Latin America, a regional framework that

marked a departure from Reagan-era anti-communist policies
and its view of Central America as a stage of the cold war. . . .
But if the accord succeeded in ending political and ideological
strife, it failed to create peaceful societies." Sara Miller Llana,
"Central American peace accord celebrates 25 years, but has
it brought peace?" *Christian Science Monitor*, August 7, 2012,
http://www.csmonitor.com/World/Americas/2012/0807
/Central-American-peace-accord-celebrates-25-years-but
-has-it-brought-peace?.

11. "The Central American crisis allowed Canada to enter into the
most volatile issue in the hemisphere—which it did in a delicate
balance between US pressure to overthrow the Sandinistas and
Latin American resistance. . . . The Central American crisis was
perhaps the principal catalyst for [Canada's] decision to join the
OAS . . . because it brought Canada closer to Latin American
ad hoc multilateralism and defined an unprecedented role for
peace-keeping and conflict resolution in the hemisphere." Brian J.
R. Stevenson, *Canada, Latin America, and the New Internationalism*
(Montreal: McGill-Queen's Press, 2000): 179.

12. Brian Stewart, "When Brian Mulroney was great," CBC News,
May 15, 2009, http://www.cbc.ca/news/canada/story/2009/05/14
/f-vp-stewart.html.

13. *Economist*, "The non-governmental order: Will NGOs democratize,
or merely disrupt, global governance?" December 9, 1999,
http://www.economist.com/node/266250.

14. Union of International Associations ed., *Yearbook of International
Organizations, 2010–2011: Statistics, visualizations and patterns,*
vol. 5 (Berlin: De Gruyter, 2010): 35.

15. Sakiko Fukuda-Parr et al., *Human Development Report, 2002:
Deepening democracy in a fragmented world* (New York:
Oxford University Press, 2002): 8, http://hdr.undp.org/en/media
/HDR_2002_EN_Complete.pdf.

16. International Federation of Red Cross and Red Crescent Societies,
"National Societies," http://www.ifrc.org/en/who-we-are/the
-movement/national-societies/ (accessed June 30, 2013).

17. BNP Paribas, "About BNP Paribas," http://www.bnpparibas.ca
/en/bnp-paribas/bnp-paribas-group/ (accessed August 15, 2013).

18. Deutsche Bank, "FAQs," Deutsche Bank Investor Relations,
https://www.db.com/ir/en/content/faqs.htm (accessed June 30, 2013).

19. HSBC, *HSBC Holdings plc Interim Report, 2011* (London: HSBC,
2011): 25, http://www.hsbc.es/1/PA_esf-ca-app-content/content
/spain/corporate/pdf/hsbc_interim_report_2011.pdf.

20. 1. Walmart Stores 2,100,000 employees; 2. Royal Dutch Shell
97,000 employees; 3. Exxon Mobil 103,700 employees; BP 79,700

employees; 5. Sinopec Group 640,335 employees; 6. China National Petroleum 1,674,541 employees; 7. State Grid 1,564,000 employees; 8. Toyota Motor 317,716; 9. Japan Post Holdings 233,000 employees; 10. Chevron 62,196 employees. CNN Money, Global Fortune 500, http://money.cnn.com/magazines/fortune /global500/2011/performers/companies/biggest/ (for employees among top 10 in 2011; accessed June 2013).

21. United Nations Economic and Social Council, "Committee on non-governmental organizations, opening resumed session, recommends consultative status for 35 applicants, postpones consideration of 10," press release, May 21, 2012, http:// www.un.org/News/Press/docs//2012/ecosoc6512.doc.htm.

22. M. Widmer et al., "The role of faith-based organizations in maternal and newborn health care in Africa," *International Journal of Gynecology & Obstetrics* 114, no. 3 (September 2011): 218–222.

23. African Religious Health Assets Program, *Appreciating Assets: The Contribution of Religion to Universal Access in Africa*, 2006 (Cape Town: ARHAP, October 2006), http://www.arhap.uct.ac.za /downloads/ARHAPWHO_execsumm.pdf.

24. Médecins Sans Frontières, "About MSF," http://www.msf.org /about-msf (accessed June 30, 2013); Jean-Hervé Bradol and Claudine Vidal, eds. *Medical Innovations in Humanitarian Situations: The work of Médecins Sans Frontières* (CreateSpace Independent Publishing Platform, 2011).

25. United Nations Global Compact, "Oxfam and Unilever on Business and Poverty," http://www.unglobalcompact.org /NewsAndEvents/news_archives/2005_09_16_b.html (accessed June 30, 2013).

26. Avaaz, "Burma Cyclone Aid Report," http://www.avaaz.org/en /burma_aid_report/7.php?cl=90108383 (accessed June 30, 2013).

27. Greenpeace International, "1982—Moratorium puts an end to commercial whaling," September 12, 2011, http://www.greenpeace .org/international/en/about/history/Victories-timeline/whaling -moratorium/ (accessed June 30, 2013).

28. Greenpeace International, "1995—Shell reverses decision to dump the Brent Spar," September 13, 2011, http://www.greenpeace.org /international/en/about/history/Victories-timeline/Brent-Spar/ (accessed August 15, 2013).

29. Partners In Health, "The HIV Equity Initiative," http://photos.pih .org/where/haiti/Haiti-HIVequity.html (accessed June 30, 2013).

30. Bill & Melinda Gates Foundation, "Foundation Fact Sheet," http://www.gatesfoundation.org/Who-We-Are/General-Information /Foundation-Factsheet (accessed August 15, 2013).

31. "What would it take to change the world? Rotary's 1.2 million members believe it starts with a commitment to Service Above Self. In more than 34,000 clubs worldwide, you'll find members volunteering in communities at home and abroad to support education and job training, provide clean water, combat hunger, improve health and sanitation, and eradicate polio." Rotary International, "About Us," http://www.rotary.org/EN/ABOUTUS /Pages/ridefault.aspx (accessed August 15, 2013).

32. "Our 46,000 clubs and 1.35 million members make us the world's largest service club organization. We're also one of the most effective. Our members do whatever is needed to help their local communities. Everywhere we work, we make friends. With children who need eyeglasses, with seniors who don't have enough to eat and with people we may never meet." Lions Clubs, "About Lions Clubs," http://www.lionsclubs.org/EN/about-lions/index.php (accessed August 15, 2013).

33. "The International Crisis Group is an independent, non-profit, non-governmental organisation committed to preventing and resolving deadly conflict." International Crisis Group, "About Crisis Group," http://www.crisisgroup.org/en/about.aspx (accessed June 30, 2013).

34. "The Centre for Humanitarian Dialogue (HD Centre) is one of the world's leading conflict mediation organisations. Since 1999, the HD Centre has been helping to prevent and resolve armed conflict, and to alleviate the suffering of those affected by violence. Independent and discreet, we work with our clients—parties to conflict—to assist them in their search for peace." Centre for Humanitarian Dialogue, "Who We Are," http://www.hdcentre.org /en/about-us/who-we-are/ (accessed August 15, 2013).

35. "The Carter Center, in partnership with Emory University, is guided by a fundamental commitment to human rights and the alleviation of human suffering; it seeks to prevent and resolve conflicts, enhance freedom and democracy, and improve health." The Carter Center, "About Us," http://www.cartercenter.org/about /index.html (accessed August 15, 2013).

36. "NDI is a nonprofit, nonpartisan, nongovernmental organization that has supported democratic institutions and practices in every region of the world for more than two decades. Since its founding in 1983, NDI and its local partners have worked to establish and strengthen political and civic organizations, safeguard elections, and promote citizen participation, openness and accountability in government." The National Democratic Institute, "Who We Are," http://www.ndi.org/whoweare (accessed August 15, 2013).

37. "A nonprofit, nonpartisan organization, IRI advances freedom and

democracy worldwide by developing political parties, civic institutions, open elections, democratic governance and the rule of law." The International Republican Institute, "Mission," http://www.iri.org/learn-more-about-iri/mission (accessed August 15, 2013).

38. "GLF exists to support political leadership and good governance around the world by making available the experience of former leaders to today's national leaders. GLF operates discreetly and in confidence, with GLF Members typically working in small teams to give frank and private advice on specific issues of concern to Heads of Government and on general governance issues." Global Leadership Foundation, "Purpose," http://www.g-l-f.org/index.cfm?pagepath=Purpose&id=22872 (accessed August 15, 2013).

39. "The Elders is an independent group of global leaders who work together for peace and human rights." The Elders, "About the Elders," http://theelders.org/about (accessed August 15, 2013).

40. Trenton Daniel, "Isaac tests the resolve of a Haitian family man," Associated Press, August 27, 2012, http://bigstory.ap.org/article/isaac-tests-resolve-haitian-family-man.

CHAPTER 6: CANADA'S POLICY TODAY

1. "Describing, much less explaining, the evolution of Conservative policy (on China) is a daunting task. Policy making has been concentrated in very few hands and its content has never been fully articulated or explained by its makers." Paul Evans, "Engagement with Conservative Characteristics: Policy and Public Attitudes, 2006–2011," in *Issues in Canada-China Relations*, ed. Pitman B. Potter (Toronto: CIC, 2011): 20, http://www.opencanada.org/wp-content/uploads/2011/11/CIC-Issues-in-Canada-China-Relations-2011.pdf.

2. Pitman Potter, "Introduction: Changing Dimensions of Canada-China Relations," in *Issues in Canada-China Relations*, ed. Pitman B. Potter (Toronto: CIC, 2011): 1, http://www.opencanada.org/wp-content/uploads/2011/11/CIC-Issues-in-Canada-China-Relations-2011.pdf.

3. Ibid.

4. Paul Evans, "Engagement with Conservative Characteristics: Policy and Public Attitudes, 2006–2011," in *Issues in Canada-China Relations*, ed. Pitman B. Potter (Toronto: CIC, 2011): 26, http://www.opencanada.org/wp-content/uploads/2011/11/CIC-Issues-in-Canada-China-Relations-2011.pdf.

5. Margaret MacMillan, *Nixon in China: The Week that Changed the World* (Toronto: Penguin Canada, 2006): 6.

6. Ibid.: 312.

7. Paul Evans, "Engagement with Conservative Characteristics: Policy and Public Attitudes, 2006–2011," *Issues in Canada-China Relations*, ed. Pitman B. Potter (Toronto: CIC, 2011): 19, http://www.opencanada.org/wp-content/uploads/2011/11/CIC -Issues-in-Canada-China-Relations-2011.pdf.

8. Ibid.

9. Ibid.

10. Ibid: 22.

11. Ibid.

12. Mark Mackinnon, "The remaking of Harper's China gambit," *Globe and Mail*, March 25, 2013, http://m.theglobeandmail.com /news/world/the-remaking-of-harpers-china-gambit/article543845 /?service=mobile.

13. John Ibbitson, "China publicly scolds Harper for taking too long to visit," *Globe and Mail*, December 3, 2009, http:// www.theglobeandmail.com/news/politics/china-publicly -scolds-harper-for-taking-too-long-to-visit/article1386656/.

14. Charles Flicker, "Next year in Jerusalem: Joe Clark and the Jerusalem embassy affair," *International Journal* 58, no. 1 (Winter, 2002/2003): 115–138, http://www.jstor.org/stable/40203815.

15. David D. Dewitt and John J. Kirton, "Canada and the Process of Peace Making in the Arab-Israel Conflict," in *Peace-Making in the Middle East: Problems and Prospects*, ed. Paul Marantz and Janice Gross Stein (Kent, UK: Croom Helm Ltd, 1985): 207.

16. "Between 1941 and 1945, five to six million Jews were systematically murdered by the Nazi regime, its allies, and its surrogates in the Nazi-occupied territories" Adam Jones, *Genocide: A Comprehensive Introduction* (Oxford: Routledge/Taylor & Francis Publishers, August 2010), http://www.genocidetext.net/gaci _holocaust.pdf.

17. Michael Brenner, "Displaced Persons after the Holocaust," in *The Holocaust Encyclopedia*, ed. Walter Lacquer (London: Yale University Press, 2001).

18. Anti-Defamation League, "Anti-Semitism on the Rise in America— ADL Survey on Anti-Semitic Attitudes Reveals 17 Percent of Americans Hold 'Hardcore' Beliefs," press release, June 11, 2002, http://archive.adl.org/presrele/asus_12/4109_12.htm; "Israeli researchers warned last month that there had been an increase in attacks against Jewish communities across Europe, reporting a 30 per cent jump in anti-Semitic violence and vandalism. . . . The study by Tel Aviv University attributed the rise in part to the economic crisis, with extremist parties taking advantage of people's frustrations about financial hardships." Tony Paterson and Charlotte Mcdonald-Gibson, "The shadow of anti-semitism

falls on Europe once more as Hungary's far-fight Jobbik party protests against World Jewish Congress meeting in Budapest," *Independent*, May 5, 2013, http://www.independent.co.uk/news /world/europe/the-shadow-of-antisemitism-falls-on-europe-once -more-as-hungarys-farfight-jobbik-party-protests-against-world -jewish-congress-meeting-in-budapest-8604656.html.

19. "At the start of 2011, more than 950,000 Israelis live within range of rocket and mortar attacks. Since the beginning of 2011, more than 330 rockets, missiles or mortars have been fired into and landed in Israel, compared to 238 for all of 2010." Israel Project, "Gaza Border Press Kit: Rocket Statistics," http://www.theisraelproject. org/site/pp.aspx?c=hsJPKoPIJpH&b=6643983&printmode=1 (accessed June 30, 2013).

20. The phrase was first and widely translated as "wiped off the face of the earth." Jonathan Steele, "Lost in translation," *Guardian*, June 14, 2006, http://www.theguardian.com/commentisfree/2006 /jun/14/post155.

21. "Palestine as a geo-political unit dates back to 3000 BC." Hasan Afif El-Hasan, "Who are the Palestinians," *Palestine Chronicle*, May 1, 2012, http://www.palestinechronicle.com/old/view_article _details.php?id=17368.

22. Maen Rashid Areikat, "Palestine, a history rich and deep, *Washington Post*, December 27, 2011, http://articles.washingtonpost.com/2011 -12-27/opinions/35288281_1_palestinians-arabs-jews.

23. *Guardian*, "The Arab-Israeli conflict: A brief history," 2011, http://www.guardian.co.uk/flash/0,,720353,00.html.

24. Ibid.

25. "Peace Talks at Camp David, September 1978," *American Experience*, PBS, http://www.pbs.org/wgbh/americanexperience /features/general-article/carter-peace/.

26. "Shattered Dreams of Peace," *Frontline*, PBS, http://www.pbs.org /wgbh/pages/frontline/shows/oslo/negotiations/.

27. *Jerusalem Post*, "Report: Kerry to officially announce resumption of peace talks," July 18, 2013, http://www.jpost.com/Middle -East/Report-Kerry-to-officially-announce-resumption-of-peace -processes-320222, July 18, 2013.

28. Nelson Mandela, "Address by President Nelson Mandela at the International Day of Solidarity with the Palestinian People," (speech, Pretoria, South Africa, December 4, 1997), http://anc.org .za/show.php?id=3384.

29. "The Palestinian official said the Security Council was divided into three groups, with only the US directly opposing Palestinian membership. Russia, China, Brazil, India, Lebanon, South Africa, Gabon and Nigeria supported the Palestinian bid and Britain,

Germany, France, Portugal and Colombia said they would abstain in any vote. Bosnia did not speak." Sheera Frenkel, "Palestinian statehood bid stillborn in Security Council," *Sydney Morning Herald*, November 12, 2011, http://www.smh.com.au/world /palestinian-statehood-bid-stillborn-in-security-council-20111111 -1nbm4.html.

30. United Nations General Assembly, "General Assembly votes overwhelmingly to accord Palestine 'non-Member Observer State' status in United Nations," press release, November 29, 2012, http://www.un.org/News/Press/docs/2012/ga11317.doc.htm.

31. "Some people see Canada as being a great even-handed referee. . . . Well, we're not a referee. We have a side." John Baird, quoted in Lee Berthiaume, "Canada is not a referee in the world, John Baird says," Post Media News, December 21, 2012, http://o.Canada.com/2012/12 /21/Canada-is-not-a-referee-in-the-world-john-baird-says/.

32. John Baird, quoted in *Toronto Sun*, "Canada is Israel's best friend: Baird," May 5, 2012, http://www.torontosun.com/2012/05/05 /canada-is-israels-best-friend-baird. His then-colleague in cabinet Peter Kent told *The Globe and Mail* that "an attack on Israel would be considered an attack on Canada." Steven Chase, "'An attack on Israel would be considered an attack on Canada,'" *Globe and Mail*, February 16, 2010, http://www.theglobeandmail. com/news/politics/ottawa-notebook/an-attack-on-israel-would -be-considered-an-attack-on-canada/article4187892/.

33. BBC News, "Hamas sweeps to election victory," January 26, 2006, http://news.bbc.co.uk/2/hi/4650788.stm.

34. CBC News, "'Not a red cent to Hamas,' MacKay says," March 26, 2006, http://www.cbc.ca/news/canada/story/2006/03/29/ottawa -hamas060329.html.

35. Gloria Galloway, "Following Israel's lead, Canada cuts aid to Hamas," *Globe and Mail*, March 30, 2006, http://www.theglobe-andmail.com/news/national/following-israels-lead-canada-cuts -aid-to-hamas/article705640/.

36. Sarah Leah Whitson, quoted in Human Rights Watch, "Lebanon/ Israel: Hezbollah Rockets Targeted Civilians in 2006 War," http://www.hrw.org/news/2007/08/28/lebanonisrael-hezbollah -rockets-targeted-civilians-2006-war (accessed June 30, 2013).

37. Quoted in Chris McGeal, "Capture of soldiers was 'act of war' says Israel," *Guardian*, July 13, 2006, http://www.guardian.co.uk /world/2006/jul/13/israelandthepalestinians.lebanon1.

38. Peter Bouckaert and Nadim Houry, *Why They Died: Civilian Casualties in Lebanon during the 2006 War*, (New York: Human Rights Watch, September 2007): 3, http://www.hrw.org/sites /default/files/reports/lebanon0907.pdf.

39. Quoted in Jane Taber, "Harper defends Israel's right to 'defend itself,'" *Globe and Mail*, July 14, 2006.

40. *National Post*, "Harper wants 'durable and lasting peace' in Middle East," August 5, 2006, http://www.nationalpost.com/news /story.html?id=978b8ac9-3d8a-4e10-95f3-438f53cbe004&k=51589.

41. Donald Barry, "Canada and the Middle East today: Electoral politics and foreign policy," *Arab Studies Quarterly* 32, no. 4 (Fall 2010): 191.

42. Barack Obama, "Full transcript | Barack Obama | Middle East speech | Washington, DC | 19 May 2011," *New Statesman*, May 19, 2011, http://www.newstatesman.com/blogs/the-staggers /2011/05/speech-washington-barack-obama.

43. Quoted in NBC News, "'We can't go back': Israeli PM rejects 1967 border proposal," May 20, 2011, http://www.nbcnews.com /id/43106082/ns/politics-white_house/t/we-cant-go-back-israeli -pm-rejects-border-proposal/.

44. Doug Saunders, "On Israel, Harper stands alone at G8 summit," *Globe and Mail*, May 25, 2011, http://www.theglobeandmail.com /news/politics/on-israel-harper-stands-alone-at-g8-summit/article 4263322/.

45. *Jewish Tribune*, "Harper Blocks 1967 lines reference in G8 statement," May 30, 2011, http://www.jewishtribune.ca /uncategorized/2011/05/30/harper-blocks-1967-lines-reference -in-g8-statement.

46. Quoted in Laura Payton, "Canada closes embassy in Iran, expels Iranian diplomats," CBC News, September 7, 2012, http://www.cbc.ca/news/politics/story/2012/09/07/pol-baird -canada-iran-embassy.html.

47. Quoted in Bruce Campion-Smith, "Canada closes Iran embassy, expels remaining Iranian diplomats," *Toronto Star*, September 7, 2012, http://www.thestar.com/news/canada/2012/09/07/canada _closes_iran_embassy_expels_remaining_iranian_diplomats.html.

48. Laura Payton, "Canada closes embassy in Iran, expels Iranian diplomats," CBC News, September 7, 2012, http://www.cbc.ca /news/politics/story/2012/09/07/pol-baird-canada-iran-embassy .html.

49. Daniel Schwartz, "Why Canada severed relations with Iran," CBC News, September 8, 2012, http://www.cbc.ca/news/world /story/2012/09/08/f-iran-canada-diplomatic-relations.html.

50. Quoted in ibid.

51. United Nations General Assembly, "General Assembly votes overwhelmingly to accord Palestine 'non-Member Observer State' status in United Nations," press release, November 29, 2012, http://www.un.org/News/Press/docs/2012/ga11317.doc.htm.

52. Canada, Czech Republic, Israel, Marshall Islands, (Federated States of) Micronesia, Nauru, Palau, Panama, United States voted against. Ibid.

53. Joanna Slater and Campbell Clark, "With UN vote, Palestinians emerge triumphant," *Globe and Mail*, November 29, 2012, http://www.theglobeandmail.com/news/world/with-un-vote -palestinians-emerge-triumphant/article5831738/?page=all.

54. Quoted in Campbell Clark, "Baird accuses UN of abandoning principles by recognizing Palestine," *Globe and Mail*, November 30, 2012, http://m.theglobeandmail.com/news/politics/baird -accuses-un-of-abandoning-principles-by-recognizing-palestine /article5811986/?service=mobile.

55. Quoted in Patrick Martin, "Baird's east Jerusalem coffee date causes diplomatic flap,"*Globe and Mail*, April 11, 2013, http:// www.theglobeandmail.com/news/politics/bairds-east-jerusalem -coffee-date-causes-diplomatic-flap/article11107856/.

56. "Canada's Foreign Affairs Minister, John Baird, is pleased to announce that Canada proudly boycotted action on a United Nations General Assembly resolution which sets out the details for a high-level meeting to commemorate the 10 year anniversary of the 2001 hateful and anti-Semitic Durban Conference." Canada Proudly Boycotts Resolution on Durban Commemorative Meeting, June 13, 2011, website of Department of Foreign Affairs, Trade and Development Canada, http://www.international.gc.ca/media /aff/news-communiques/2011/161.aspx.

57. "Growing discontent among Arab nations over the Harper government's pro-Israel stand is prompting joint talks on retalia-tion." Campbell Clark, "Disgruntled Arab states look to strip Canada of UN agency," *Globe and Mail*, May 2, 2013, http:// www.theglobeandmail.com/news/world/disgruntled-arab-states -look-to-strip-canada-of-un-agency/article11672346/.

58. Those explanations range from the deep personal commitment, rooted in admiration of the accomplishments of Israel and the "horrors of the Nazi era" expressed by John Baird (John Baird, "Why Israel holds such a special place in my heart," *National Post*, November 20, 2012, http://fullcomment.nationalpost. com/2012/11/20/john-baird-why-israel-holds-such-a-special -place-in-my-heart), through the strong support for Israel of some Evangelical Christians (Marci McDonald, *The Armageddon Factor: The Rise of Christian Nationalism in Canada*, Random House Canada, 2011), through a domestic political strategy described by Stephen Harper as "unit[ing] social conservatives of different denominations and even different faiths," which "won the respect—and support—of a large segment of Canada's Jewish

community." (Michelle Collins, "How the Jewish vote swung from red to blue," *Embassy*, February 11, 2009, quoted in Donald Barry "Canada and the Middle East Today: Electoral Politics and Foreign Policy," Probe International, http://probeinternational.org/library /wp-content/uploads/2012/07/sPLUASQV001P01A001911.pdf.

59. Paul Wells, "Canada and Quebec unite on EU Free Trade Accord," *Maclean's*, July 30, 2007.

60. "In 2007, the Government of Canada (GoC) announced its intention to re-engage with Latin America and the Caribbean and to make the Region a top international priority." Office of the Inspector General, *Evaluation of the Americas Strategy* (Ottawa: DFAIT, January 2011), http://www.international.gc.ca/about-a _propos/oig-big/2011/evaluation/tas_lsa11.aspx?lang=eng&view=d.

61. "At the Asia-Pacific Economic Cooperation summit in Honolulu on Nov. 12, Obama announced the US and eight other countries— not including China—agreed to complete a Trans-Pacific Partner- ship trade accord within a year." Margaret Talev, "Obama's Asia pivot puts US approach to China on new path," Bloomberg, November 19, 2011, http://www.bloomberg.com/news/2011-11-18 /obama-s-asia-pivot-puts-u-s-approach-to-China-on-new-path.html.

62. J.L. Granatstein, "Ottawa needs a defence policy, Conservative or otherwise," *National Post*, December 7, 2012, http://fullcomment .nationalpost.com/2012/12/07/j-l-granatstein-ottawa-needs-a -defence-policy-conservative-or-otherwise/.

The Conference of Defence Associations made the same case more politely: "For too long there has been too little public discussion of the emerging international security environment and of Canada's defence and security needs in the years ahead." It published a report with sixteen recommendations "for the reform of defence thinking and defence planning": "Vimy Paper 2012: The Strategic Outlook for Canada," *Small Wars Journal*, February 21, 2012, http://smallwarsjournal.com/blog/the-strategic-outlook -for-canada.

Doug Saunders, "Sweden's big immigration idea: the 'Canada model,'" *Globe and Mail*, updated September 10, 2012, http://www.theglobeandmail.com/news/world/worldview/swedens -big-immigration-idea-the-canada-model/article618559/. The changes also have critics (Loretta Ho and Harbi Natt, "Q&A with Audrey Macklin: Emergent trends in Canadian immigration policy," Global Migration Research Institute, University of Toronto, December 12, 2012, http://munkschool.utoronto.ca /ethnicstudies/2012/12/qa-leading-immigration-expert-describes -emergent-trends-in-canadian-immigration-policy/); but the government has been activist and innovative ("Canada experiencing 'unprecedented' changes to immigration policy: experts," iPolitics, March 16, 2013, http://www.ipolitics.ca/2013/03/16/canada -experiencing-unprecedented-changes-to-immigration-policy-experts/.

65. "We are a country of the Americas . . . . Re-engagement in our hemisphere is a critical international priority for our Government. Canada is committed to playing a bigger role in the Americas and to doing so for the long term." Stephen Harper, quoted in Office of the Prime Minister, "Prime Minister Harper signals Canada's renewed engagement in the Americas," press release, July 17, 2007, http://www.pm.gc.ca/eng/media.asp?id=1760.

66. Bill Curry and Shawn McCarthy, "Canada formally abandons Kyoto Protocol on climate change," *Globe and Mail*, December 12, 2011, http://www.theglobeandmail.com/news/politics/Canada -formally-abandons-kyoto-protocol-on-climate-change/article 4180809.

67. Paul Heinbecker, "It's not just the drought treaty. Canada is vanishing from the United Nations," *Globe and Mail*, April 1, 2013, http://www.theglobeandmail.com/commentary/its-not-just -the-drought-treaty-Canada-is-vanishing-from-the-united-nations /article10600939/.

68. Barry Wilson, "Canada leaves UN drought treaty," *The Western Producer*, April 4, 2013, http://issuu.com/westernproducer/docs /20130404.

69. Stephen Harper, "Stephen Harper on International Co-operation" (remarks, House of Commons, Ottawa, March 28, 2013), http:// openparliament.ca/debates/2013/3/28/stephen-harper-4/only/.

70. Stephen Harper, award acceptance speech, Appeal of Conscience Foundation, New York, September 27, 2012, http://www.cbc.ca /m/touch/politics/story/2012/09/28/pol-stephen-harper-award -speech.html.

71. Canadians for Peacekeeping, "Canada and UN Peacekeeping," July 2012, http://peacekeepingcanada.com/wp-content/uploads /2010/03/PKO-Eng-2012.pdf.

72. Campbell Clark, "Canada rejects UN request to lead Congo mission," *Globe and Mail*, April 30, 2010, http://www.theglobe- andmail.com/news/politics/Canada-rejects-un-request-to-lead -congo-mission/article1386861/.

73. Simon Donner, "How Canada has changed since the 1992 Rio summit," Maribo, http://simondonner.blogspot.ca/2012/06/how -canada-has-changed-since-1992-rio.html (accessed June 30, 2013).

74. Rod Mickleburgh, "'Radical ideological agenda' easy to spot from downtown Toronto," *Globe and Mail*, January 12, 2012, http:// www.theglobeandmail.com/news/british-columbia/radical-ideological -agenda-easy-to-spot-from-downtown-toronto/article1358280/.

75. "[Conservative MP Brad] Trost said he and 'many' other MPs
helped spearhead efforts to round up petitions 'to defund Planned
Parenthood. 'Let me just tell you, and I cannot tell you specifically
how we used it, but those petitions were very, very useful and they
were part of what we used to defund Planned Parenthood because
it has been absolute disgrace that that organization and several
others like it have been receiving one penny of Canadian taxpayers
dollars,' Trost said." Tonda MacCharles, "Anti-abortion groups
shaped Tory funding policy on Planned Parenthood," *Toronto
Star*, April 21, 2011, http://www.thestar.com/news/canada
/2011/04/21/antiabortion_groups_shaped_tory_funding_policy
_on_planned_parenthood.html. In September 2011, Planned
Parenthood's funding was renewed, but only in countries where
abortion is largely illegal. Laura Payton, "Planned Parenthood's
Canadian funding renewed," CBC News, September 22, 2011,
http://www.cbc.ca/news/politics/story/2011/09/22/pol-planned
-parenthood-funding.html.

76. Gerald Caplan writes of a "reversal, by Stephen Harper, of a
60-year consensus shared by all previous governments about the
central role of civil society in Canada. Every previous government
has funded civil society groups and NGOs even when they espoused
policies that contradicted the government's own. . . . it has been
one of the quiet glories of Canadian democracy that our governments have often backed groups that criticized them or had competing priorities. No more. With Stephen Harper, you either buy the
party line or you get slapped down. That's what happened to
KAIROS . . . the Canadian Council For International Co-operation . . .
Match International. . . . [and] many, many dozens . . . of other
worthy organizations." "KAIROS case is a reminder of the real
Harper agenda," *Gerry Caplan's Blog*, rabble.ca, February 20,
2011, http://rabble.ca/blogs/bloggers/gerry-caplan/2011/02/kairos
-case-reminder-real-harper-agenda.

77. GlobeScan, http://www.globescan.com/commentary-and-analysis
/press-releases/press-releases-2012/84-press-releases-2012/186
-views-of-Europe-slide-sharply-in-global-poll-while-views-of-China
-improve.html.

78. Human development reports for the last twenty-four years
are available here: United Nations Development Programme,
"24 years of Human Development Reports," Human Development
Reports, http://hdr.undp.org/en/reports/ (accessed June 30, 2013).

79. "Even more alarming was the fact that the defeat itself had been
conferred by an impressively wide margin. Under UN rules, the
minimum requirement for election is 2/3 of those present and
voting—in this case, 127 votes. Germany won a seat on the first

round with 128 votes. That was expected. The Germans were universally regarded as a shoo-in. In the second round, however, out of 191 votes cast, Portugal received 113 (just 14 votes short of the 127-vote minimum), while Canada attracted only 78—a mere 40 percent of the total and 49 votes short of the minimum. It was so obvious at that stage that Canada had no hope of overtaking its rival that its delegation then withdrew from the race and conceded the victory to the Portuguese. The withdrawal was far from selfless. It simply made an embarrassing third round of voting unnecessary." Denis Stairs, "Being Rejected in the United Nations: The Causes and Implications of Canada's Failure to Win a Seat in the UN Security Council" (Calgary: CDFAI, March 2011), http://www.cdfai.org/PDF/Being%20Rejected%20in%20the %20United%20Nations.pdf.

80. Security Council Report, "SC Election GAOR Plenary Part II," January 12, 1946, http://www.securitycouncilreport.org/atf /cf/%7B65BFCF9B-6D27-4E9C-8CD3-CF6E4FF96FF9%7D /SC%20Election%20GAOR%20Plenary%20Part%20II.pdf.

81. Denis Stairs, "Being Rejected in the United Nations: The Causes and Implications of Canada's Failure to Win a Seat in the UN Security Council" (Calgary: CDFAI, March 2011), http:// www.cdfai.org/PDF/Being%20Rejected%20in%20the%20United %20Nations.pdf.

82. Ibid.

83. "All industrialized nations, with the exception of the United States and Canada, laid the ground for a treaty by offering ambitious national emissions reductions and providing considerable amounts of money for climate policy in developing countries." Radoslav S. Dimitrov, "Inside UN Climate Change Negotiations: The Copenhagen Conference," *Review of Policy Research* 27, no. 6 (November 2010): 795–821, http://politicalscience.uwo.ca/faculty/dimitrov/climate %20negotiations%20RPR.pdf.

CHAPTER 7: PUBLIC INTEREST COUNTRY/PRIVATE INTEREST GOVERNMENT

1. Quoted in Fannie Oliver, "Harper hopes next Francophonie summit is held in country with 'democratic standards,'" *Globe and Mail*, October 14, 2012, http://www.theglobeandmail.com /news/politics/Harper-hopes-next-francophonie-summit-is-held -in-country-with-democratic-standards/article4611677/.

2. For example, women did not have the vote in Canada until 1918, and First Nations peoples did not have the vote until 1960.

3. *Encyclopedia of Human Rights*, s.v. "Helsinki Accord and CSCE/OSCE."

4. Ibid.

5. Ibid.

6. "We are deeply concerned about the plight of African peoples who are suffering from famine and drought. . . . We shall continue to supply emergency food aid. In addition, we shall intensify our cooperation with African countries to help them develop their economic potential and a longterm food strategy, based on their own agricultural programs. We are prepared to promote increases in food production by supplying agricultural inputs such as seed, pesticides and fertilizers, within the framework of agricultural development projects. . . . Political obstacles in the countries concerned should not be allowed to stand in the way of the delivery of food to the hungry." G7, "The Bonn Economic Declaration: Towards Sustained Growth and Higher Employment," (declaration, G7 Summit, Bonn, Germany, May 4, 1985), http://www.g8.utoronto.ca/summit/1985bonn/communique.html.

7. Canadian diplomat William H. Barton founded The Barton Group, "a major clearing house for views on disarmament matters among Western countries." Chris Cline, "Carleton presents Leadership in Philanthropy Award to William H. Barton," press release, Carleton University, April 8, 2013, http://newsroom.carleton.ca/2013/04/09 /carleton-presents-leadership-in-philanthropy-award-to-supporter -william-h-barton/.

8. Maurice Strong, a Canadian, was secretary general of the United Nations Conference on the Human Environment during the 1970s.

9. Canadian Louise Arbour was a United Nations High Commissioner of Human Rights from 2004 to 2008.

10. Translation Bureau, Public Works and Services Canada, http://www.btb.termiumplus.gc.ca/tpv2alpha/alpha-eng.html ?lang=eng&i=1&index=ent&srchtxt=megaphone%20diplomacy (for definition of megaphone diplomacy; accessed June 30, 2013).

11. Kim Richard Nossal and Leah Sarson, "About Face: Explaining Changes in Canada's China Policy 2006–2012," (paper presented to the Annual Meeting of the Canadian Political Science Association, University of Victoria, June 6, 2013), http://www.cpsa-acsp .ca/papers-2013/Nossal.pdf.

12. As major examples: the Kelowna Accord and the practice of working co-operatively with indigenous people; the Kyoto Accord and Canada's general leadership on domestic and international environmental standards; the National Roundtable on the Environment and the Economy; the Canadian Wheat Board; the long-gun registry; arm's length organizations like the International Centre on Human Rights and Democratic Development, and the general practice of co-operation with civil society; CIDA's emphasis on Africa and fighting poverty.

13. The case of KAIROS is a telling example of how the Harper
    government deals with NGOs whose practices do not match its
    priorities and how it prevaricates about foreign policy priorities it
    knows will not be popular: "Disregard for the rule of law and
    democratic process has also characterized the government's
    handling of its now infamous decision to cut funding to KAIROS in
    late 2009. The organization, which represents 11 Canadian church
    groups engaging in human rights, poverty reduction, and educa-
    tion advocacy across the developing world, had its overseas budget
    slashed after it publicly criticized Israeli Defence Forces' bombing
    of a Gaza City health clinic. . . . Immigration Minister Jason
    Kenney first told an Israeli audience that the cut was in response to
    KAIROS' views on Israel, while the government insisted the funding
    cut was not related to the organization's views. In April and
    October 2010, Bev Oda, the minister overseeing CIDA, told
    Parliament that her department had made the decision to cut
    KAIROS' funding because the group's work no longer fit with CIDA's
    objectives. Then a document surfaced in which it appeared CIDA
    had approved continued KAIROS funding, only to have the recom-
    mendation reversed by the insertion of a handwritten "not." Oda
    thereupon stated that the document had been altered at her own
    direction." Maria Gergin, "Silencing Dissent: The Conservative
    Record," Canadian Centre for Policy Alternatives, April 6, 2011,
    http://www.policyalternatives.ca/publications/commentary
    /silencing-dissent-conservative-record (accessed June 30, 2013).

14. The list of Crown corporations and other instruments of direct
    government action is long, diverse and traverses both the country
    and all political parties that have held office, including the
    Progressive Conservative and Social Credit parties, which the
    present government claims as its roots. As one example, the
    Alberta government of Peter Lougheed created the Alberta Energy
    Company Limited, "in which it initially held a 50 percent interest,"
    "as an investment vehicle for ordinary citizens in the development
    and utilization of public resources owned by those citizens."

15. From 1998 to 2002, Mr. Harper was president of the National
    Citizens Coalition, whose website describes it as Canada's largest
    non-partisan organization for the defence and promotion of free
    enterprise, free speech and government that is accountable to its
    taxpayers," http://nationalcitizens.ca/; Mr. Kenney was president and
    CEO of the Canadian Taxpayers Federation, whose website describes
    it as a citizens advocacy group dedicated to "lower taxes, less waste
    and accountable government," http://www.taxpayer.com/about/.

16. Mr. Harper had resigned from Parliament then, and was speaking
    in his capacity as vice-president of the National Citizens Coalition.

CBC "Harper defends remarks to U.S. conservative movement," last updated Thursday, January 12, 2006, http://www.CBC.ca/story /Canadavotes2006/national/2006/01/12/Harper-quotes060112.html.

17. "I see myself as a citizen of the world," World Values Survey Data Bank, "World Values Survey (2005–2008)," http://www.world valuessurvey.org/.

18. Ibid. When the question was "Do you strongly agree?" the responses were US, 20.60 percent; Canada, 29.40 percent; Japan 14.60 percent; Australia, 21.90 percent; Sweden, 18.40 percent; Switzerland, 31.80 percent.

19. The Centre for Law and Democracy now ranks Canada at 55th out of 93 nations on granting journalists access to government documents. Arnold Amber, "Plague of government secrecy throttles Canadians' freedom," *Toronto Star*, May 3, 2013, http://www.thestar.com/opinion/commentary/2013/05/03/plague _of_government_secrecy_throttles_canadians_freedom.html.

20. Department of Foreign Affairs, Trade and Development, "Canada's Economic Action Plan," http://actionplan.gc.ca/en/initiative /department-foreign-affairs-trade-and-development (accessed June 30, 2013).

21. For example, Bill C-45 was 445 pages long and contained changes to 64 pieces of legislation. Laura Payton, "Budget bill's pension changes to save $2.6B over 5 years," CBC News, October 18, 2012, http://www.cbc.ca/news/politics/story/2012/10/18/pol -omnibus-budget-implementation-bill-part-two.html.

22. Mitchell William Sharp, *Foreign Policy for Canadians* (Ottawa: Queen's Printer, 1970).

23. The Mulroney government published a white paper on defence and a green paper on foreign policy. Henry Perrin Beatty, *Challenge and Commitment: A Defence Policy for Canada* (Ottawa: Dept. of National Defence, 1987); Joe Clark, *Competitiveness and Security: Directions for Canada's International Relations: Green Paper* (Ottawa: Secretary of State for External Affairs, 1985).

24. André Ouellet, *Canada in the World: Government Statement* (Ottawa: Government of Canada, 1995).

25. Pierre Stewart Pettigrew et al., *A Role of Pride and Influence in the World* (Ottawa: DFAIT, 2005).

CHAPTER 8: WHY WE HAVE A FOREIGN POLICY

1. A study by the Conference Board of Canada found that the richest 10 percent of the world's population receives 42 percent of total world income, while the poorest 10 percent of the population receive 1 percent of total world income. "Even though the US

currently has the largest rich-poor income gap among these
countries, the gap in Canada has been rising at a faster rate,"
said Anne Golden, president of the Conference Board of Canada,
quoted in Tavia Grant, "Income inequality rising quickly in
Canada," *Globe and Mail*, September 13, 2011, http://www.the
globeandmail.com/report-on-business/economy/economy-lab/daily
-mix/income-inequality-rising-quickly-in-canada/article2163938/.

2.   The challenge of accounting for Second World War civilian and
military casualties, and the range of estimates of the total number
of casualties are explained in *Encyclopaedia Britannica Online*,
s.v. "World War II," http://www.britannica.com/EBchecked/topic
/648813/World-War-II (accessed June 30, 2013).

3.   "France, the country which can claim to have invented the idea of
cultural diplomacy, still puts about one third of its foreign affairs
budget into cultural and academic relations (at one point recently,
that one third was the equivalent in spending power of the total
Canadian Foreign Affairs budget)." Robin Higham, "The World
Needs More Canada. Canada Needs More Canada," in *The
Handing Down of Culture, Smaller Societies and Globalization*,
ed. Jean Paul Baillargeon (Toronto: grubstreet editions, 2002).

4.   Ibero-American General Secretariat, pamphlet, Madrid, http://
segib.org/documentos/esp/ingles_web_hojas.pdf.

5.   "Confucius Institutes are now operating with more than 350
educational institutions in 106 countries. The Confucius Class-
room program designed for foreign primary and secondary school
students is developing at an even faster pace, with more than
500 such classrooms already set up worldwide." Wen Xian, Zhang
Yang and Zhengqi, "New visa policy sets barriers for Confucius
Institutes in US (3)," *People's Daily*, May 25, 2012, http://english
.peopledaily.com.cn/203691/7827580.html.

6.   In Canada alone there are 13 Confucius Institutes, all overseen by
China's national government. "The services at the institute are for
students, businesses, and community organizations who want to
learn more about China and want to do business there. . . . The
Asia–Pacific region is the major growth region for the next 20 to
30 years, which makes the opening of our Confucius Institute
timely." Colin Dodds, president of Saint Mary's University, quoted
in Carol Moreira, "Year of the Dragon," *Progress Magazine*,
July 23, 2012, http://www.progressmedia.ca/article/2012/04/year
-dragon.

7.   The Arab Spring is a series of revolutionary protests and uprisings
beginning on December 17, 2010, with the self-immolation of
Mohamed Bouazizi in Tunisia and spreading to Algeria, Lebanon,
Oman, Mauritania, Yemen, Jordan, Saudi Arabia, Egypt, Syria,

Morocco, Sudan, Palestine, Iraq, Bahrain, Libya, Kuwait and the Western Sahara. As of June 30, 2013, governments have been overthrown in Tunisia, Libya, Egypt and Yemen.

8. The Revolutions of Eastern Europe (also called the Fall of Communism) began in Poland in 1989 and spread rapidly to other Eastern European nations. All former soviet countries had moved to an electoral system of some form by the end of 1991. Romania was the only country to overthrow its communist regime violently.

9. In December, 2005, Evo Morales became the first indigenous leader to be elected president of Bolivia. In 2009, a new constitution reflecting indigenous rights and equality was endorsed in a referendum. "'Brothers and sisters, the colonial state ends here,' President Morales, an Aymara Indian, told crowds in front of the presidential palace in La Paz after results emerged." BBC News, "Bolivians 'back new constitution,'" January 26, 2009, http://news.bbc.co.uk/2/hi/americas/7849666.stm.

10. Bloomberg, "Wen warns on China tensions in final speech as premier: Economy," May 5, 2013, http://www.bloomberg.com /news/2013-03-05/china-sets-7-5-goal-for-2013-growth-with -3-5-inflation-target.html.

11. "The least ethnically fractionalized countries are South Korea, Japan and North Korea. Turning to linguistic fractionalization. . . . The least diverse countries are South Korea and North Korea, followed by Yemen." Alberto Alesina et al., "Fractionalization," *Journal of Economic Growth* 8 (2003): 155–94.

12. The Commonwealth includes more than fifty independent sovereign states, representing roughly one-third of the world's population.

13. The members of the committee were the foreign ministers of Australia, Canada, Guyana, India, Nigeria, Tanzania, Zambia and Zimbabwe (later joined by Malaysia).

14. Bryan McDonald, "The Global Landmine Crisis in the 1990s," in *Landmines and Human Security: International Politics and War's Hidden Legacy*, ed. Richard A. Matthew, Bryan McDonald and Kenneth R. Rutherford (Albany: State University of New York Press, 2004): 24–26.

15. Ibid.: 22.

16. Ibid.

17. Andrew Robinson, "Canada's Credibility as an Actor in the Middle East Peace Process: The Refugee Working Group 1992-2000," *International Journal: Canada's Journal of Global Policy Analysis*, Summer 2011, p. 699 http://ijx.sagepub.com/content/66/3.toc.

18. Ibid.

19. Rex Brynen and Jill Tansley, "The Refugee Working Group of the Middle East Multilateral Peace Negotiations," *Israel-Palestine*

Journal 2, no.4 (Autumn 1995), http://prrn.mcgill.ca/prrn/papers/brytan.html.

20. Andrew Robinson, "Canada's Credibility as an Actor in the Middle East Peace Process: The Refugee Working Group, 1992–2000," *International Journal* 66, no. 3 (Summer 2011): 703.

21. Rex Brynen, "Canada's Role in the Israeli-Palestinian Peace Process," in *Canada and the Middle East: In Theory and Practice*, ed. Paul Heinbecker and Bessma Momani (Waterloo: Wilfred Laurier University Press, 2007): 79.

22. Foreign Affairs, Trade and Development Canada, "Middle East Peace Process: Introduction to the Refugee Working Group," http://www.international.gc.ca/name-anmo/peace_process-processus_paix/refugees-refugies/index.aspx?lang=eng (accessed June 30, 2013).

23. This private sponsorship provision had been entered into the Act at the request of the Jewish Immigration Aid Society in hopes of providing more assistance to Soviet Jews wishing to enter Canada. While initially seen by some as a way for the government to offload the responsibility to pay for refugee claimants, the humanitarian crisis unfolding with the Indochinese people greatly changed the significance of the clause. See Howard Adelman, *Canada and the Indochinese Refugees* (Regina: L.A. Weigl Educational Associates, 1982): 85.

24. Employment and Immigration Canada, *Indochinese Refugees: The Canadian Response, 1979–1980* (Ottawa: Ministry of Supply and Services, 1982): 15.

25. Ibid: 8.

26. "Government's Response to the Report by the Standing Committee on External Affairs and National Defence Concerning the Honourable David MacDonald's Report on the African Famine and Canada's Response," Library and Archives Canada, Joe Clark fonds, MG26 R 5-1, vol. 10, file 6.

27. David MacDonald, *No More Famine: A Decade for Africa* (Hull: Canadian Emergency Coordinator / African Famine, 1986): 23.

28. According to the IMF, Brazil's GDP per capita rose from $5,000 in 1990 to $11,000 in 2013; India went from $900 GDP per capita in 1990, to $4,000 GDP per capita in 2013. International Monetary Fund, http://www.imf.org/external/pubs/ft/weo/2012/01/weodata/index.aspx (for India and Brazil GDP per capita; accessed June 30, 2013).

CHAPTER 9: CANADA AND THE UNITED STATES

1. The Order-in-Council, approved by Governor General Edward Schreyer, read as follows: "His Excellency the Governor in Council, on the recommendation of the Secretary of State for

External Affairs, is pleased hereby to authorize the Secretary of State for External Affairs to derogate from the provisions of Article Six of the Canadian Passport Regulations (Order-in-Council CP 1973-17, January 9, 1973) and to issue passports strictly to those US diplomatic representatives and their wives who are under the protection of the Canadian Embassy in Tehran."

2. An explanation of the events in Tehran can be found in Robert Wright, *Our Man in Tehran* (Toronto: HarperCollins Canada, 2010).

3. The full text of the Declaration of Independence may be found in the US government archives online: http://www.archives.gov /exhibits/charters/declaration_transcript.html.

4. "In about a Quarter of an Hour the Enemy gave way on all Sides, when a terrible Slaughter ensued from the quick Fire of our Field Pieces and Musquetry." Serjeant-Major of Gen. Hopson's Grenadiers, *A Journal of the Expedition up the River St. Lawrence* (Boston, November 1759), http://www.militaryheritage.com /quebec1.htm.

5. Quoted in Winston Churchill, *The Unrelenting Struggle* (Boston: Little, Brown, 1942): 363.

6. John Diefenbaker argued that "the diplomatic ostracizing of Cuba by the Western powers could serve only to eliminate her options and drive her into the Soviet orbit." John G. Diefenbaker, *One Canada: The Memoirs of the Right Honorable John G. Diefenbaker; The Years of Achievement, 1957–1962*, vol. 2 (Toronto: Macmillian, 1976): 174.

7. "Between 1964 and 1969 total motor production in Canada rose by 85 percent and labour productivity in the assembly sector rose by over 60 percent." Maureen Irish, *The Auto Pact: Investment, Labour and the* WTO (New York: Kluwer Law International, 2004).

8. *Dictionary of Canadian Biography*, s.v. "Pearson, Lester Bowles," http://www.biographi.ca/en/bio.php?id_nbr=7988 (accessed June 30, 2013).

9. The United States did not recognize the People's Republic of China until 1979. Charles Burton, "The Canadian Policy Context of Canada's China Policy since 1970," in *The China Challenge: Sino-Canadian Relations in the 21st Century*, ed. Vivienne Poy and Huhua Cao (Ottawa: University of Ottawa Press, 2011).

10. Environment Canada, "Canada–United States Air Quality Agreement," http://www.ec.gc.ca/air/default.asp?lang=En&n= 83930AC3-1 (accessed June 30, 2013).

11. CBC Digital Archives, "1985: Canada opts out of 'Star Wars,'" http://www.cbc.ca/archives/categories/politics/international -politics/general-23/canada-opts-out-of-star-wars.html (accessed June 30, 2013).

12. "During his tenure in external affairs, Green was an advocate of nuclear disarmament and sponsored UN resolutions that furthered that goal." *Canadian Encyclopedia Online*, s.v. "Howard Charles Green," http://www.thecanadianencyclopedia.com/articles /howard-charles-green (accessed June 30, 2013).

13. For further information about Canada's role in the region see Brian J. R. Stevenson, *Canada, Latin America, and the New Internationalism* (Montreal: McGill-Queen's Press, 2000).

14. I met with ambassadors from the Contadora group in November 1984 and again in January 1985 during my visit to Mexico. It was during these meetings that Canada was asked to lend assistance to the Contadora process. "Points which could be used in an interview by Mr. Gerry Weiner to the Round Table on Negotiations for Peace in Central America," September, 28, 1985, DFAIT Archives, RG25 (14492), vol. 24, file 20-AMRICA-CEN.

15. "Canada and Central America: fireworks and foreign policy," private note to the author from John Graham, who had been Director General of Latin America and the Caribbean from 1983-1988, January 25, 2008.

16. Jonathan Lemco, "Canada and the Peacekeeping Process in Central America," *Canada and the Crisis in Central America* (New York: Praeger, 1991), 125.

17. I summarized Canada's policy toward the Central American peace process in "Statement by the Right Honourable Joe Clark, Secretary of State for External Affairs, to the 42nd Session of the General Assembly of the United Nations," September 22, 1987, Library and Archives Canada , Joe Clark fonds, MG26 R 5-4, vol. 11, file 34.

18. For example, the relationship between Turkey and the United States is becoming increasingly essential. Bariskan Unal, Mehmet Toroglu and Hasan Oymez, "Washington getting ready to host Turkish PM Erdogan," *Turkish Press*, May 14, 2013, http://www.turkishpress.com/news.asp?id=385028.

19. Jorge Heine is quoted in Campbell Clark, "Solid Americas strategy would reap big rewards for Canada," *Globe and Mail*, May 24, 2011, http://www.theglobeandmail.com/news/national/time-to -lead/solid-americas-strategy-would-reap-big-rewards-for-canada /article598260/.

20. Because American broadcasters are private, and often local, there is little access to the comprehensive and objective reporting that is standard fare on many public broadcasters, such as the BBC, TV5Monde or CBC.

CHAPTER 10: THE POWER OF PREVIOUS THINKING

1. International Joint Commission, "Role of the IJC," http://www.ijc
    .org/en/backgroundX/ijc_cmi_nature.htm (accessed June 30, 2013).

2. United Nations, "The United Nations Convention on the Law of
    the Sea (A historical perspective)," http://www.un.org/Depts/los
    /convention_agreements/convention_historical_perspective.
    htm#Third%20Conference (accessed June 30, 2013).

3. Government of Canada, Canada Treaty Information, http://
    www.treaty-accord.gc.ca/search-recherche.aspx?type=10&page=
    TLA (for total number of treaties; accessed June 30, 2013).

4. One of the first issues on my desk as foreign minister in 1984
    was a request by Mexico for Canadian advice on how they might
    prepare to join GATT.

5. "A quantitative inventory of five African states (Ethiopia, Ghana,
    Madagascar, Mali and Sudan) compiled by the International
    Institute for Environment and Development (IIED), the Food and
    Agricultural Organization (FAO), and the International Fund for
    Agriculture and Development (IFAD), documented a total of
    2,492,684 hectares of approved land acquisitions from 2004 to
    early 2009. That is almost half the arable land of the United
    Kingdom and three times the arable land of Norway." Howard
    Mann, "Foreign land purchases for agriculture: what impact on
    sustainable development?" *Sustainable Development Innovation
    Briefs* 8 (January 2008), http://www.un.org/esa/dsd/resources/res
    _pdfs/publications/ib/no8.pdf.

6. "Despite [its] elaborate corporate governance network, Enron was
    able to attract large sums of capital to fund a questionable business
    model, conceal its true performance through a series of account
    and financial maneuvers, and hype its stock to unsustainable
    levels. . . . The problems of governance and incentives that
    emerged at Enron can also surface at many other firms and may
    potentially affect the entire capital market." Paul M. Healy and
    Krishna G. Palepu, "The Fall of Enron," *Journal of Economic
    Perspectives* 17, no. 2 (Spring 2003): 3–26.

7. The London Interbank Offered Rate (Libor) "determines the prices
    that people and corporations around the world pay for loans or
    receive for their savings. It is used as a benchmark to set payments
    on about $800 trillion-worth of financial instruments, ranging
    from complex interest-rate derivatives to simple mortgages." In
    2012, it was revealed that traders at Barclay's and other UK and
    international banks worked with rate-setters to fix advantageous
    rates to increase profits and mitigate losses. *Economist*, "The
    rotten heart of finance," July 7, 2012, http://www.economist
    .com/node/21558281.

8. "Poverty reduction accelerated in the early 2000s at a rate that has been sustained throughout the decade, even during the dark recesses of the financial crisis. Today we estimate that there are approximately 820 million people living on less than $1.25 a day. This means that the prime target of the millennium development goals—to halve the rate of global poverty by 2015 from its 1990 level—was probably achieved around three years ago. Whereas it took 25 years to reduce poverty by half a billion people up to 2005, that same feat was likely achieved in the six years between then and now." Laurence Chandy and Geoffrey Gertz, "With little notice, globalization reduced poverty," YaleGlobal Online, July 5, 2011, http://yaleglobal.yale.edu/content/little-notice-globalization-reduced-poverty.

9. Supachai Panitchpakdi, *The Least Developed Countries Report, 2009: The State and Development Governance; Overview* (Geneva: UNCTAD, 2009), http://unctad.org/en/docs/ldc2009overview_en.pdf.

10. In 2011 China's accumulated investment in Africa reached more than $40 billion. Xan Rice, "Chinese investment: The money is welcome but more controls are needed," *Financial Times*, June 19, 2012, http://www.ft.com/cms/s/0/d8f41dd6-b4a6-11e1-bb2e-00144feabdc0.html#ixzz26nalhgw2. Since 2005, China has spent an estimated $75 billion on financial investments in South America. This is "more [investment] than the World Bank, US Export Bank and the Inter-American Development Bank combined." In the past five years, bilateral trade between China and South America jumped more than 160 percent, rising from $68 billion in 2006 to $178 billion in 2010. Chris Arsenault, "The dragon goes shopping in South America," Al Jazeera, December 21, 2011, http://www.aljazeera.com/indepth/features/2011/12/2011121216211335042 5.html.

11. Martyn Davies, *How China Is Influencing Africa's Development* (Paris: OECD, April 2010), http://www.oecd.org/dev/perspectiveson globaldevelopment/45068325.pdf.

12. Ibid.

13. Jack Perkowski, "Get ready for more China overseas investment," *Forbes*, October 3, 2012, http://www.forbes.com/sites/jackperkowski/2012/10/03/get-ready-for-more-china-overseas-investment/.

14. Ibid.

15. "Soon after his ascent to power, Deng introduced 'Socialism with Chinese characteristics,' which combined central planning with a market economy." Mallory Factor, "How Deng Xiaoping, architect of China's rise, defined the decade," *New York Daily News*, December 30, 2010, http://www.nydailynews.com/opinion/deng-xiaoping-architect-china-rise-defined-decade-article-1.475194.

16. *Economist*, "The visible hand," January 21, 2012, http://www.economist.com/node/21542931.

17. Fernando Menéndez, "The Counterbalance in America's Backyard," *Foreign Policy*, May 28, 2013, http://www.chinausfocus.com/foreign-policy/the-counterbalance-in-americas-backyard-2/.

18. Telephónica, "Latin American millennials welcome future with optimism and confidence, Telephónica survey reveals," June 6, 2013, http://survey.telefonica.com/pt-br/latin-american-millennials-welcome-future-with-optimism-and-confidence-telefonica-survey-reveals/#sthash.QF2CxJIu.dpuf.

19. Ibid.

20. "At the September 2012 UN General Assembly . . . presidents Juan Manuel Santos of Colombia, Otto Pérez Molina of Guatemala and Felipe Calderon of Mexico urged the world organization to recognize the glaring shortcomings of prevailing approaches to drug control and initiate a far-reaching review of options." Peter Hakim and Kimberly Covington, Politica Externa, June 21, 2013, http://www.thedialogue.org/page.cfm?pageID=32&pubID=3337.

21. Godfrey Mwakikagile, *Nyerere and Africa: End of an Era* (New Africa Press, 2006): 15.

22. Franklyn Lisk, "The African Union after 10 years: Successes and Challenges," University of Warwick, http://www2.warwick.ac.uk/newsandevents/expertcomment/the_african_union/ (accessed June 30, 2013).

23. Alex de Waal, "Contesting Visions of Peace in Africa: Darfur, Ivory Coast, Libya" (lecture, University of Limerick, Limerick, Ireland, May 2012), http://sites.tufts.edu/reinventingpeace/2012/05/11/contesting-visions-of-peace-in-africa-darfur-ivory-coast-libya/.

24. The East African Community (EAC), Southern African Development Community (SADC), Common Market for Eastern and Southern Africa (COMESA), and Economic Community of West African States (ECOWAS).

25. "At the track one or inter-governmental level, the process of Asia-Pacific Economic Cooperation (APEC) began in Canberra in 1989. . . . track two or unofficial-level dialogues proliferated at a remarkable pace. . . . The first effort was the North Pacific Cooperative Security Dialogue (NPCSD), which ran from 1990 to 1992, with representatives from all eight North Pacific states, including North Korea." David Capie, "Rival Regions? East Asian Regionalism and its Challenge to the Asia-Pacific," 1994, http://www.alternative-regionalisms.org/wp-content/uploads/2009/07/capie_rivalregions.pdf (The North Pacific Co-operative Security Dialogue was a Canadian initiative, taken when I was

Secretary of State for External Affairs, at the instigation of
Professors David Dewitt and Paul Evans).

26. Jayant Menon, "How to multilateralise Asian regionalism,"
    East Asia Forum, January 6, 2013, http://www.eastasiaforum.
    org/2013/01/06/how-to-multilateralise-asian-regionalism/.

27. Ibid.

28. Rosemary Foot, "The Role of East Asian Regional Organizations
    in Regional Governance: Constraints and Contributions," article,
    Carnegie Endowment for International Peace, June 7, 2011,
    http://carnegieendowment.org/2011/06/07/role-of-east-asian
    -regional-organizations-in-regional-governance-constraints-and
    -contributions/1kqn.

29. Ibid.

30. "China and India . . . together will account for 38% of the
    global gross investment in 2030," World Bank press release,
    "India: By 2030 India and China will dominate global saving
    and investment, says new World Bank report," June 3, 2013,
    http://www.worldbank.org/en/news/press-release/2013/06/03
    /india-by-2030-india-and-china-will-dominate-global-saving
    -and-investment-says-new-world-bank-report.

31. Humanitarian Crisis Response, part of the Asian Regional
    Initiative, Center for Strategic and International Studies,
    http://csis.org/program/humanitarian-crisis-response.

32. *Economist*, "The lion kings?" January 6, 2011, http://www
    .economist.com/node/17853324.

33. Matthew Goodwin, *Right Response: Understanding and Counter-
    ing Populist Extremism in Europe* (London: Chatham House,
    2011), http://www.chathamhouse.org/sites/default/files/r0911
    _goodwin.pdf.

34. For example, "the number of hate groups counted by the Southern
    Poverty Law Center (SPLC) last year reached a total of 1,018, up
    slightly from the year before but continuing a trend of significant
    growth that is now more than a decade old." Mark Potok, "The
    'Patriot' Movement Explodes," *Intelligence Report*, Spring 2012,
    no. 145, http://www.splcenter.org/get-informed/intelligence-report
    /browse-all-issues/2012/spring/the-year-in-hate-and-extremism.

35. "Analysis carried out in this report indicates that international
    trade in counterfeit and pirated products could have been up to
    USD 200 billion in 2005. This total does not include domestically
    produced and consumed counterfeit and pirated products and the
    significant volume of pirated digital products being distributed via
    the Internet. If these items were added, the total magnitude of
    counterfeiting and piracy worldwide could well be several hundred
    billion dollars." Secretary General of the OECD, *The Economic*

Impact of Counterfeiting and Piracy: Executive Summary (Paris: OECD, 2007), http://www.oecd.org/industry/industryandglobalisation /38707619.pdf.

36. "Since 1992, a total of 270 UN civilian staff members and 2,468 uniformed personnel have been killed as a result of malicious acts, including murder, bombings, landmines, and hijacking. Of the 270 civilians killed, locally-recruited staff comprise the majority—215, or eighty percent. This is largely consistent with the overall proportion of national to international UN staff. In the past, this violence represented isolated incidents or was the result of being in the wrong place at the wrong time. But, as noted, it appears that this is more and more the result of deliberate targeting." Lakhdar Brahimi et al., *Towards a Culture of Security and Accountability: Report of the Independent Panel on Safety and Security of UN Personnel and Premises Worldwide* (New York: United Nations, June 2008): 14, http://www.un.org/News/dh/infocus/terrorism /PanelOnSafetyReport.pdf.

37. Robert R. Fowler, *A Season in Hell: My 130 Days in the Sahara with Al Qaeda* (Toronto: HarperCollins Canada, 2011): 314.

38. Voice of America, "Gorbachev's foreign policy changed map of Europe," February 21, 2011, http://www.voanews.com/content /gorbachevs-foreign-policy-changes-map-of-europe-117417398 /135993.html.

39. Quoted in ibid.

40. Robert Legvold, "The Revolution in Soviet Foreign Policy," *Foreign Affairs* 68, no. 1 (1988/1989): 82–98.

41. "The impact of technology and globalization was profound for my generation. . . . I could access the international without leaving the comfort of my own home." Jennifer Welsh, *At Home in the World* (Toronto: HarperCollins, 2004): 6.

42. The KOF Index of Globalization, which has been measuring cultural, political and economic globalization since 1970, has shown that the world has become increasingly more connected and globalized up until the financial crisis of 2008, which saw a levelling out due to economic pressures. Social globalization is estimated by personal contact (international telephone traffic, transfers, tourism, foreign population and international letters), information flows (Internet users, television ownership, trade in newspapers) and cultural proximity (number of McDonald's restaurants, number of Ikea shops and trade in books). KOF Index of Globalization Index, http://globalization.kof.ethz.ch/aggregation/ (for globalization data; accessed June 30, 2013).

43. China recently reasserted the need to fight against being colonized by Western culture. "We must clearly see that international hostile

forces are intensifying the strategic plot of westernizing and dividing china, and ideological and cultural fields are the focal areas of their long-term infiltration." President Hu Jintao, quoted in Edward Wong, "China's president lashes out at Western culture," *New York Times*, January 3, 2012, http://www.nytimes.com/2012/01/04/world/asia/chinas-president-pushes-back-against-western-culture.html.

44. *Economist*, "Busted trust," January 23, 2012, http://www.economist.com/blogs/newsbook/2012/01/faith-world-leaders.

45. Transparency International is a global movement whose vision is "a world in which government, politics, business, civil society and the daily lives of people are free of corruption." Founded in 1993 through the initiative of Peter Eigen, a former regional director for the World Bank who was offended by the systemic corruption he encountered, it is active in more than 100 countries today. Its work has led directly to international anti-corruption conventions, prosecution of corrupt leaders and seizure of their illicit wealth, and standards holding companies accountable for their behaviour at home and abroad, among other reforms. Together, the organization and its local affiliates work to raise awareness about corruption and bring about change. Since 2005, its chair has been Huguette Labelle of Canada. Transparency International Canada, "Overview," http://www.transparency.ca/1-Overview/Overview.htm (accessed June 30, 2013).

46. Publish What You Pay is a global network of civil society organisations which fights for systematic public disclosure of extractive industry revenues and contracts. Their network includes more than 650 human rights, development, environmental and faith-based organizations in more than 30 countries. Publish What You Pay, "Objectives," http://www.publishwhatyoupay.org/about/objectives (accessed June 30, 2013).

47. The Open Society Foundations work to build societies with governments that are accountable and open to public participation of all people. They seek to strengthen the rule of law; respect for human rights, minorities and a diversity of opinions; democratically elected governments; and active civil society that helps keep government power in check, with a high priority on marginalized communities. Open Society Foundations, "Mission & Values," http://www.soros.org/about/mission-values (accessed June 30, 2013).

48. The International Aid Transparency Initiative (IATI) is a voluntary, multi-stakeholder initiative established to help implement the transparency commitments made at the Accra Agenda for Action. International Aid Transparency Initiative, "About," http://www.aidtransparency.net/about (accessed June 30, 2013).

49. For example, "Countries facing the greatest challenges have made
    significant progress towards universal primary education. Enrolment
    rates of children of primary school age increased markedly in sub-
    Saharan Africa, from 58 to 76 per cent between 1999 and 2010."
    Ban Ki-moon et al., *The Millennium Development Goals Report,
    2012* (New York: United Nations, 2012), http://mdgs.un.org/unsd
    /mdg/resources/static/products/progress2012/english2012.pdf.

50. "mHealth, the use of mobile technologies to improve health out-
    comes, is a swiftly evolving field with innovative technological
    advances occurring daily. While it is a relatively new health strategy,
    83% of UN member states report offering at least one type of mHealth
    service." United Nations, "mHealth: Mobile Technologies to Improve
    Health," RIO+20 United Nations Conference on Sustainable
    Development, http://www.uncsd2012.org/index.php?page=view
    &type=700&nr=85&menu=23 (accessed June 30, 2013).

51. Cell phones have become a catalyst for innovative development
    programs across Africa. For example, they have improved the
    bureaucracies of governments, including Tanzania, where cell
    phones and digital pens are used to send crop data from small
    municipalities to the capital. In Kenya, mobile phones serve as a
    form of banking, otherwise unavailable to many residents, allowing
    users to send money via mobile money transfers to relatives across
    the country. This is not a silver bullet for development, but it has
    and will have dramatic political, social and economic influences
    across the continent. Jenny C. Aker and Isaac M. Mbit, "Mobile
    Phones and Economic Development in Africa," *Journal of Economic
    Perspectives* 24, no. 3 (Summer 2010): 207–232, http://sites.tufts
    .edu/jennyaker/files/2010/09/aker_mobileafrica.pdf.

52. Twenty-two of the worst affected countries in sub-Saharan Africa
    have reduced HIV incidence by more than 25 percent in the last
    eight years, according to UNAIDS. *Guardian*, "Millennium develop-
    ment goals: Tracking progress on HIV/Aids," September 22, 2010,
    http://www.guardian.co.uk/global-development/2010/sep/22
    /millennium-development-goals-hiv-aids; "When former president
    Jimmy Carter, in conjunction with the World Health Organisation
    and the US Centres for Disease Control and Prevention, spearheaded
    the effort to eradicate the [guinea worm disease] in 1986, there
    were 3.5m new cases of guinea worm disease a year across
    21 countries. So far this year there have been 391 new cases
    worldwide—down from 807 this time in 2011, according to
    the CDC." Alyssa A. Botelho, "Guinea worm disease poised to
    be eradicated within a few years," *Guardian*, September 4, 2010,
    http://www.guardian.co.uk/global-development/2012/sep/04
    /guinea-worm-disease-eradicated-soon.

CHAPTER 11: TWENTY-FIRST CENTURY ALLIANCES

1.   Paul Heinbecker, "The UN is the forum for peace and prosperity," *Ottawa Citizen*, December 3, 2012, http://www2.canada.com /ottawacitizen/news/archives/story.html?id=640d2569-ccbe-45ff -b674-727288759260&p=1.

2.   Raymond Torres, "High unemployment and growing inequality fuel social unrest around the world," interview, International Labour Organization, April 27, 2012, http://www.ilo.org/global /about-the-ilo/newsroom/news/WCMS_179430/lang--en/index.htm.

3.   Kaiser Family Foundation, Global Health Facts, http://kff.org /global-indicator/population-under-age-15/ (for youth population; accessed June 30, 2013); Population Reference Bureau, *2012 World Population Data Sheet* (Washington: PRB, 2013), http://www.prb.org/Publications/Datasheets/2012/world-population -data-sheet/data-sheet.aspx.

4.   Theo Sparreboom et al., *Global Employment Trends for Youth, 2012*, (Geneva: ILO Publications, 2012), http://www.ilo.org /wcmsp5/groups/public/---dgreports/---dcomm/documents /publication/wcms_180976.pdf.

5.   Ibid.

6.   UN—Water Decade Programme on Advocacy and Communication, "Water and urbanization," press release, http://www.un.org /waterforlifedecade/swm_cities_zaragoza_2010/pdf/03_water _and_urbanisation.pdf; WaterAid, "Turning slums around: The case for water and sanitation," discussion paper, October 2008, http://www.wateraid.org/~/media/Publications/water -sanitation-slums.pdf.

7.   Stewart M. Patrick, "The other culprit that's making natural disasters deadlier: Cities," *Atlantic*, August 15, 2012, http:// www.theatlantic.com/international/archive/2012/08/the-other -culprit-thats-making-natural-disasters-deadlier-cities/261172/#.

8.   Ibid.

9.   The precise definition by the OECD for ODA is: "Flows of official financing administered with the promotion of the economic development and welfare of developing countries as the main objective, and which are concessional in character with a grant element of at least 25 percent (using a fixed 10 percent rate of discount). By convention, ODA flows comprise contributions of donor government agencies, at all levels, to developing countries ("bilateral ODA") and to multilateral institutions. ODA receipts comprise disbursements by bilateral donors and multilateral institutions. Lending by export credit agencies—with the pure purpose of export promotion—is excluded." OECD, "Glossary of Statistical Terms," http://stats.OECD.org/glossary/detail.asp ?ID=6043 (accessed June 30, 2013).

10.   Olav Kjørven et al., *The Global Partnership for Development: Making Rhetoric a Reality; MDG Gap Task Force Report, 2012* (New York: United Nations, 2012): 8, http://www.un.org/en /development/desa/policy/mdg_gap/mdg_gap2012/mdg8report 2012_engw.pdf.

11.   Ibid.: 11.

12.   Homi Kharas, *Coming Together: How a New Global Partnership on Development Cooperation was Forged at the Busan High Level Forum on Aid Effectiveness (ARI)* (Madrid: Real Instituto Elcano, December 2011), http://www.realinstitutoelcano.org/wps/portal /rielcano_eng/Content?WCM_GLOBAL_CONTEXT=/elcano /Elcano_in/Zonas_in/ARI%20164-2011.

13.   "While international migrants accounted for small proportions of the population of many countries in both 1990 and 2005, the number of countries where the share of migrants exceeded 10 per cent increased from 73 in 1990 to 79 in 2005 (figure 1). Only 30 of these countries had populations of at least one million in 1990 but, by 2005, their number increased to 35. In 2005, countries with at least 20 million inhabitants where international migrants constituted high shares of the population included Australia (20 per cent), Canada (19 per cent), France (11 per cent), Germany (12 per cent), Saudi Arabia (26 per cent), Spain (11 per cent), Ukraine (15 per cent) and the United States (13 per cent). In 2005, countries with at least 20 million inhabitants where international migrants constituted high shares of the population included Australia (20 per cent), Canada (19 per cent), France (11 per cent), Germany (12 per cent), Saudi Arabia (26 per cent), Spain (11 per cent), Ukraine (15 per cent) and the United States (13 per cent)." United Nations, Department of Economic and Social Affairs, Population Division, *International Migration Report, 2006: A Global Assessment* (New York: United Nations, 2009), http://www.un.org/esa/population/publications/2006 _MigrationRep/fullreport.pdf.

14.   "There are an estimated14 million refugees living outside their country of citizenship, representing about 7 percent of the world's migrants." Jeni Klugman et al., *Human Development Report, 2009: Overcoming barriers; Human mobility and development* (New York: Palgrave Macmillan, 2009), http://hdr.undp.org/en /media/HDR_2009_EN_Complete.pdf.

15.   One organization that understands the value of managing diversity is the Forum of Federations: "The Forum of Federations runs training and knowledge sharing programs to address governance challenges in existing and emerging federations, as well as in devolved and decentralized countries." Forum of Federations,

"What We Do," http://www.forumfed.org/en/what/index.php (accessed June 30, 2013).

16. "Created in 1988 as a non-profit, charitable organization, the Canadian Institute for Conflict Resolution (CICR) provides training and intervention programs in Canada and internationally in Austria, Rwanda, Bosnia and Herzegovina, Sudan, Taiwan and other countries." Canadian Institute for Conflict Resolution, "About," http://www.cicr-icrc.ca/en/about (accessed June 30, 2013).

17. As of December 5, 2012, 160 countries had ratified the treaty, according to Human Rights Watch. Human Rights Watch, "Landmine Ban: Poland final EU member to join," press release, December 7, 2012, http://www.hrw.org/news/2012/12/07 /landmine-ban-poland-final-eu-member-join.

18. Now the Office for Security and Co-operation in Europe (OSCE).

19. "For the first time, environmental issues commanded attention at such a high level of international governance. . . . Respect for Sweden as a neutral and progressive country. . . . allowed the members of the Swedish delegation to lead the preparatory process. . . . Much of the success of the Stockholm Conference was to a certain degree a product of its Secretary-General, Maurice Strong. A Canadian industrialist and businessman with an avid interest in international affairs. . . . Strong was appointed Secretary General of the Conference in 1970 because of his skills as a coordinator, collaborator, and convener." Maria Ivanova. "Moving forward by looking back: Learning from UNEP's history," in *Global Environmental Governance: Perspectives on the Current Debate*, ed. Lydia Swart and Estelle Perry (New York: Center for UN Reform Education, 2007), http://environmentalgovernance.org/cms/wp-content/uploads /2009/06/Ivanova_Designing-UNEP_2007.pdf.

20. Mexico, 1975; Copenhagen, 1980; Nairobi, 1985; Beijing, 1995.

21. The Community of Portuguese Speaking Countries.

22. The Organisation of Islamic Cooperation claims 57 member states across four continents. Organisation of Islamic Cooperation, "About OIC," http://www.oic-oci.org/oicv2/page/?p_id=52&p _ref=26&lan=en (accessed June 30, 2013).

23. Human Rights Watch, "Indonesia," in *World Report, 2012* (New York: Human Rights Watch, January 2012), www.hrw.org /world-report-2012/world-report-2012-indonesia.

24. Daniel Fisher, "Detroit tops the 2012 list of America's most dangerous cities," *Forbes*, November 18, 2012, http://www.forbes. com/sites/danielfisher/2012/10/18/detroit-tops-the-2012-list-of -americas-most-dangerous-cities/.

25. Matt Richtel, "US online gambling policy violates law, WTO rules,"

New York Times, March 26, 2004, http://www.nytimes.com/2004
/03/26/technology/26gamble.html.

26. The predicament faced by Tuvalu is detailed in this report:
Australian Bureau of Meteorology and Commonwealth Scientific
and Industrial Research Organisation, *Climate Change in the
Pacific: Scientific Assessment and New Research*, vol. 2 (Canberra:
Bureau of Meteorology; Highett, Australia: CSIRO, 2011),
http://www.pacificclimatechangescience.org/wp-content/up-
loads/2013/06/PCCSP_Report_Vol2_FULL_120202.pdf. Tuvalu
rejected the result of the Copenhagen climate summit in 2009,
claiming it would fail low-lying countries that face a grave future
if global warming causes sea levels to rise. ABC News, "Future
not for sale: climate deal rejected," December 20, 2009,
http://www.abc.net.au/news/2009-12-19/future-not-for-sale
-climate-deal-rejected/1185014.

27. Bruce Campion-Smith, "Canada and Britain embassy-sharing pact
called 'nickel and dime' diplomacy," *Toronto Star*, September 24,
2012, http://www.thestar.com/news/canada/2012/09/24/canada
_and_britain_embassysharing_pact_called_nickel_and_dime
_diplomacy.html.

28. Government of Canada, "Canada-Australia Consular Services
Sharing Agreement," http://travel.gc.ca/about/assistance/consular
/framework/canada-australia (accessed June 30, 2013).

29. Kevin P.Q. Phelan, "From an Idea to Action: The Evolution of
Médicins Sans Frontières," in *The New Humanitarians: Inspiration,
Innovations, and Blueprints for Visionaries*, ed. Chris E. Stout
(Westport, CT: Praeger Publishers, 2009).

30. The partnerships were between Plan Canada and Iamgold in
Burkina Faso, World University Service of Canada and Rio Tinto
Alcan in Ghana, and the Canadian Hunger Foundation and Placer
Dome in Papua New Guinea. Rick Westhead, "Donors closing
wallets to Canadian charities who work with CIDA, mining
companies," *Toronto Star*, January 31, 2013, http://www.thestar
.com/news/world/2013/01/31/donors_closing_wallets_to_canadian
_charities_who_work_with_cida_mining_companies.html.
Rosemary McCarney president and CEO of Plan Canada strongly
defended the partnership: "We . . . believe in the power of the
project to help youth and their communities, and to lift generations of Burkinabés out of poverty. . . . We have more than
75 years of experience in developing countries and so we know
that mining is a constant reality in these nations. Therefore, we
are taking the lead in learning all we can from this experience
rather than watching from the sidelines. . . . When well-designed,
transparent, regulated, responsibly-managed and aligned with

national poverty reduction plans, mining investments can provide significant opportunities for job creation, poverty alleviation and long-term growth." Rosemary McCarney, letter to the editor, *Toronto Star*, February 3, 2013, http://www.thestar.com/opinion /letters_to_the_editors/2013/02/03/plan_canadas_commitment.html.

31. Section 15 of the Charter of Rights and Freedoms contains guaranteed equality rights and prohibits discrimination. *Constitution Act, 1982* (80) 1982, c. 11 (U.K.), Schedule B.

32. Section 35 of the Constitution provides protection for the treaty rights of First Nations peoples of Canada. It is not technically a part of the Charter of Rights and Freedoms, coming immediately following in the Constitution, but it is closely associated with the Charter. *Constitution Act, 1982* (80) 1982, c. 11 (U.K.), Schedule B.

33. Quoted in David R. Morrison, *Aid and Ebb Tide: A History of CIDA and Canadian Development Assistance* (Ottawa: North-South Institute, 1988): 69.

34. Ibid.: 21.

35. The CLC is the united front for trade unions in Canada. They were instrumental in the formation of the NDP and support them exclusively; they also fought aggressively against the free trade agreement.

36. Unilever and Oxfam have continued to work together for poverty reduction. For example, in 2010 they announced a plan to help farmers in developing countries join the supply chain of the company. Kamal Ahmed, "Unilever backs small farmers," *Telegraph*, December 26, 2010, http://www.telegraph.co.uk/finance/newsbysector /retailandconsumer/8224339/Unilever-backs-small-farmers.html.

37. Robert J. Crawford and N. Craig Smith, *Unilever and Oxfam: Understanding the Impacts of Business on Poverty* (Paris: INSEAD-EABIS, 2008), http://www.eabis.org/fileadmin/eabis_uploads /Resources/Project_outputs/Mainstreaming_CR_-_Cases_PDFs /Unilever_Oxfam_Insead.pdf

38. "I met President Reagan on January 17, 1984, just before I was sent to Moscow by the White House on a back channel mission. After this successful mission, I met with him twenty-one more times over the next four years of his second term and taught him the Russian Proverb, Doveryai no Proveryai (Trust but Verify), which he loved and used often." Suzanne Massie, "The Reagan Years, 1984–88," http://www.suzannemassie.com/reaganYears.html (accessed June 30, 2013).

39. "GLF exists to make available, discreetly and in confidence, the experience of former leaders to today's national leaders." Global Leadership Foundation, "Purpose," http://www.g-l-f.org/index. cfm?pagepath=Purpose&id=22872 (accessed June 30, 2013).

40. F.W. de Klerk, "A Recipe for Freedom," (speech, Democracy Lab, Washington, March 5, 2012), http://www.g-l-f.org/index.cfm ?PAGEPATH=&ID=41493.

41. Ibid.

42. The Assembly of First Nations, the Native Council of Canada, the Inuit Tapiriit Kanatami and the Métis National Council.

CHAPTER 12: NATIONAL CONVERSATIONS

1. The outside members invited to ASEAN are Australia, Canada, the European Union, Japan, New Zealand and the United States.

2. Food Banks Canada, *HungerCount, 2012* (Toronto: Food Banks Canada, 2012), http://www.foodbankscanada.ca/getmedia/3b946e 67-fbe2-490e-90dc-4a313dfb97e5/HungerCount2012.pdf.aspx.

3. In 1973, The Inuit Tapirisat of Canada (Inuit Tapiriit Kanatami) began a study of Inuit land use. Eventually this culminated in the 1999 Nunavut Act which created the Territory of Nunavut, settling the Nunavut land claims and enabling self-government for the Inuit people. Government of Nunavut, "The Creation of Nunavut," http://www.gov.nu.ca/files/Creation%20of%20 Nunavut.pdf (accessed June 30, 2013).

4. Thomas L. Friedman, "The whole truth and nothing but," *New York Times*, September 6, 2011, http://www.nytimes.com /2011/09/07/opinion/friedman-the-whole-truth-and-nothing -but.html?_r=o.

5. Nunavut had not yet been established.

6. The Assembly of First Nations, the Native Council of Canada, the Inuit Tapiriit Kanatami and the Métis National Council.

7. "Perhaps their greatest contribution was to change the political climate of the country through the emphasis upon reconciliation and accommodation which emerged from these conferences." Ronald L. Watts, "Processes of constitutional restructuring the Canadian experience in comparative context," (working paper, Kingston: Queen's University, 1999): 6, http://www.queensu.ca /iigr/WorkingPapers/watts/wattsrestructure.pdf.

8. "The Citizens Assembly on Electoral Reform was an independent, non-partisan group of 160 randomly selected British Columbians, assembled [in 2003] to examine the British Columbia provincial electoral system." Memory BC: The British Columbia Archival Network, "British Columbia. Citizens' Assembly on Electoral Reform," http://www.memorybc.ca/british-columbia-citizens -assembly-on-electoral-reform (accessed June 30, 2013).

9. In 2007, "Quebec Premier Jean Charest announced the creation of a special commission, headed by prominent academics Gérard

Bouchard and Charles Taylor. The mandate of the Bouchard -Taylor commission is to conduct extensive public consultation on the issue of reasonable accommodation throughout Quebec." Mick Wall, "The Quebec debate on reasonable accommodation," Centre for Constitutional Studies, University of Alberta, January 16, 2008, http://www.law.ualberta.ca/centres/ccs/news/?id=15 (accessed June 30, 2013).

10. Canadians spend more time online than anybody else in the world—an average of 45 hours per month. Canadian Internet Registration Authority, "Canada Online," Factbook 2013, http://www.cira.ca/factbook/2013/index.html (accessed June 30, 2013).

11. "The Canadian International Council (CIC) . . . is an independent, member-based council [of] . . . a broad constituency of Canadians who believe that a country's foreign policy is not an esoteric concern of experts but directly affects the lives and prosperity of its citizens." Canadian International Council, "About the CIC," http://opencanada.org/about/ (accessed June 30, 2013).

12. "The Canadian Defence & Foreign Affairs Institute is a charitable, independent, non-partisan, research institute with an emphasis on Canadian foreign policy, defence policy, and international aid." Canadian Defence & Foreign Affairs Insititute, "About CDFAI," http://www.cdfai.org/aboutcdfai.htm (accessed June 30, 2013).

13. "The Carnegie Endowment for International Peace is the oldest international affairs think tank in the United States. . . . It is known for excellence in scholarship, responsiveness to changing global circumstances, and a commitment to concrete improvements in public policy." Carnegie Endowment for International Peace, "The Global Think Tank," http://carnegieendowment.org /about/?lang=en (accessed June 30, 2013).

ACKNOWLEDGEMENTS

A book is both a solitary and team effort. I first proposed an idea about Canada and the modern world to Random House Canada publisher Anne Collins four years ago and her enthusiasm and positive response ensured it was finally written and published. Craig Pyette, Senior Editor at Random House Canada, was my Sherpa, and my spur, and his skill, perspective and patience helped shape my thinking and writing. I owe them both a great debt, and want also to thank several of their colleagues at Random House, including particularly Sarah Moscovitch, researcher, Scott Sellers, Director of Marketing Strategy, Louise Dennys, Executive Publisher, Five Seventeen, the book's designer, Brittany Larkin, the book production co-ordinator, and Terra Page, the typesetter, whose extraordinary efforts kept us on schedule.

A number of other individuals have helped me research and build my case, and I want especially to acknowledge the insight and advice of Dr. Megan Bradley, Katherine Reichel, Dr. Erin Crandall, Denise Van Der Kamp, Heather Hughson and Malcolm Ferguson, as well as the support of the Institute for the Study of International Development and the Department of Political Science, of McGill University.

Finally, Maureen, and Catherine and her family, redefined the terms "patience" and "understanding" these past four years and, as always,

I consider myself very lucky to have their support, suggestions and help.

In the end, of course, this is my work, and I accept full responsibility for the arguments and interpretations, and any errors.

INDEX

JOE CLARK was elected in 1979 as Canada's sixteenth and youngest prime minister. During the Mulroney government, he served as minister of external affairs from 1984 to 1991 and as president of the Privy Council and minister responsible for constitutional affairs from 1991 to 1993. After several years away from public life he was elected again to the House of Commons in 2000, where he represented Calgary Centre until leaving politics in 2004. He now works as a political and business consultant in Ottawa, where he lives with his wife, Maureen McTeer.